Four Phenomenological Philosophers

In this book, Christopher Macann guides the student through the major texts of the four great figures of the phenomenological tradition – Edmund Husserl, Martin Heidegger, Jean-Paul Sartre and Maurice Merleau-Ponty. Each chapter is devoted to one of the four thinkers.

Since studying phenomenological philosophy under Ricoeur, Christopher Macann has published *Kant and the Foundations of Metaphysics, Presence and Coincidence* and a translation of Theunissen's *Der Andere*. His most recent work is *Martin Heidegger* in the Routledge series *Critical Assessments of the Leading Philosophers*. He has taught at the universities of Paris, California and Pennsylvania; he is a research fellow of the Alexander von Humboldt Foundation and is currently Professor of Philosophy at Regent's College in London.

Four Phenomenological Philosophers

Husserl, Heidegger, Sartre, Merleau-Ponty

Christopher Macann

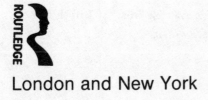

London and New York

First published 1993
by Routledge
11 New Fetter Lane, London EC4P 4EE

Simultaneously published in the USA and Canada
by Routledge
29 West 35th Street, New York, NY 10001

© 1993 Christopher Macann

Typeset in 10 on 12 point Palatino by Witwell Ltd, Southport
Printed in Great Britain by Clays, St Ives plc

British Library Cataloguing in Publication Data

A catalogue record for this book is available from the British Library

Library of Congress Cataloging in Publication Data

Also available

ISBN 0-415-07353-7 (hbk)
    0-415-07354-5 (pbk)

To the students I have taught
over many generations and in several countries
– without whom I should not have had a life

Contents

Preface

This book has been written for the student, more specifically for students in an English speaking world which, for many years, has been dominated by analytical philosophy. My basic aim is to put into the hands of the reader, and within the compass of a single volume, a work enabling beginning students of phenomenology to find their way through the major texts of what will, I believe, in retrospect, be seen as one of the (if not *the*) most important philosophical traditions of the century.

My concern with the needs of students has dictated the format of the book. In my estimate, the four figures I deal with count as the most important phenomenological philosophers of this century – with no other figure falling into quite the same category of original, constructive thinking. Three of these four figures (Heidegger, Sartre and Merleau-Ponty) each wrote one major work in which the substance of their phenomenological thinking is represented. In order to keep the cost of this book down to a minimum, I have therefore deliberately chosen to ignore the other, often extensive, philosophical writings of these three figures. With Husserl, however, such a policy cannot be pursued. And so I have tried to cover all the texts which tackle the issues with which the student is required to be familiar.

From personal experience, I know how difficult it is to move from an analytical foundation to a comprehension and assimilation of continental philosophy. If I was ever able to make this shift when I went from an undergraduate training at Oxford to a graduate training in Paris, it was by dint of a deliberate decision, in my second year at Paris, to *pretend* I knew no philosophy at all, and so to begin all over again. This policy of deliberate ignorance made it possible for me to approach phenomenology with a fresh eye, free of the biases of my analytical background. Hence, I believe that the broadening of the scope of English-speaking philosophy will result not from analytical philosophers acquiring a late 'taste' for phenomenological philosophy but from students of philosophy being exposed to the phenomenological tradition at about the same time that they are introduced to contemporary analytical philosophy and so *before* the point at which their minds set, irreversibly, in the mould of language, truth and logic.

For generations, phenomenology has been presented to students in the English-speaking world in the language and idiom of analytical philosophy, and therefore not merely in a language and idiom *alien*, but actually *antithetical*, to the spirit of phenomenology – partly, no doubt, with a view to diminishing the significance of phenomenological philosophy. In view of the fact that the greatest phenomenological philosophers are now routinely classified amongst the greatest philosophers of the century, such an approach can no longer be sustained.

This book is therefore not meant to replace a reading of the texts, either in the original German or French versions or in one or other of the many excellent translations which are at present available, but has been written to help students find their way through these always difficult, and often also long, texts. It is a textbook in the strict and literal sense of that word, that is, a book designed to help students come to terms with the *texts*.

Chapter 1

Edmund Husserl

Edmund Husserl was born in 1859 in Prossnitz, a village in Czechoslovakian Moravia which, at that time, formed a part of the Austrian Empire. He initially studied mathematics and physics at Leipzig and Berlin but his transfer to the University of Vienna inaugurated a shift in interest towards philosophy. In 1886, he went to the University of Halle, where he became an assistant under Stumpf. But in 1900 he received an invitation to join the philosophy faculty at Göttingen, where he subsequently became professor in philosophy. In 1916 he obtained a full professorship at Freiburg im Breisgau, where he remained until his retirement. The last years of his life were overshadowed by Nazi politics, though his death, in 1938, saved him from witnessing the war unleashed with Hitler's invasion of Poland.

The philosophical development of Edmund Husserl, the founder of twentieth-century phenomenological philosophy, can be divided into three main periods, the first period of his pre-transcendental or epistemological phenomenology, the middle period of his fully transcendental phenomenology and the last period of his so-called 'genetic' phenomenology. Although our attention will be concentrated on the middle period of his properly transcendental phenomenology, we shall nevertheless present Husserl's thinking in terms of these three phases.

There is no one work which stands in the same relation to the Husserlian philosophy that *Being and Time*, *Being and Nothingness* and *Phenomenology of Perception* stand in relation to the thinking of their respective authors. Inevitably, therefore, we shall be obliged to take account of a number of texts stemming from different periods in Husserl's development.

HUSSERL'S EPISTEMOLOGICAL PHENOMENOLOGY

The point of departure

Husserl came to philosophy from mathematics, a fact which is reflected in the very title of his first published work – *The Philosophy of Arithmetic*. Though he later came to qualify some of the theses presented in his first major work, it is worth noting that the approach he adopts here sets the stage for the entire further development of his thinking. For in this, his first attempt to account philosophically for the seemingly unequivocal 'objectivity' of a branch of the mathematical sciences, he already seeks to steer a course between *psychologism* and *logicism*. Indeed such an attempt may be taken to characterize the epistemological status of the first period in his philosophical development.[1] For later he will come to see that a properly phenomenological philosophy cannot be developed along the lines of a simple mediation between the two pillars of epistemological philosophy, namely, the *a priori analytic* and the *a posteriori synthetic* (represented in Logical Positivism by the twofold way in which propositions are said to be verifiable – as analytically or as empirically true or false), but calls instead for something in the way of a transcendental turn.

Psychologism, the view that the laws of knowledge can be derived from an understanding of the basic facts of psychic life, was a position represented by J. S. Mill and which had been taken up by such German predecessors of Husserl as Wundt, Sigwart and Lipps. Logicism, a position assumed by Natorp, Shröder, Voigt, and of course Frege, began as a reaction to psychologism, a reaction in which Husserl thought of himself as participating.

It lies outside the scope of this commentary to attempt a comparison of Husserl's *Philosophy of Arithmetic* with Frege's *Foundations of Arithmetic*. But the antagonism between the two conceptions of arithmetic can be very easily seen in their respective attitudes towards the two critical concepts 'zero' and 'one'. For Frege (and Russell after him), the entire number series can be generated from these two fundamental concepts.

For Husserl, on the other hand, 'zero' and 'one' are not concepts of number at all, and for the simple reason that, for Husserl, a number can only be generated by way of the (logical) concept of a 'something in general' and the (psychological) concept of 'collective connection'. But the apprehension of *one* object requires no collective synthesis, or immediate apprehension of 'togetherness' – and the same holds even more evidently of zero. From the very beginning, therefore, Husserl required that the objectivity of even the most 'logical' of objectivities be traced back to the structures of consciousness in and through which it first became possible. Fundamental notions such as 'equality', 'similarity', 'whole and part', 'plurality and unity' were regarded by Husserl as incapable of formal-logical definition. Rather, the validity of these notions had to be exhibited in concrete synthetic activities and through a disclosure of the types of abstraction through which they were generated. In his review of Husserl's *Philosophy of Arithmetic*[2] Frege could only regret the intrusion of psychological considerations into logic, a criticism which Husserl took seriously and against which he sought to defend himself.

Perhaps the best way to assess the significance of Husserl's attempt to avoid the charge of 'psychologism' is with reference to the work of Brentano and Meinong, the former a generation or so older than himself, the latter more or less a contemporary. From Brentano, Husserl drew the principle that all consciousness, by its very nature, is a consciousness 'of', in other words, is intentional. However, the complementary side of Brentano's intentional analyses, his concern with the immediate apprehension of psychic data in consciousness, proved too empirical for Husserl.[3]

Retaining Brentano's emphasis upon psychic life as the real foundation of conscious activity, Meinong sought to liberate Brentano's 'phenomenology' from empiricism through an appeal to ideality. Though still taking his stand in a descriptive psychology,[4] Meinong sought to overcome the empiricism of his starting point in the evidences of internal perception through a characteristic disconnection of 'higher order' objectivities, objectivities which can, however, be built up on this same psychic basis. The unreality or ideality of the object, for Meinong, is marked out by the characteristic of 'intentional inexistence'. With Meinong, the emphasis accorded to the unreality of the psychic object led to a multiplication of ontological regions, each with its own distinctive mode of representation, that is, with its own distinctive way of positing its object as ideal or inexistent.[5]

By eliminating the realism inherent in Brentano's descriptions of psychic life, Husserl's phenomenology moves beyond the limits of an empirical psychology. By replacing Meinong's *negative* concept of ideality, characterized essentially by inexistence and, as such, standing out in stark contrast against the real psychic contents upon which it is based, with a more *positive* concept, Husserl's phenomenology opens the way to a quite distinctive, eidetic analysis. What now ensures the invariability of the intentional object is not (as it was with Meinong) the invariability of the psychic content to which it is related. On the contrary, this psychic content, qua lived experience, can, with Husserl, undergo all kinds of variations, just as long as the wealth of psychic modifications is directed towards an object whose invariability is guaranteed by its ideality.

The *Logical Investigations*

The *Logical Investigations* are divided into a Prolegomena and six subsequent Investigations, of which the sixth is by far the longest. The general movement of these six researches is from the formal to the material, from the abstract possibility of a science of sciences, through an investigation of meaning and its relation to language, to a concrete analysis of the structures of consciousness and their relation to experience and to the knowledge of that which is given in experience.

However, for purposes of convenience, we shall not attempt to present the *Logical Investigations* Investigation by Investigation. Instead, the substance of this long and often elaborate work will be conveyed with reference to six guiding themes: (1) the controversy between formalism and psychologism, (2) language as the expression of meaning, (3) the correlational character of consciousness, (4) eidetic intuition, (5) the pure ego and finally (6) truth and knowledge.

To some extent these themes arise in the course of the *Logical Investigations* in the same order in which they will be dealt with here, but only to some extent. In particular, the Sixth Investigation, the last and the longest, tends to pull together the themes of all the preceding Investigations under the one all-embracing head of a phenomenology of truth and knowledge.

The Prolegomena begins by raising the same issue as that examined earlier in *Philosophy of Arithmetic*. As before, Husserl's aim is to steer between the Scylla of *formalism*, for which logic exists as a technology of thought ultimately dependent upon certain arbitrarily (or at least conventionally) established concepts and procedures, and the Charybdis of *psychologism*, for which the laws of logical thought are in the end reducible to psychological laws governing the actual functioning of the human psyche. The Prolegomena assumes an anti-formalist position, because logical formalism disregards altogether the psychic life in which logical objectivities arise and through which they are sustained in being by, for example, a repetition of the same logical procedures on different occasions. It also assumes an anti-psychologistic position, because psychologism disregards, or rather regards as secondary, the ideal objectivities of formal thought (by making them depend upon certain concrete acts of counting, inferring etc). From a present day standpoint, it would seem that the principal objection to Husserl's procedure would stem from the formalist direction. But in Husserl's own day, psychologism offered the most persuasive account of the origin of logical thinking. It is for this reason that the critique of psychologism takes up the greater part of the Prolegomena.

Logic, especially in the very broad sense in which Husserl understands this term, obviously presupposes language, and indeed a quite special conception of language. The unusual feature of Husserl's concern with language is that, for him, language is, first and foremost, the medium in which *meanings* are expressed and communicated. This implies that meaning is in some sense *prior* to language and can therefore only be attained, in its phenomenological purity, through a series of exclusions.

He begins to operate these exclusions in the First Investigation, by distinguishing signs (*Zeichen*), on the one hand, from indications (*Anzeigen*), on the other. Sign is the most general term. For every sign is a sign of something. But not every sign signifies. By a sign in the sense of an 'indication', Husserl tells us he means an object or state of affairs whose existence indicates the existence of a certain other object or state of affairs, in the sense that belief in the existence of the former constitutes a motive for belief in the existence of the other. Thus clouds may serve as indications of the imminent arrival of rain, symptoms as indications of the presence of a disease, a certain geological formation as an indication of the presence of oil and so on. The point of drawing this distinction is to exclude indications (*Anzeigen*) from the general province of expressions, properly so-called, that is, the province of that whose function it is to signify, to give expression to.

Husserl then goes on to distinguish, within the general province of signifying signs, that is linguistic expressions, a physical aspect from that aspect through which the expression is endowed with meaning. By the physical aspect of an expression, Husserl means the physiognomical gestures required for speech or writing, the contexts in which these gestures take place, as well as the outward manifestations of an expression – in the case of speech, audible sounds, in the case of writing, visible marks. All of this is incidental to the function of signification which is disclosed in and through those acts which, as it were, animate the lifeless sounds and marks in question. Any statement, whether spoken or written, can function as an expression, and so also can any part of such a statement, the concepts or phrases of which it is made up. But a statement is only an expression in so far as it is viewed from the standpoint of what it seeks to express, from the standpoint therefore of an outward ex-pression (pressing out) of something in itself inward and hidden, not merely the meaning as such but the meaning just as it is intended by the very meaning-giving consciousness in question.

Conversely, when I understand an expression uttered by someone else, necessarily my understanding is predicated upon a sensational apprehension (of the sounds emitted). But the understanding of the meaning is not reducible to this sensory input which, in the act of understanding, is immediately transcended towards the signification, what the sounds are taken to express. In order to reinforce the ideality of his conception of signification, Husserl takes note of, in order to rule out as irrelevant, expressions in which something other than the expression of an objective intention is meant by the speech act in question. Acts which are not primary bearers of signification, the kind of acts Austin called 'performative', acts through which desires, wishes, commands are expressed, together with the various forces (perlocutory/illocutory) which accompany such speech acts, also fall under this head. In so far as, by saying, I *do* something (by saying 'I promise', I actually *do* promise), what is done transcends the parameters of an objective expression – as do such accidental aspects of an expression as those whose meaning is dependent upon the person and the occasion of utterance. At the same time, Husserl will insist that occasional expressions, such as demonstratives, do also contain a core objective sense over and above that subjective sense which comes to them from the occasion of utterance. He who says 'I' means, in general, 'whoever is uttering the expression', and this no matter how variously that pronoun may refer to different people in actual contexts of utterance. Pure logic deals solely with those ideal unities which Husserl calls 'significations', and which have to be conceived in abstraction from the real variations attendant upon the differences of person, place and circumstance.

In the Fifth Investigation Husserl carries his phenomenology of language to its logical conclusion with reference to a *function of nomination*. In the case of names, and provided we add the article to the relevant noun or noun complex, a position of existence is normally implied. Just as a name is used to affirm the existence of a thing which, as such, can feature as the subject of a predicative judgment, so a whole phrase can function in this nominal manner, in which case it requires completion in a judgment which furnishes a predicate. Between a statement of fact, employed as a judgment, and a naming of this statement of fact which, as such, requires completion through further predication, a difference of essence prevails, for example between 'It is raining' and 'that it is raining will please the farmers'. Thus, in general, nominating presentations differ from judgments, and positing presentations which affirm existence from non-positing presentations.

This appeal to the function of nomination has two results. First, it enables Husserl to treat states of affairs (expressed in complex expressions) as modifications of an act of simple nomination. Thus 'S is P' is convertible into the 'being P of S' or 'that S is P'. Second, inherent in the function of nomination we find an objective reference, and this even before the introduction of questions concerning truth and intuitive fulfilment. It is this objective reference which provides a basis for the notion of an 'objectivating act'.

The discussion is then extended in such a way that the critical concept of an objectivating act can be employed to clarify and amplify the initially vague notion of intentionality. An objectivating act (§41) is the primary bearer of matter. As such, it is what links the 'unreal' life of consciousness with a reality distinct from consciousness. Every intentional *Erlebnis* is either itself an objectivating act or has such an act at its base – for example, if it expresses a *desire* for some state of affairs. Since, in the final analysis, objectivating acts have been shown to be nominating acts, the unity of intentional life can ultimately be founded in language, not in the sense that it is reducible to the latter but in the sense that we can have no access to intentional *Erlebnisse* save by way of corresponding forms of expression in and through which the *Erlebnisse* in question are objectified.

But the function of signification, the *meaning-giving* acts of consciousness together with their expression in language, cannot be considered independently of what is signified, the *meant* – and here we come to our third heading. An examination of the subjectively determined life of consciousness would be meaningless if it did not stand in relation to its intentionally determined objectivities. It is this correlation 'meaning–meant' which governs the entire course of the *Logical Investigations*. It should, however, be noted that, on both sides, the common category of reality has been suspended from the start, in the first case in the name of what is actual ('reell' not 'real', or what will later be known as the 'noetic') and in the second in the name of what is ideal ('ideell', or what will later be known as the 'noematic'). Whereas certain of the Investigations, such as the First and the Fifth, will concentrate primarily upon the meaning-giving side of consciousness itself, others, such as the Second, the Third and the Fourth, will focus on the meant and the intentional idealities which are objectified thereby. Even when one side of the correlation is examined without reference to the other, it should therefore always be borne in mind that this exclusion is purely artificial, an exclusion performed for the purposes of analytical convenience, and therefore one which in no way undermines the correlational character of Husserl's phenomenological investigations.

Turning to the side of the meant, to the intentionally

signified rather than the signifying activity of consciousness, we find, first of all, Husserl's own novel conception of 'ideational abstraction'. The Second Investigation is specifically devoted to the problem of abstraction. Husserl's phenomenological theory of abstraction is mostly directed against two views, the metaphysical hypostasis of the real existence of kinds quite independent of consciousness, and the psychological hypostasis of the real existence of kinds in consciousness, more specifically, in and through a psychological process by which the mind moves from the apprehension of particulars to the comprehension of general ideas derived from particulars. The former position is of course that of Platonic realism, which successfully defends the objectivity of essences but in so doing fails to trace them back to their sources in consciousness. The latter position is mostly illustrated and critiqued with reference to British empiricism, which successfully traces the universality of general ideas back to a function of consciousness but fails to recognize the ideal objectivity of the essences derived by way of just such a procedure of abstraction.

Husserl more or less disregards Platonic realism and devotes virtually the whole of the Second Investigation to a critique of the psychologism implied in the empiricist doctrine of abstraction. Husserl's starting point is a phenomenological observation to the effect that the act of apprehension by means of which an individual is intended is radically different from that by which a kind or species is intended and that all attempts to account for the passage from the former to the latter presuppose, in the end, precisely what they seek to prove. Thus, for Locke, the abstraction of the general idea 'red' is arrived at by leaving out of account all those respects in which several red objects differ in order to hold on to that respect in which they are similar. But the concept of similarity (or even of respect) which is in question here itself presupposes the very comprehension (of the essence 'red') which it is supposed to account for. Nothing is gained by turning from Locke to Berkeley or Hume. For although the latter admit the particularity of the idea 'red' (qua content of consciousness), they still account for its generality through a representative capacity (whereby it is made to stand indifferently for all objects 'of the same kind') which itself again presupposes the essence ('same kind') in question.

Ideational abstraction is the beginning of what Husserl will later call *eidetic intuition*, a type of intuition which is to be met with even in the foundations of logical thought, where it assumes the form of a *categorial intuition* (Sixth Investigation). By comparison with the act of signifying, which is concrete and specific, ideational abstraction points towards the possibility of an apprehension of abstract and non-specific universals which, as such, form the basis of what Husserl means by the *meant* – that ideal object which functions as the correlate of the meaning-giving activities of consciousness.

Returning to the act side of consciousness we find, especially in the Fifth Investigation, a different set of analyses concerned with a characterization of consciousness and of the *concept of the ego* appropriate to a phenomenological investigation. Husserl begins with a threefold definition of consciousness:

1 consciousness as the complex of actual (reell) components belonging within the empirical ego and subject to a flux;
2 consciousness as the internal perception of psychic acts;
3 consciousness as a global designation for all kinds of psychic acts or intentional *Erlebnisse*.

Husserl eventually opts for a version of the third and broadest conception of consciousness but only by way of a preliminary critique of the first two conceptions.

The first conception of consciousness as a fluxional complex has to be disburdened of its empirical connotations. This is done, first, by refusing the presupposition of an objective reality and, in accordance therewith, by denying the legitimacy of the division of reality into two spheres, the external and the internal. The appearance of the thing is not the appearing thing. The former is a psychological datum (to which there corresponds a physical conception of the thing itself), the latter a phenomenological given. Moreover, the popular conception of *Erlebnisse* as what an individual lives through in terms of worldly events has also to be discarded. Further, the concept of the psychic ego which follows therefrom, the concept of an ego whose unity is made up of a connection of phenomenal properties and whose reality depends upon the existence of these same properties, must be distinguished from the phenomenologically purified notion of the 'I'. The latter is more or less identical with the unity of fluxional consciousness and so stands in no need of a superior egological principle.

The second and more reflective concept of consciousness (as rooted in a specific act of internal perception) is then in turn dismissed in so far as it falls prey to the default of an infinite regression – a concept of consciousness rooted in an act of reflection which itself requires a higher consciousness still to reflect on it. Here Husserl appeals approvingly to Kantian apperception as the source of a concept of the 'I' as that which, as subject, can never be made an object of consciousness. Such a concept of the 'I' requires not merely the elimination of the empirical ego but also of the body, and for the same reason, that they both belong to an objectified conception of the self.

This preliminary examination of the first two misconceptions opens the way to an investigation of the third and broadest conception of consciousness as the phenomenologically purified unity of all intentional *Erlebnisse*. We are now in a position to appreciate that the pure 'I' cannot be objectified even though the relation of consciousness to its objects can and indeed *must* be objectified if anything like a phenomenological analysis of the contents of consciousness is to be possible. Before such an analysis can be undertaken, however, the concept of 'content' has to be purged of certain critical ambiguities.

In the first place, by content might be meant both the actual content (the lived experiences themselves) and the intentional content (that towards which such actual contents are directed). The actual (reell) content is the precursor of what will later be known as the *noesis* and is identified here in order that there be no confusion when Husserl engages in the more significant analysis of the intentional content. On the side of the intentional content, however, further distinctions are needed; first and most obviously, the distinction between the object *which* is apprehended and the object *as* it is apprehended. Only the latter is pertinent to a phenomenological investigation of contents.

But second, within the general sphere of the intentional object as it is apprehended, it is necessary to distinguish between the *matter* of an intentional act and its *quality*. The matter of an intentional act indicates the content of an act as that which makes an act about this rather than some other objectivity. The quality of the act indicates the way in which the objectivity in question is posited, as affirmed, questioned, desired, imagined etc. Obviously, the same matter can be qualified in different ways and vice versa. The same state of affairs can be successively affirmed, denied, desired, imagined and so on. And a series of imaginatively qualified acts can have a different 'matter' in each instance.

Finally, in the Sixth Investigation, the last and the longest, the individual strands which have been separately investigated along the way are woven back together around the themes of truth and knowledge. For, strictly speaking, until now the course of the analyses has been guided by the question of signification not that of truth. But truth rests not just on the coherence and meaningfulness of linguistic expressions but on the relation of language to reality, the presence of the thing itself. To be sure, the intentionality of consciousness was already pointing in this direction, more especially since the investigation of intentionality revolved around the disclosure of objectivating acts. But the reality towards which intentionality pointed had hitherto merely been presumed. It is this presumptive orientation towards truth and knowledge which now becomes the explicit theme of a series of analyses.

Husserl begins by recuperating a distinction alluded to earlier. For already in the First Investigation Husserl had drawn attention to a distinction between an empty *intention of signification* and the *intuitive fulfilment* of that empty intention. What I mean when I use the expression 'dog' is meaningful, both to myself and to others, even in the absence of the dog. However, in the end such an expression remains empty, or vacuous, unless it is (or at least could be) fulfilled through an appropriate intuition which presents the object in question. In the broader context of the Sixth Investigation this means that what an expression expresses, that is, its content, now calls for a threefold distinction between the content as intentional sense or meaning, the content as fulfilling that sense through, for example, sense experience and the content as object. In analytic epistemology, this relation is picked up through a theory of verification which itself presupposes the distinction of self and world, language and reality, and therefore also understanding and sensibility. Phenomenological epistemology, however, is able to execute its analyses without any such metaphysical presuppositions by merely elucidating (*Aufklären*), not explaining (*Erklären*), the lived experiences through which knowledge becomes possible. To the Kantian question of the condition of the possibility of knowledge Husserl replies with an exposition of the *coincidence* (not correspondence) which necessarily obtains between signifying acts and the intuitive acts through which the former find their fulfilment.

An example will help to clarify what Husserl has in mind; the statement: 'a blackbird is flying off' – said in the face of the relevant perception. The statement is about a perception and is intuitively fulfilled through it. But the signification does not depend upon it, as is clear from the fact that the same statement made in the absence of the relevant experience would at least be intelligible. Just as obviously, the word-sound does not contain the meaning, since the same statement made in an incomprehensible language would be meaningless. Rather, through the utterance of a word-sound combination, a signification is intended which receives its intuitive fulfilment from the actual perception. In case I am someone else, at least two sets of intuitions are required for knowledge to be possible, the intuitive apprehension of the word-sound (which must then be endowed with meaning) and the intuitive apprehension of the perception intended by the one uttering the word-sound combination. That in certain cases Husserl is prepared to admit imagination as an appropriate intuitive fulfilment is indicative of the 'interiority' of phenomenological analyses. (One can almost hear Wittgenstein complaining: how can I check the validity of a knowledge claim in this case? By producing a second image to confirm the first? Would this not be like buying a second copy of the same newspaper to check the truth of the first?)

To this simple, phenomenological model of knowledge, a model based upon a series of distinctions between the act of intentional signification, the verbal expression, the intuitive fulfilment of this intention and the resulting knowledge, Husserl then adds a number of additional complications. First, there can be a temporal lag between the act of expression and that of fulfilment or of confirming knowledge. The static structural model of knowledge requires completion by a more dynamic model which allows for such lags. This is especially true in the case of fulfilment through a manifold of so-called adumbrations, the object first from this side and then from that. Just as important, the existence of such lags allows for the opposite of confirmation. Husserl employs the term 'non-concordance' to express the possibility of anticipated intuitions not materializing as expected and so giving rise to doubts about the perception or even to outright dis-qualification of the knowledge-claim.

The first part of the Sixth Investigation concludes with a chapter (V) on evidence. Evidence is defined in terms of fulfilment, more specifically, in terms of a series of approximations to the ideal of a final fulfilment. An intention of signification may be regarded in itself as possessing no fulfilling intuitive content. An imaginative fulfilment represents a certain degree of fulfilment which, at the other extreme, is perfectly represented by the givenness in itself of the object. Where an intention of signification has procured final fulfilment through an ideally complete perfection the genuine *adequatio rei et intellectus* is provided for. In turn (§38) evidence points to being in the sense of the truth of the evidence. But the 'is' of being and of the evidence through which the object or state of affairs is given, in itself, is quite different from that by means of which a predicate is attributed to a subject. In other words, truth as idea is based upon the idea of adequation, or of an objectifying signification which finds its fulfilment through such an adequation, while the latter in turn points beyond itself to something (truth as being) which exists as the foundation for the possibility of just such an adequation. This correlation (truth *as idea* and truth *as being*) makes it impossible to hypostasize a reality existing independent of consciousness. For being itself is, or can be, given in the truth of evidence in an originary way.

The second part of the Sixth Investigation is largely devoted to the famous issue of *categorial intuition*. A good way to come to terms with this notion is to see it as a reformulation of the Kantian problem of *a priori synthetic* judgments. Husserl's solution is to extend the notion of formal intuition, which, in Kant, is restricted to mathematical objectivities bearing on spatial and temporal forms, to a much wider sphere. This wider sphere encompasses, first, an 'abstractive ideation' which 'creates' generalities such as 'red'. We are already familiar with this order of formal intuition from the Second Investigation. The sphere of categorial intuition also includes the act of predication which creates a categorial fulfilment for an 'is' for which no corresponding element is to be found in sensible intuition.

Thus the statement 'the cat is on the mat' requires intuitive material for the 'is' as well as for the 'cat' and the 'mat'. In the third place, categorial intuition is needed to account for terms such as 'all', 'some', 'none' – terms which feature as logical operators.

Two other major features of this theory of categorial intuition should be noted. First, the theory incorporates a concept of founding which permits Husserl to establish what might be called an *epistemological hierarchy*. At the lowest level we find significations relating to particular objects of sensible intuition. These provide the basis for the entire hierarchy and make it possible for Husserl to talk of his phenomenology as an 'empiricism'. Founded in such basic sensible intuitions, we find higher order generalities such as those depicted in concepts of properties. The 'abstractive ideation' through which such generalities are brought into being cannot dispense with sensible singularities but is not reducible to the singularities which form the lowest order of the hierarchy.

Finally, and perhaps most significantly, we find an upper level of pure logical objectivities. Expressions such as 'This E is P', 'Some S is not P', 'All S is P' include components which have *no sensible fulfilment*. These are (a) the 'is' as used in its predicative not its positional form and (b) the terms 'some', 'all', 'and', 'not' etc. To take (a) first, Husserl insists: 'It is not in a reflection on judgments or rather on their intuitive fulfilments but in these intuitive fulfilments themselves that the origin of such concepts as 'state of affairs' and of 'being' (in the sense of the copula) is to be sought; it is not in the acts qua objects but in the objects of these acts that we find the foundation for that act of abstraction which makes these concepts possible' (§44). Categorial intuition gives these new objectivities not through any act of reflection upon lower order objectivities but through an act of fulfilment which is analogous to that operative in ordinary sensible intuition.

With reference to the second type (b) of purely logical objectivity, Husserl could have argued that concepts such as 'some', 'all', 'and', 'not' are mere symbols void of intuitive meaning. But he does the very opposite, seeking an intuitive analogue for such categorial forms in a distinctive categorial intuition. Categorial intuition is therefore that form of intuition in which these new objectivities are actually given in person. Thus such Kantian categories as 'unity', 'plurality', 'totality', 'ground-consequent', 'substance-attribute' and so on find their intuitive fulfilment in a distinctively categorial intuition. To be sure, acts such as those of conjunction and disjunction are founded in objects given simultaneously, but the categorial form is not reducible to these objects nor to any association which consciousness automatically establishes between them. For it is not A and B or A or B itself which has to be explained but the 'being-together' of A and B or the 'one of the two' of A and B. For all that, supersensible, or categorial, intuition is still founded in sensible intuition even though it engenders objects of a different order altogether. The founded acts upon which categorial intuition is based could not exist without the founding acts of sensible intuition.

Let us take as a second instance the specific case of the notion of identity. For Husserl, the origin of this notion is to be sought in sensible perception and the intuitive fulfilment connected with such a first order intuition. The manner in which, for instance, the parts of a serial perception presenting different sides of an object fuse and coincide to form the presentation of one and the same thing offers a first instance of the notion of *sameness*, a notion which merely functions here as an organizing principle in the course of perception. However, through an act of 'abstractive ideation', it is always possible to make this unifying function the object of an explicit idea – thereby engendering the abstract idea of *unity*. In turn, the idea of unity can furnish the foundation for a yet higher order 'categorial abstraction' which yields the logical principle of *identity*.

We should not be in any doubt as to the largeness of the claims Husserl makes on behalf of his investigations. From a Husserlian standpoint, the pure laws of thought which a phenomenological elucidation brings to light are not in any way dependent upon the contingencies of the human understanding. Any rational understanding capable of living through acts of thought in some way or other would eventually be brought to recognize these *a priori* laws of thought. For this very reason there is no need of any metaphysical explanation for the congruence of the course of nature with the nature of our understanding. For this essential congruence is itself brought to light in the work of phenomenological elucidation.

HUSSERL'S TRANSCENDENTAL PHENOMENOLOGY

As René Schérer, one of the most acute critics of Husserl's *Logical Investigations*, repeatedly observes, many of the difficulties of this, his first major work, can be traced to the absence of an explicit concept of the reduction. Not until *Ideas I* does Husserl work out in detail the two main ideas which are fundamental to his transcendental phenomenology, the idea of the reduction and the complementary idea of a sphere of immanence or of immanental consciousness. Prior to the detailed working out of these ideas, however, we do find two subsidiary texts which lead in this direction: *The Idea of Phenomenology* (where we find an 'epistemological' reduction (whose ancestry he traces back to Descartes) and *The Phenomenology of Internal Time Consciousness*.

The Idea of Phenomenology is one of those texts (like *Cartesian Meditations*) which is mostly introductory but which does also include one new and significant contribution – in this case, the idea of 'immanence'. Critical to an understanding of the significance of this idea is the distinction between a first and *preliminary* conception of the immanent–transcendent distinction and a second and *conclusive* conception of this same distinction. The starting point for the entire series of analyses is the question: how it is possible for consciousness to reach its object? A first answer to this question is offered in terms of the phenomenologically inadequate distinction of the inner and the outer. The immanent is *in me*, the transcendent *outside of me*. In order to preserve this distinction from the naivety of a conception of the mind as a sort of receptacle for conscious contents Husserl draws a distinction between *reale* and *reelle Immanenz*. Real immanence in the sense of 'reale', treats the psyche as a domain of objects like any other, and indeed divides up the whole of reality into two distinct domains, the internal and the external. On the other hand, actual immanence, in the sense of 'reell', considers every objectivity from the standpoint of that consciousness for which it exists and by which it therefore has to be experienced in that specifically Husserlian sense in which by experience is meant *lived experience* (*Erlebnis* not *Erfahrung*). Whatever is actually lived out – perceived, thought, imagined, remembered – is, in so far as it is a lived experience, free from doubt. The indubitability of immediate self-givenness goes along with the concept of immanence, even in this preliminary sense of the term. To put it in the simplest terms, this first conception of the distinction between the immanent and the transcendent suffices to substitute for the epistemologically naive subject–object distinction a more sophisticated distinction between act and object. Due to the intentionality of consciousness, the act side of consciousness cannot be regarded as a self-enclosed sphere of subjectivity since the life of consciousness is always (actively) directed towards its object.

The trouble with this first concept of immanence is that it excludes too much. Whatever exists in such a way that it is not an actual item of the on-going life of consciousness must be excluded from the sphere of immanence and so becomes transcendent to consciousness. This means, as Husserl points out, that 'the cognition belonging to the objective sciences, the natural sciences and the sciences of culture and on closer inspection also the mathematical sciences, is transcendent. Involved in the objective sciences is the doubtfulness of transcendence, the question: How can cognition reach beyond itself? How can it reach a being that is not to be found within the confines of consciousness?' (p. 3). The seemingly incidental reference to the dubiousness of the mathematical sciences is the key here. For as purely formal, the mathematical sciences contain nothing material. Their objects are themselves universal essences and so can themselves be given with that indubitability which characterizes any apprehension of essences within the life of consciousness. This means that essences are absolutely given even though they are not actually immanent. From which Husserl concludes: 'No longer is it a commonplace and taken on face value that the absolutely given and the actually immanent are one and the same. For that which is universal is absolutely given but is not actually immanent. *The act of cognizing* the universal is something singular. . . . *The universal itself* which is given in evidence (*Evidenz*) within the stream of consciousness is nothing singular but just a universal, and in the actual (*reellen*) sense it is transcendent' (pp. 6–7).

As a result, it turns out that the above concept of the actually (*reell*) immanent is only a limiting case of a much wider concept of immanence – and the same holds of the concept of transcendence. From this Husserl draws two conclusions: first, that the concept of absolute self-givenness has now to be replaced by the more adequate criterion of *evidence*; second, this broader concept of immanence is now required to include what Husserl will also call *'reelle Transzendenz'*. The phenomenological reduction already suffices to exclude what is really (*real*) transcendent. But so far from wanting to exclude the entire sphere of the actually (*im reellen Sinne*) transcendent, it is the task of a phenomenological philosophy to include within the sphere of immanence *the entire field of objective correlates*, more specifically, all those (ideal) objectivities which can now be comprehended from the standpoint of their essential structure. The very task of phenomenology can now be conceived as the analysis of those systems of correlation which obtain between the diversity and multiplicity of actually given lived experiences and the essential structures which are posited as the ideal objects of just such a manifold of lived experience. From the standpoint of this new concept of immanence, what was previously regarded as transcendent (transcendent to the life of consciousness) must now be treated as immanent, and as such available for an analysis whose descriptions operate within the scope of the criterion of indubitable self-evidence. To put it in more Cartesian language, the sphere of immanence now no longer merely includes the Ego and the *cogito* (*or cogitatio*) but also that of the *cogitatum* (or *cogitationes*).

Whereas *The Idea of Phenomenology* can be treated as an introductory text, this is not the case with *The Phenomenology of Internal Time Consciousness* of 1905 which, if we include the supplements added between the years 1905 and 1910, makes a major contribution to phenomenological philosophy in one quite specific domain, that of time consciousness. The importance of this study cannot be exaggerated because, in a certain sense, the phenomenology of time consciousness is the phenomenology of consciousness *per se*, since all conscious contents are, to speak in Kantian language, given subject to the condition of time. By way of introduction, three points should be made. First, though little space is devoted to the reduction, it does figure at the outset under the rubric of an exclusion (*Ausschaltung*) of objective time, the time with which we reckon, which we 'tell' in the normal sense of that word. Second, the disclosure of an ultimate and absolutely constitutive flux of consciousness does represent a preliminary introduction to the notion of a specifically transcendental dimension of consciousness, the notion which will bear the main weight of a so-called 'transcendental' phenomenology. Third, about the same time that Husserl was making his breakthrough to the notion of an ultimately constitutive flux of consciousness, another major thinker, Henri Bergson, was also laying the foundations for his own distinctive type of philosophical analysis on a rather similar basis, the disclosure of a flux of consciousness and, in conjunction therewith, a 'profound ego'.

Ignoring the second part devoted to Addenda and Supplements, Husserl's *Phenomenology of Internal Time Consciousness* falls into three sections, a first section devoted to the reduction and a brief critique of Brentano's path-breaking study of time, a second section devoted to the analysis of immanental time consciousness and a third section devoted to an analysis of the ultimately constitutive flux of consciousness. It is noteworthy that many of the secondary studies on this work ignore or fail to come to terms with the third section.[6]

Although an examination of this extremely difficult final section falls outside the bounds of this study, I have devoted a considerable amount of attention to it in a section of my *Presence and Coincidence* and would simply like to reiterate here two conclusions which I drew in that book; first, that in a certain sense the theory of the flux represents the *crux* of the entire theory of internal time consciousness since it is in and through the flux that temporal objectivities are ultimately to be constituted, and second that, in my view, the theory of the flux not only represents the point at which Husserl's general method of constitution breaks down but that it does so in such a way as to point towards an alternative ontological analysis of time – the very kind of analysis undertaken later by Heidegger. All that we can cover here are the basic structures of Husserl's immanental analyses of time consciousness, the analyses contained within the second section.

Husserl begins his analyses with the example of a melody. A melody consists in the sounding of a succession of tones. Husserl gives the name 'primal impression' or 'originary data intuition' to the instantaneous sounding of a tone in the now. But in order that a succession of such sounds be grasped in the unity of a melody the preceding tones have to be retained as the playing proceeds on to the succeeding. Husserl calls 'retention' or 'primary remembrance' this feature of the act of apprehension which results in my still being aware, in the now of the contemporaneous sounding of a tone, of previous moments in the succession of sounding tones. Moreover, and especially if the melody is one with which I am familiar, in addition to the retention of preceding tonal moments I am able to anticipate those to come. Husserl calls 'protention' that aspect of the act of apprehension which permits me to anticipate tonal moments yet to come. My ability to grasp the sequence of sounds in the unity of a melody is thus dependent upon this dual orientation of intentions, *retentional* (directed towards the past) and *protentional* (directed towards the future).

Retention and protention are acts operative in the present (more correctly, acts contributing to the whole operation taking place in the present), acts which, so to speak, extend the scope of the present to cover the immediate past and the immediate future, the 'just having been' and the 'about to be'. These acts now have to be contrasted with acts which take us *explicitly* back to the past or on into the future. Husserl himself tends to accord far less consideration to acts oriented towards the future and indeed has no specific name for the complement of memory. However, in the interests of maintaining the balance between the two sets of acts, the term 'pre-diction' will be coined to cover the opposite of memorial reproduction. Whereas 'retention' and 'protention' are acts of presentation, 're-production' and 'pre-diction' may be called acts of re-presentation. In the present, the past is re-produced in memory or pre-viewed in prediction. Whereas presentation operates on the basis of actual impressions, representation operates on the basis of what Husserl calls 'phantasy', that is, the ability of consciousness to presentify an object or an event, in image, and so in its actual absence. However, it is important to note that there is an actuality of representation in phantasy just as there is an actuality of present experience. For it is in the actual present of representative phantasy that I re-present a past or a future present.

With this proviso, let us now turn our attention to the act upon which Husserl concentrates his attention, the act of re-production. Instead of living along the succession of tones constitutive of the melody I can, after the melody has been played, or even while it is still playing, return in memory to the first tone and then reproduce the whole sequence again 'in my mind'. Husserl sometimes calls this 'secondary remembrance', in contrast to 'primary remembrance', which is retention. The first tone is no longer given in actuality but it is reproduced in phantasy. Further, with the passage to the second tone, and ever thereafter, the same structure of retention and protention which pertains to the original lived experience now also pertains to the representation. With the representation of the second tone, there is a retention of the first and a protention of the third and so on. However, whereas originally consciousness is subjected to the actual course of the primal impressions, here consciousness is 'free' to run the melody through as fast or as slowly as it pleases, to stop at any point, return to the beginning again, execute variations and so on. Nevertheless, just as in the case of an original presentation, the unity of the melody, as represented, is attributed to the structures of retention and protention (appropriately modified to accommodate the different demands of representation).

Despite the fact that acts of reproduction may have the same contents as former acts of retention, the modification by means of which an original 'now' is changed into one that is past is absolutely different from the modification by means of which an original 'now' is reproduced. For the former takes place, as it were, 'of its own accord', whereas the latter modification is one which consciousness effects 'of itself'. Within the sphere of reproduction in general, it is also important to distinguish between phantasy and recollection. I can imaginatively represent a remembered melody, that is, simply make it present to me now in image, or I can represent it in such a way that a reference to the past is implied. In what does the difference consist? Obviously, I cannot go back to the past to check on the actual occurrence of what I remember, so the difference must lie in the way in which the melody is represented. The act of consciousness by which an image is represented as having been or as having taken place is something different from the act by means of which it is 'neutrally' posited. Recollection not only posits what is reproduced but in so doing gives it a position in time (more or less explicitly) with regard to the present. Phantasy, on the other hand, only remembers as a current performance which brings with it no explicit relation to the past. Thus, in running through a remembered melody, I do not need to recall the occasions on which it was heard in the past and may indeed have entirely forgotten the past contexts which made the current performance possible.

But is there any genuinely original experience in which the reality of the past can be affirmed as presently given to consciousness, in which, in other words, it is possible to have 'insight' into the past? Husserl not only thinks that there is, but draws the further conclusion that this experience furnishes the only adequate evidence for our belief in the existence of a past in which events actually took place in a manner corresponding to that in which they are remembered to have taken place. In the actual present in which certain past contents are still retained and so are, in this sense, still actually perceived, I can reproduce these same contents in such a way that there results a certain *coincidence* of retained and reproduced contents. The reproduced contents, as empty intentional representations, find their evidential fulfilment in the retained contents.

Moreover, something similar may be assumed to take place in the case of protentions. Husserl tells us that a prophetic consciousness is conceivable, one in which each character of the expectation, of the coming into being stands before our eyes. Thus the indeterminateness of pre-vision should not be taken as the *a priori* mark of distinction, especially since a memory may be very vague. This symmetry as between re-production and pre-diction means that a prophetic representation could also be made to coincide with its protentional anticipation in a manner analogous to that which takes place in the past. And yet the analogy is by no means exact. For protention does not see into the future as retention sees into the past. The note anticipated may not materialize, or may be replaced by another note. For this reason, Husserl places the main emphasis upon the modes of fulfilment. Because the actual realization of the tone *succeeds* the expectation rather than preceding it, the actual sounding of the tone is always a *fulfilment* or confirmation of the empty intention, which it cannot be in the case of memory, whether of the primary or of the secondary kind.

From an immanental analysis of retention and protention, together with reproduction and pre-diction, Husserl moves on to an immanental investigation of the constitution of temporal objects themselves (as opposed to an analysis of the structures of apprehension which make such a constitution possible). By immanental temporal objects, Husserl means such 'things' as temporal periods, temporal durations and temporal sequences, taken in and of themselves, as opposed to merely being read off the intentional activity of consciousness. We shall not follow Husserl any further into his analysis of immanent temporal objects, let alone his investigation of the flux with its correlated concepts of 'longitudinal' and 'latitudinal' intentionality, all of which are dealt with in some detail in the relevant sections of *Presence and Coincidence*.

Ideas I

Ideas I was first published in 1913 as the leading article of the first issue of Husserl's *Jahrbuch für Philosophie und Phänomenologische Forschung* and is one of three texts which go by the name of *Ideas toward a Pure Phenomenology and Phenomenological Philosophy*, the other two being entitled *Ideas II* and *Ideas III* respectively. *Ideas II*, though never published in Husserl's life time, is an extremely interesting (though structurally flawed) work which comes closer than any other of his texts to an attempt at a systematic presentation of phenomenological philosophy. *Ideas III* is a meta-theoretical text which reflects briefly upon such issues as the relation of phenomenology to psychology or to ontology. Though we shall concentrate upon *Ideas I*, a word should also be said about *Ideas II*.

Ideas I is divided into four parts: a first part which represents, in effect, a recapitulation of the themes of *Logical Investigations*, a second part which deals with the natural attitude, the reduction and the disclosure of a sphere of pure consciousness, a third part devoted to immanental analyses with particular reference to the correlational structures noesis–noema and a fourth and final part devoted to a restoration of (transcendent) reality, the reality placed in suspense with the reduction. However, before we begin, a word of warning! The student would be well advised to start with Part II rather than Part I (especially Chapter 1) since the recuperation of earlier themes is difficult to understand independently of the texts in which they are dealt with in detail.

The chapter on fact and essence antecedes Husserl's distinction of a transcendental domain and so, implicitly, harks back to a pre-transcendental phenomenology whose eidetic categories and connections, however, are necessary for the establishment

of a transcendental phenomenology. Husserl begins by pointing out that natural knowledge is based on facts which become
known through experience. In accordance with factual
knowledge of this kind, we find factual sciences, the so-called
natural sciences. Facts about the world refer in the end to
individual objects whose existence (Dasein) and whose being
such and such (Sosein) are accidental or contingent. However,
correlated with individual objects and the factual configurations in which they figure, we find essential objects which are
given in configurations of an essentially pre-determined or pre-
determinable kind. Just as perceptual intuition gives us (more
or less adequately) corresponding natural objects, so essential
intuition gives us (more or less adequately) essential objects.
Whereas perceptual intuition gives objects which are supposed
to exist (in space and time), essential intuition gives us objects
whose existence is not presupposed even though it may very
well be illustrated or exemplified with regard to specific
instances. And this is why the intuitive exemplification of the
eidos or pure essence can take place just as well in phantasy or
acts of imaginative intuition.

Although the intuition of individuals is radically different
from the intuition of essences, a connection obtains between
them such that for every essence there corresponds a series of
possible individuals as its factual instances and, conversely, for
every individual experience an essence can be intuited which
exhibits what is purely general in the individual. Thus the
intuition of a red instance can always be transformed into the
intuition of the essence 'red' while the latter can always be
intuitively illustrated through the exhibiting of an instance,
either in perception or phantasy. Just as a connection of this
kind holds between factual and essential intuition, so a connection of a corresponding kind holds between sciences of fact and
sciences of the essence. And just as the intuition of individuals
is intrinsically different from the intuition of essences, so the
eidetic sciences can be developed in complete independence
from the factual sciences, even though the truths at which the
former arrives are, in principle, always applicable to the latter.

Every concrete empirical object can be located within a
highest material genus which demarcates the region within
which all objects of the same kind are to be found. The concept
of a regional essence lies at the root of the concept of a regional

ontology. To every regional ontology there corresponds an eidetic science which furnishes, *a priori*, a variety of knowledge pertaining to all possible objects located within that region. Thus an eidetic science of physical nature in general can be distinguished from any particular science which takes physical objects as its material, and the unrestricted *generality* of the laws which can be formulated on the basis of an observation of objects of the relevant kind has to be sharply distinguished from the unconditional *necessity* of the laws which can be formulated on the basis of an insight into the essence of physical nature in general.

In addition to the eidetic sciences which can be developed on the basis of regions which serve to demarcate material ontologies, there are eidetic sciences which can be developed upon the basis of purely formal regions, that is, regions of objects to which nothing in reality corresponds. Thus the region 'object in general' gives rise to the formal ontology of logic, just as the region 'number in general' gives rise to a formal ontology of arithmetic. Formal ontologies and the eidetic sciences connected with them can be developed quite independently of any material ontology since the regions in question do not, properly speaking, demarcate regions so much as the *pure form* of a region in general. However, those formal ontologies based upon the pure form of a region in general are, in principle, always applicable to the ontologies based upon material regions and, in general, the progress made by a material science is linked to the extent to which it has been able to apply bodies of knowledge drawn from the formal ontologies to its own material region.

From the foregoing, the notion of an 'epistemological hierarchy' can readily be confirmed. Every essence takes its place in a graded series of essences. Moving downward, we reach the lowest order eidetic singularities. Moving upward, we arrive at a highest genus which is such that it has no further genus above it. However, the formal essences (together with the sciences based upon them) cannot be thought of as superimposed upon the material essences and in such a way that, for instance, the purely logical concept of an 'object in general' could be regarded as a highest genus under which we could range any specific region of material being. For the procedure of *formalization* is quite distinct from that of *generalization*. To generalization, on the way up, there corresponds *specialization*, on the way down. But to formalization there corresponds what Husserl calls *de-formalization*, namely, the application of purely logical laws through the assigning of concrete values to the variables in question (§13).

For example, a red percept can always be subsumed under the essence 'red'. The essence 'red', however, is a dependent object (a moment) which cannot exist without reference to the essence 'material thing'. In turn the essence 'material thing' can be subordinated to higher order essences and, in the end, to spatiality in general. But the transition from the highest genus 'space' to the 'Euclidean manifold' is not a generalization but a formalization of the former. In other words, the transition from the highest genus of a material ontology to the cor-responding formal ontology is not to be thought of as an extension of the process whereby lower order differences are subordinated under a higher order genus. For the procedure of formalization is *sui generis* and so operates quite independently of that of generalization. In other words, the construction of general laws, such as the law of gravity, are intended to bring empirically observable events under certain prescribed rules. Connected therewith, but entirely independent of the latter, is a procedure whereby bodies of mathematical knowledge are applied to such laws, thereby facilitating the exact formulation of such laws and making possible precise predictions with regard to the events to which such laws apply. Whereas the essential knowledge based upon the differentiation of regional ontologies might, along Kantian lines, be called *'a priori* syn-thetic', the essential knowledge based upon the differentiation of formal ontologies will have to be called 'analytic'.

The second chapter (which we shall pass over) is devoted to the misconceptions to which naturalism (empiricism/posit-ivism) leads, misconceptions which are avoided with the suspension of the natural attitude. Part II, Chapter 1, briefly specifies what is meant by the thesis of the natural attitude and also shows how this thesis can be overcome. The natural attitude is that in which I operate as a human being in a world which I assume to exist distinct and independent of me. This world contains a multitude of objects which are supposed to be identifiable in terms of spatial and temporal determinations and which possess, in addition, numerous value predicates such as the useful, the beautiful and so on. Although I live in this world as a 'wakeful' consciousness I need have little or no awareness of myself as such, though consciousness of self is always a possibility available to the natural self. Other 'subjects' are there too for me with the same immediacy that I am there for myself. I take it for granted that they too are consciousnesses, aware of the same world as that in which I live, and aware of it in much the same way as myself. All of the above undergoes a radical alteration with the suspension of the natural attitude.

It is critical to Husserl's conception of the reduction, or *epoche*, that it should be rigorously distinguished from Cartesian doubt. I do not doubt, still less deny the existence of the world in which I find myself. Indeed, after the suspension, I continue to take it in much the same way as it appeared to me before. Only, everything that goes to make up the character of the world as a taken for granted reality is now made explicit, in as much as I 'bracket', 'disconnect', 'make no use of', 'put out of action' the theses which sustained it. Indeed, the thesis of the natural attitude first becomes a thesis through the reduction.

Chapter 2 of Part II inaugurates the re-direction of attention towards the central topic of phenomenology – consciousness. That it does so by slow steps is indicated from the first by talk of pure consciousness as a 'phenomenological residuum' – what is left over after the reduction or reductions. Husserl briefly refers to a multiplicity of reductions all of which fall under the general concept of a 'phenomenological reduction' – though at this point he does little to specify the distinct character of each of these reductions. The disengagement of consciousness from the whole (psycho-physical) being as a residuum is then further developed with reference to a distinctive feature of consciousness, its directedness towards specific objects or its intentionality. The intentional relation is then further specified in two ways. On the side of the object, the *cogitatum* splits up into figure and ground, what consciousness is explicitly focused upon and the marginal potentiality which surrounds this focal actuality. On the side of the subject, the *cogitatio* refers back to an Ego which is involved in the act of conscious awareness. This backward reference is then reinforced with a distinction between immanent and transcendent perceptions. Any *cogitatio*, say the perception of an object, can itself become the object of a higher order reflective act which makes of this consciousness (of the object) an object of reflective consciousness. In so doing the earlier reference to transcendent reality is replaced with an immanental relation (see §38). What interests Husserl about these immanentally directed experiences is their 'self-containedness' – what he will later call the 'absolute' character of consciousness as opposed to the merely 'relative' character of that transcendental reality which can only exist for consciousness.

This distinction between the immanent and the transcendent occupies Husserl for the rest of the chapter. The object itself is transcendent to consciousness. This means that it can only be given inadequately or incompletely through aspects (*Abschattungen*) which point on towards patterns of possible completion, and this of necessity. Whereas the transcendent object is only given *phenomenally*, the immanental 'object' is given *absolutely*. This means that whereas I can always be mistaken about what is supposed to exist in reality, I can in principle never be mistaken about the experience itself through which the former manifests itself to me. In other words, the immanent experience features as the indubitable foundation for any (dubitable) affirmation of existence, though, it must be said, this indubitable foundation is accessible to me and to me alone.

Chapters 3 and 4 of Part II carry the idealistic implications of Husserl's transcendental phenomenology further still. Whereas in naive, unreflective consciousness, we are carried along by the intentional relation and so come to accord real being to that which is intended as the correlate of consciousness, in the reflective attitude the focus is transferred from the object itself to the intentional relation in and through which the object is posited as such. Through just such a change in the focus of attention, consciousness is seen to be the absolute with regard to which the natural world enjoys a purely relative being. Husserl will even go so far as to suppose an annulment of the world which leaves consciousness unaltered. In such a case, Husserl claims, everything would remain the same, whereas the annulment of consciousness would bring with it the annulment of the world. Precisely because consciousness is a self-contained and self-sufficient realm, causal laws can only be held to obtain between worldly events, not between the world and consciousness.

Chapter 4 pursues the directive of absolute idealism with a

reversion to the theme of the phenomenological reduction(s), this time in the light of the concept of transcendence. Whatever is transcendent to consciousness must be suspended, its meaning as (independently) real (or independently valid) being discredited. This applies first and foremost to both the physical and the human sciences. Just as the physical object no longer possesses any real being independent of consciousness, so consciousness cannot itself be set up as a bit of nature, a psychic constituent. Still less can the psycho-physical nature 'Man' be accepted as a phenomenological given. Qua transcendent, the reality of God must also be suspended and, with a certain, significant qualification, the same holds even of the Ego.

For in §57, Husserl does move beyond the (*non-egological*) position assumed in the *Logical Investigations* where the Ego is nothing more than the unity of its phenomenologically purified contents (a unity which cannot be further explained or elucidated). Now Husserl makes use of an *egological* but *non-constituted* concept of the 'I' to which he gives the name 'Pure "I" '. Assuming a more Kantian position, he recognizes the self-identical and unitary character of the Ego even while he denies (with Hume) that the Ego could ever be encountered as an experience or an idea. The description 'non-constituted transcendence' or 'transcendence in immanence' (§57) is important here because it gives expression to a position which Husserl will modify later (Cartesian Meditations IV) when he attempts to *constitute* the transcendental Ego. At this point, however, though recognizing the necessity of assuming the Ego as a foundation, he denies the possibility of constituting what has, admittedly, to be assumed as a 'transcendence in immanence'.[7]

The further suspension of the eidetic sciences is only a reworking of the position already assumed in the *Idea of Phenomenology* where he distinguishes between a limitative and an extensive concept of immanence. From the more sophisticated standpoint of the extensive conception, formal objects are as transcendent to consciousness as material objects and may naively be assumed to exist in the same taken for granted manner as material objects. In every instance the naivety involved is that of positing the object in question out of relation to consciousness, out of relation to that from and through which it draws its meaning, which meaning is con-

stitutive of the type of being which it is taken to possess. Thus
the goal of all these suspensions is, in effect, the same, to draw
attention to the correlational character of consciousness and
thus to open the way for the more exact descriptions (of the
relevant systems of correlation) which will form the centre of
Husserl's analyses in Part III.

The core of Part III (and I would also say of the entire work)
is to be found in Chapters 3 and 4 (of Part III), devoted to the
specification of *noetico–noematic* structures. However, there are
two preliminary chapters which lead up to the investigation of
noesis and *noema*, the first of which deals mostly with methodological issues connected with the possibility of an *eidetic*
science of consciousness while the last deals with the nature of
the consciousness which must be presupposed by such a
science. The key word is correlation, the importance of which is
made quite clear at the beginning of Chapter 2 where Husserl
talks, almost in ontological terms, of a radical division of Being
into two main spheres – Being as consciousness or
transcendental Being, and Being as 'declaring itself in consciousness' or transcendent Being.

The preliminary methodological considerations dealt with in
Chapter 1 serve more than anything else to bring out the visual
orientation of Husserl's phenomenology – and this has been a
point at issue with his critics. The Cartesian language of
intuition, bringing to intuitive self-givenness, clarification etc.,
is marshalled with a view to justifying the phenomenological
method of investigation, and the complementary element – the
faithful expression of the essences brought to light in this
manner – is simply presented as going without saying. After
fifty years of intense concentration upon the phenomenon of
language it is no longer possible for us to speak with such
assurance of giving expression to the essential structure of
experience. However, for our introductory purposes it will
suffice to accept Husserl's definition of phenomenology as 'a
descriptive theory of the essence of pure transcendental experiences . . . which has its own justification' (§75).

The phenomenological method is a method of transcendental
reflection, and a considerable amount of time is spent establishing and justifying the relevant concept of reflection. First,
reflection in the phenomenological sense is not to be confused
with what might be called 'natural' reflection, that is, a

reflective procedure through which the self becomes an (and one might almost say *the*) object of reflection. Phenomenologically speaking, consciousness is not to be regarded as one domain of reality among many others (that is, the psyche). Rather, it is the foundation of reality in its entirety. Second, as we have already seen, phenomenological reflection involves a peculiar and quite specific transformation of consciousness. Instead of going along with the positing of an object (in the natural attitude), I make the intentional relation to the object an object of investigation. I ask myself how the object in question comes to be posited with the meaning which adheres to it as an object of such and such a kind. Instead of imagining or remembering, I make the *act* of imagining or remembering the *object* of a specific phenomenological investigation with a view to specifying the essence of imaginative or memorial consciousness. Instead of living in an emotion (joy, let us say), I make the emotion a reflective object. In so doing, I do of course modify the very nature of the emotion in question but this very modification can, in turn, become the object of a yet higher order reflective act. Third, though an experiencing Ego must be presupposed, it cannot be made an object of enquiry. While accompanying all acts of reflective awareness, it cannot itself be made the object of such acts.

Starting from the most subjective' components of consciousness, Husserl introduces a new notion to clear up an earlier confusion. What was somewhat ambiguously referred to in the (Sixth) *Logical Investigations* (and also in the *Philosophy of Arithmetic*) as 'primary contents' are now called *hyletic data*. They are those sensory contents which lie below the threshold of intentional consciousness and which are required to give intentional consciousness an anchorage in reality, to prevent intentional consciousness being a creation rather than a constitution. Since intentional consciousness, by its very nature, is meaning-giving, there has to be something underlying such a consciousness which restricts the scope of its meaning-giving activity and ties it down to quite specific contents, the sensory data which, for example, become available in ordinary perception – though also in raw feels and sensations. The complement of this concept of the *hyle*, or of 'formless material', is that of the *morphe*, or 'immaterial form'. The *morphe* is nothing but that phase of the *hyletic* data which is, so to speak, animated by a meaning-bestowing act, an act which, qua intentional, is directed towards its object.

The *morphe* is formed matter in so far as this formation is referred back to that material (*hyletic*) bedrock of sensory experience out of which it arises and to which it is tied down. The *noesis* is this same formed matter in so far as it is referred on to the object which is intended thereby. With this concept of the *noesis*, or noetic data, we therefore stand at the threshold of the central doctrine of *Ideas I*, the study of the correlational structures of transcendentally reduced consciousness.

Chapter 3 introduces the notion of *noetico-noematic* correlations. In order to understand the point of the famous example of the blossoming apple tree (§88) which Husserl uses to illustrate the transformation that consciousness undergoes as a result of adopting the transcendental stance, it would be as well to consider this transformation with reference to each of three elements – experience, intentionality, reflection. In each instance we shall distinguish the naturalistic conception of the element in question from its phenomenologically proper equivalent. In the natural attitude, experience is taken to be a presentation of the object (or the world) as it is in itself, that is, of the object as a substance possessing properties of one kind or another. In the phenomenologically reduced attitude, this naturalistic concept of experience (*Erfahrung*) becomes the more phenomenologically proper concept of *Erlebnis* or, as it usually translated, 'lived experience'. The German concept of *Erlebnis* brings out the sense in which, phenomenologically speaking, experiencing is a dynamic process in which the Ego is engaged, not a static presentation of what simply exists. Second, whereas in the natural attitude the Ego is simply supposed to posit its objects as existing distinct and independent of consciousness, in the phenomenologically reduced attitude, positional consciousness becomes an explicitly intentional consciousness, that is, an implicitly or explicitly reflective consciousness 'of'. In other words, it is not the object itself so much as the intentional relation to the object which now becomes the focus of attention. Finally, whereas in the natural attitude reflection intervenes only as a specific re-direction of attention (from the object to the subject), in the phenomenologically reduced attitude, all consciousness is implicitly, if not explicitly, reflective in character. In so far as a phenomenological investigation is always and invariably directed towards the immanental contents of consciousness it is already, at least implicitly, reflective. But, of course, instead of simply investigating memorial consciousness as such, I may always choose to make any given memory the object of a higher order reflective act through which it becomes a memory reflected upon, with a view, for instance, to bringing to light the meaning-bestowing activity of remembering rather than focusing on the memory as such.

We are now in a position to understand the radical transformation which the word 'real' undergoes as a result of a *noetico–noematic* analysis of experience. In the natural attitude a 'real' person (understood to be a psycho-physical unity) is said to perceive a 'real' object in the sense of an object whose existence (Dasein) and properties (Sosein) in no way depend upon the subject to which it appears. In the phenomenologically reduced attitude, this naive concept of reality undergoes a twofold referential transformation. On the one hand, what is real (*real*) is referred back to the consciousness to which it appears and so becomes an actual (*reell*) noetic component of lived experience. On the other hand, what is real (*real*) is referred on to the meaning which it exhibits and so becomes an ideal (*ideell*) noematic component of the intentional object.

Let us now turn to Husserl's famous example of the blossoming apple tree which I am perceiving with pleasure in the garden. 'From the natural standpoint the apple-tree is something that exists in the transcendent reality of space, and the perception as well as the pleasure a physical state which we enjoy as real human beings. Between the one and the other real being (*Realen*), the real man or the real perception on the one hand, and the real apple-tree on the other, there subsist real relations' (§88). From a phenomenological standpoint all this undergoes a radical alteration. The perception becomes an actual (*reell*) perceiving whose object is an ideal (*ideal*) meaning, the perceived as such. The lived experience is unreal, in the sense that it features as an *actual* component of a consciousness which is no longer to be thought of as a psychic reality. The perceptual meaning is unreal also, in the sense that it features as an *ideal* intentional object. The tree plain and simple can burn away but the meaning of this perception cannot burn away since it has no real properties. On the one hand, we have a real

object and real experiences through which it is said to be given;
on the other, an ideal object and the purely immanental
experiences through which it is given. But, and this is
absolutely critical to an understanding of Husserl's own quite
characteristic idealism, it does not follow from the above that
we are now confronted with two realities, a natural reality and
a phenomenologically reduced reality, a transcendent and an
immanent reality. The second conception of reality is not added
on to the first nor does it complement it in any way
whatsoever. Rather it is brought to light as a way in which the
former *can* be analysed and, moreover, in which the former *has
to be* analysed if it is ever to be possible for us to comprehend the
way in which the natural world comes to acquire the very
meaning which it is ordinarily simply assumed to possess.

Chapter 4 continues the preceding analyses in greater detail.
While Husserl confirms the correlational character of *noetic* and
noematic analysis he also acknowledges the possibility of independent investigations on the one side or the other, that is, a
description of *noetic* experiences, on the one hand, or *noematic*
forms, on the other. More important, it now becomes clear that
the essence of the distinction between the two sides lies in the
distinction between a pole of unity and a pole of diversity. 'The
noematic field is that of the unitary, the noetic that of the
"constituting" variety factors (*Mannigfaltigkeiten*)' (§98).

A transition to a new series of analyses is called for by the
introduction of a level theory of consciousness. Take an example which Husserl himself employs (§§100, 101): We remember
a visit to the Dresden picture gallery. This memory features as
a modification of a previously enacted perception or sequence
of perceptions. Tomorrow, however, I can remember my
memory of the visit, thereby inaugurating a modification of a
memorial modification and so on. Or again, I can here and now
imagine myself in the Dresden gallery, imagine my meeting
someone I know in the gallery and so on. This imaginative
modification will differ in an essential manner from the
memorial modification, even though it too has its foundation in
an original presentation. Further complications can readily be
introduced. I can remember seeing a picture of a picture gallery.
And in this picture there may, in turn, be a picture of a picture
gallery, and so on. Moreover, I may also remember the pleasure
I experienced on seeing the picture. The pleasure which, at the

time perhaps merely accompanied my viewing in an implicit way, now becomes the explicit theme of a specific positional act, an act whereby the pleasure itself becomes the object of an intentional act. Needless to say, all these modifications and ramifications can be pursued along two alternative, though connected, lines, the *noetic* and the *noematic*, the experiential manifold in and through which the objectivities in question are posited and those same objectivities themselves – the remembered object, the imagined object, the objectified pleasure etc.

That the foregoing analyses can be conducted at various levels and that these levels are built up one upon the other in turn implies that there is, or at least might be, a foundational level, a *ne plus ultra* beyond which one could not go, at least on the down side. Husserl introduces the Greek term *'doxa'* to meet this need. A *'doxic'* belief character is one which confers upon its corresponding object that 'sense of reality' which ordinarily pertains to, for instance, visual perception. The acts through which something is present as seen are called 'thetic' acts, that is, acts which posit Being. Such acts can of course be subject to modal modification. What is simply taken as being can become dubious or only possible or probable, doubtful or uncertain. These doxic modalities – doxic because they imply a positional stance, modalities because they effect a modification – clearly rely upon an 'unmodalized' basic thetic act which Husserl calls the 'originary belief' (*Urglaube*) or protodoxa (*Urdoxa*). It is this 'protodoxa' which lies at the root of the logical modification which goes by the name of negation. For negation is the cancelling of a more primordial affirmation, an affirmation which is implied in any primary thetic act even though it may not be made explicit as such. In turn, negation can be applied to modify the other modalities, thus resulting in such correspondingly negative modalities as the im-possible, the im-probable, the un-certain and so on.

An extremely important modification follows the presentation of the former, the so-called neutrality modification (§109). The importance of the neutrality modification lies in the fact that it is more or less equivalent to the reduction itself. It is said to be quite different from negation in that it involves a 'withholding of performance', a 'setting out of action', a 'bracketing'. By comparison with the position of positional consciousness, the neutrality modification results in a 'sup-positing' which makes available a 'sup-positional' consciousness, the very consciousness, in effect, which is required by any properly phenomenological investigation. By virtue of the fact that mere supposal posits nothing, affirmation can itself be regarded as a modification, the modification, namely, of a mere supposition – thereby making it possible to place affirmation and negation on a par as two alternative modifications of the same act of 'supposing'. That the neutrality modification is indeed closely related to the procedure of a specifically phenomenological investigation is further confirmed by the connection Husserl draws between supposition and phantasy, the 'mental act' most fruitfully employed in any properly phenomenological analysis.

The neutrality modification cancels the natural tendency of consciousness to believe in the existence of what is posited. But there is another and quite different way in which consciousness may be marked by inefficacy. Any actual positional consciousness, or even any 'sup-positional' consciousness, is usually surrounded by a vague and indeterminate sphere of potential positings (or 'sup-positings') whose very potentiality is made manifest in the possibility of transforming them from an indeterminate but determinable background into the foreground of an actual positing (or 'sup-positing'). This notion of potential positing is of particular importance in the affective, appetitive and volitional fields (§116) since the *noematic* correlates of these *noetic* acts can only come to light through a reflective transformation of consciousness. Thus a desire for something is originally experienced as part of the directedness of consciousness towards the desired object. Only through an appropriately reflective transformation, for instance the cancelling of the *protodoxa* through the requisite neutrality modification, is the desire itself able to become the object of a higher order positing. More important still, the entire sphere of value theory, the axiological sphere, can only be brought to light through just such a transformation of potential into actual theses. In other words, the desiring, willing etc. activity which lies at the root of evaluation and which is ordinarily thought of as purely 'subjective' can itself be made an object of consciousness through the requisite 'objectifying' acts. These objectifying acts bring into being corresponding objects, the values themselves, which can then be subject to an 'objective' analysis.[8]

Husserl ends this chapter with a series of sections devoted to 'logical' questions, questions concerning meaning and expression, but also questions concerning the synthetic unities that are required for meaningful configurations such as those implied by linguistic utterance. We find here the distinction between polythetic and monothetic acts (§119). The many-rayed, polythetic act of aggregation (expressed in the logical operator 'and') or of alternation (expressed in the logical operator 'or') can be transformed into a one-rayed monothetic act which produces its corresponding objects – the logical operators 'and' and 'or'. Indeed, any sentence takes words with individual meanings and joins them in the synthetic unity of a complete expression. Moreover, along noetico–noematic lines, the analysis of the expressing of meaning has to be distinguished from the analysis of the meaning expressed.

Since these issues have already been considered in some detail, we shall not pursue them further. Instead we shall bring our presentation of *Ideas I* to a close with an exposition of Part IV, the part devoted to Reason and Reality.

Let us first remind ourselves of the point at which we have arrived. Starting from the *noetic–noematic* correlation, it is possible to move backwards in the direction of consciousness along two lines, the *hyle* (which provides the material for *noetic* animation) and the Ego (which furnishes the ultimate foundation for any intentional analysis – so much so that Husserl will call it the absolute with regard to which the world is merely relative). But what about the other direction? If *noetico–noematic* analyses completely fulfil the ambition of a phenomenological philosophy, is there any need to move beyond the self-enclosed limits of an immanental analysis? To worry about any ulterior reference to what is real (*real* not *reell*)? And yet, intentional consciousness is defined as consciousness 'of', that is, 'of' something which is not itself a constituent of consciousness. Is this self-transcending objective consistent with the directive of a purely immanental analysis? But if an attempt is not made to come to terms with the self-transcending objective of intentionality then how can we prevent the division of reality into two, the 'objectivity' which forms the basis of the natural attitude and the 'objectivity' which forms the basis of the phenomenologically reduced attitude? How can we prevent the characterization (and implicit dismissal) of phenomenology as a new form of idealism? What then will become of the claim advanced on behalf of phenomenology to be a 'radical empiricism'?

The answer to these questions lies in a further, transcendental reference. To put it in Kantian language (and where else could Husserl have got his notion of the 'determinable X'?), the *natural* object which, in the context of an immanental analysis, became the *transcendent* object, now becomes the *transcendental* (or transcendentally constituted) object by virtue of an investigation into Reason and Reality.

Starting with the *noematic* pole of a perceptual correlation, we note that the *noema* possesses a content and that this content points beyond itself to the object. However, strictly speaking, at this point we are not entitled to the notion of an object *per se*, only to that of a 'something = X' which is referred to by means not of one but of a whole collection of *noemata*. By virtue of its being the self-same with regard to a number of *noematic* predicates, the pure X separates itself off from all actual or possible predicates. *What* the object is is given by the cluster of *noematic* predicates, each of which represents an essential characteristic. But *that* the object is is given by the fact that these otherwise various *noematic* predicates coincide, are given as grouped around a central nucleus. To put it otherwise, with reference to this notion of the something = X, the *noematic* object of our earlier immanental analyses can now become the transcendentally constituted object, thereby fulfilling the ultimate objective of any phenomenological investigation, to show how the world we ordinarily take for granted is actually built up in consciousness and through the meaning-giving activities of a consciousness which, qua constitutive, must also be transcendental.

So much for Reality; now for Reason.

The entire last part of *Ideas I* is devoted to an exalted declaration of faith in the power of phenomenologically enlightened Reason. There are two sides to this declaration of faith: on the one side, a re-statement of fundamental principles, and on the other, a sketch of a programme which will only be carried through elsewhere. The key term in the phenomenology of Reason is that of 'evidence' or self-evidence. Husserl starts by contrasting *assertoric* seeing, perceptual awareness of things in the ordinary sense, from *apodeitic* seeing, a seeing into (*einsehen* or *Einsicht*) the essence of things. He suggests a highest genus evidence (*Evidenz*) under which both assertoric (sight) and apodeitic (insight) seeing would be subsumed. But, from the standpoint of phenomenological rationality, the point of these distinctions is, of course, to point the way towards an assimilation of the factual (assertoric) under the essential (eidetic) (see §145). This is no more than a conclusive re-statement of the thesis that formed the starting point for the entire book, the distinction of fact and essence together with the (phenomenologically motivated) subordination of the former to the latter.

Connected with the principle of evidence we find that of adequacy, which latter brings with it two subsidiary themes, that of a tracing back of mediate to immediate positings and, in the final analysis, to positings in which what is posited is brought to primordial self-givenness and that of a fundamental distinction between positings which can, in principle, be adequately given by comparison with those which are, in principle, inadequately given. Husserl is referring here, of course, to the fact that a real thing can only be given by aspects and that it is, in fact, impossible for us to run through all the adumbrations specifying every possible aspect of a thing from every possible perspective. Interestingly, Husserl appeals to Kant to draw from the Critical philosophy a concept of the *Regulative Idea* which will rectify this shortcoming. Though the infinite series of adumbrations can never be carried through in fact, it can be specified as a rational requirement for full and complete self-givenness and this rational requirement can be fixed in the concept of a regulative idea. In turn, this furnishes Husserl with a new way of stating the distinction between the immanent and the transcendent. 'Thus it remains as a result that the Eidos True-Being is correlatively equivalent to the Eidos Adequately given-Being and Being that can be posited as self-evident; and this, moreover, in the sense either of finite givenness or of givenness in the form of an Idea. In the one case Being is "immanent" Being, Being as a completed experience or noematic correlate of experience; in the other case it is transcendent Being, i.e., Being whose "transcendence" rests precisely in the infinitude of the noematic correlate which it demands as ontical "material" ' (§144).

The programme outlined at the end of *Ideas I* can be summed up in one word or word-phrase – regional ontology. Within the realm of what can be thetically posited, numerous regional ontologies can be distinguished, ranging from the purely formal, at one end of the spectrum, to the sheerly material, at the other. In addition, a programme for the articulation of axiological ontologies based upon the spheres of feeling and the will is also outlined. True to the spirit of the Critical philosophy, however, Husserl too gives it as his conviction that 'the problems of Reason in the doxic sphere must have precedence over the problems of axiological and practical Reason' (§139).

Ideas II

Ideas II is divided into three parts, a first part devoted to the constitution of material nature, a second part devoted to the constitution of animal nature and a third part devoted to the constitution of the spiritual world (*geistigen Welt*). This threefold division actually conceals a fourfold level theory of being. The four regions of being in question are Matter (*Materie*), Body (*Leib*), Mind (*Seele*) and Spirit (*Geist*). Thus *Ideas II* not only represents an extensive working out of the project of regional ontology, it is in a sense Husserl's one and only attempt at a *systematic* ontology. For, obviously, the four regions in question are regions which not merely belong to the being of human being but which, together, exhaustively characterize the being of human being. To be sure, by matter Husserl means not merely the physical body but also material nature in general, just as by *Leib* he means not only my own body but animal nature in general. By the same token, the region of spirit comprehends not only the spirituality of the self (the transcendental Ego) but also that of its products, whether social or cultural.

This discrepancy between a threefold division of the book and a fourfold regional ontology explains what might otherwise seem odd locations of the topics. Thus, the initial presentation of the own body as *aesthetic* falls under the heading of matter (Part I, Chapter 3) while the later presentation of the own body as *kinaesthetic* falls under the head of animal nature (Part II, Chapter 3). Again, the initial presentation of the *pure I* falls under the head of animal nature (Part II, Chapter 1) while the later presentation falls under the head of the spiritual world (Part III, Chapter 20). More curious still, the transition from a solipsistic to an intersubjective constitution of the regions of being in question seems to occur three times over, a first time at the end of the first part (§18) – *Übergang von der solipsistischen zur intersubjektiven Erfahrung* – a second time at the end of Part II and a third time at the beginning of Part III.

In fact, these oddities reflect a structural defect in the entire conception of *Ideas II*, the failure to resolve which may have been the main reason why this work was never published in Husserl's life time. As four distinct regions of being, the constitution of matter, animate body, psyche and spirit call for constitutional studies of a kind analogous to those already carried through for formal thought, natural objects, time and so on. But as regions of being intrinsic to the very constitution of human being itself, these four regions have to be *presupposed* in order to account for the being of the one engaged in the work of transcendental constitution. But how can the phenomenologist carry through a self-suspension when the very regions to be suspended are those presupposed by the existence of the phenomenologist himself?

Matter is the lowest level in the ontological hierarchy whose constitution is in question here. And yet the transcendental constitution of matter presupposes at least a transcendental Ego, which itself belongs within the realm of spirit. Again, from a strictly objective standpoint, animate body refers to the whole realm of the animalistically animate, and so makes no special reference to that specific kind of body which characterizes (and distinguishes) the rational animal. In this sense, supplementary animate predicates can be added to those which serve to characterize material body. But this ownness characteristic cannot simply be viewed from the outside. For in order to know what it means to be a body (and therefore to find myself in a position to constitute the own body) I have to refer myself to the way in which I 'rule and govern' in that body which is my own. Worse, as the locus of the so-called sense organs, this body has to be presupposed as the condition of any sensible awareness whatsoever and therefore also of the awareness of anything like animate bodies. Moving one step up the ladder, the concept of the psyche (*Seele*) proves to be a hybrid notion. On the one hand and, as it were, from the 'outside', psyche arises as the end result of a process of what might be called 'subjectification' (Husserl sometimes calls it 'introjection'), that is, the reading into animate bodies of supplementary psychic predicates. But on the other hand and, as it were, from the 'inside', psyche arises as the end result of a process of what might be called 'objectification', that is, the mundanization of the transcendental Ego. How else can one explain the otherwise strange location of a chapter on the pure I in the midst of an investigation of animal nature (Part II, Chapter 1)? Indeed, at the start of §22, we find a passage which reads as a kind of *epoche*, performed this time not with regard to a suspension of the world but with regard to a suspension of the self in the name of a constitutive abstraction from the body. 'Let us carry through', Husserl suggests, 'a self-perception in such a way that we abstract from the body (*Leib*). We then find ourselves as a spiritual I related to a stream of *Erlebnisse*, that is, as an I whose states are not to be located in the body' (*Ideen II*, §22, S. 97).

Nowhere are these structural difficulties more evident than at the very end in the last chapter entitled 'The Ontological Priority of the Spiritual by Comparison with the Natural World'. From the standpoint of foundational dependence, the natural world has priority since it is the lowest region and, as such, the one upon which all the other higher regions are based. But in the order of constitutional dependence, the spiritual world has priority – as the title of this chapter implies – since the entire programme of constitutional analysis itself belongs within the realm of the spiritual and, moreover, the realm of a spiritual world which recognizes the legitimacy of the transcendental project. But that is not the end of it. For the third part opens with a chapter on the opposition between the natural and the spiritual world. The analysis of the natural world was, of course, done from a transcendental standpoint, that is, from a standpoint which presupposes the reduction and which is therefore, in a fundamental sense, solipsistic. But the personal world is defined as the one in which we find ourselves when we live with one another. The solipsistically constituted world (*Welt*) of the scientific researcher is therefore something quite different from the intersubjectively constituted environment (*Umwelt*) of the person, even when the person in question is one whose professional preoccupations are those of transcendental reflection.

Perhaps the most interesting sections of *Ideas II* are those devoted to an attempt at a constitution of the own body, interesting not merely because they fill a gap in the spectrum of Husserl's previous analyses but because they confront Husserl with special problems which, in my estimate, he is unable to resolve satisfactorily. The constitution of *material nature* does not represent a problem but nor does that of the *psyche*. In both cases the transcendental Ego is able to adopt with regard to the region of being in question that difference which is enshrined in the doctrine of presence, the difference of consciousness from what it is conscious 'of'. But how can I, the constituter, establish with regard to the body that distance characteristic of the intentional relation when the body to be constituted is my *own body*, since the phenomenon in question only manifests itself as such in so far as I *am* it, *coincide* with it? As soon as I establish with regard to my body that distance which is the necessary prerequisite for any intentional investigation whatsoever one of two things happens: either my body gets transformed into a *physical* body (and as such a body which can be analysed along the same lines as any other physical body) or my body gets transformed into a *psychic* body (which, at best, floats ambiguously between the physical and the psychological – the so-called psycho-somatic unity – at worst, gets dragged down into the realm of the psychological). Either way, the ownness of the body is lost sight of, ceases to be a possible theme for a phenomenological analysis. Since I have devoted a section of *Presence and Coincidence* to the problem of the constitution of the own body, I shall leave it to the interested reader to refer to the above text for a more detailed examination of this question.

Cartesian Meditations

Chronologically speaking, *Cartesian Meditations* belongs within the period of Husserl's so-called 'genetic' phenomenology. I propose to deal with it here, first because, as yet another introduction, the first four of these Meditations is largely taken up with a restatement of the basic themes of phenomenological philosophy, and second because the fifth, the one in which Husserl breaks through to new ground, takes as its theme a region of being which fills a gap in the preceding investigations, especially those of *Ideas II*, where it is assumed without ever being properly dealt with. This gap is of course that represented by the theory of intersubjectivity.

Cartesian Meditations began as a couple of lectures which Husserl delivered at the Sorbonne on 23 and 25 February 1929. These two lectures were then extended into five sets of analyses. The first four Meditations largely deal with material already presented elsewhere. But in the celebrated Fifth Meditation, by far the longest and most complex, Husserl breaks new ground in the direction of a phenomenological theory of intersubjectivity. The Fifth Meditation is itself, however, only a summary of material which is at present collected in the three volumes of the *Husserliana* devoted to the theme of intersubjectivity.

Before I move to the Fifth Meditation, I should like to say a word about the fourth. For in the fourth, Husserl attempts something which he has not attempted before, a constitution of the transcendental Ego itself. We have already noted the two phases through which Husserl's thinking on the subject of the Ego has moved, the first phase of a pre-transcendental concept of phenomenologically purified consciousness (which is not yet, properly speaking, a concept of the Ego) and a second phase of the 'Pure Ego' (where, for the first time, the Ego becomes a theme in its own right). However, he will still call the Ego, at this point, a 'non-constituted transcendence'. Only later does he seek to constitute what earlier had been left a non-constituted and non-constitutable pre-condition for phenomenological analyses of one kind or another.[9]

In *Presence and Coincidence* I have explained why, in my estimate, the project of a transcendental constitution of the transcendental Ego must fail. Rather than repeating myself here I would prefer to draw the reader's attention to another development, a development which helps to bring out the sense in which this text already belongs to the third period of so-called 'genetic' phenomenology. In §32 Husserl begins by saying that 'this centring Ego is not an empty pole of identity'. This is of course precisely what the Ego had been in the previous, fully transcendental phases of his thinking. To the Ego as *identical pole* Husserl now adds the Ego as *substrate of habitualities*, by which he means to correct the emptiness of the previous conception of the Ego as pole with the fullness of an ongoing existence in which, through innumerable constitutional activities, the Ego, as the correlate of whatever objectivities get constituted, thereby itself gets constituted, or rather acquires corresponding qualities and attributes. The concreteness of this new concept of the Ego is then carried to its ideal extreme by calling this concretized, personal Ego, *a monad*. The radicality of this description (in its explicit reference to Leibniz) should not be underestimated. When Husserl says 'the problem of explicating this monadic ego phenomenologically must include all constitutional problems without exception', he means exactly what he says; that, for him, 'the phenomenology of this self-constitution coincides with phenomenology as a whole' (§33, p. 68). To put it otherwise, and somewhat more crudely, the world is contained in consciousness, not consciousness in the world.

But how, one might ask, is such a seemingly extravagant claim to be supported? The answer lies along lines which cannot be followed up here, the lines indicated in his manuscript material devoted to 'passive genesis'. Husserl's *Analysen zur passiven Synthesis* undoubtedly belongs to the third period of his genetic phenomenology, and as such will be considered in a moment. Suffice it to say that by this time Husserl has realized that his starting point in the natural attitude is inadequately primordial, that a world has already been constituted by the time transcendental phenomenology begins its reflections and constituted not in a characteristically reflective manner but precisely in an opposite, and characteristically unreflective, manner. For the first time Husserl will talk of 'early infancy' and of the genuinely primordial constitutional operations that go on at this time. But he will not let the exploration of these constitutional operations be taken over by the discipline which would seem best equipped to tackle it, empirical psychology. On the contrary, he stresses the fact that even the passive formation of ever new syntheses of meaning is regulated by 'eidetic laws' (§38, p. 79). Even when he recognizes the paramount importance of the principle of association (§39) he still insists that 'association is not a title merely for conformity to empirical laws . . . but a title for a conformity to eidetic laws on the part of the constitution of the pure ego' (§39, p. 81). In other words, the concreteness which Husserl now hopes to achieve, and through which moreover he hopes to be able to account for the constitution of the Ego itself, is a concreteness which is to be attained through a movement of return to an origin more original than that which forms the starting point for his transcendental phenomenology (the natural attitude) and which, nevertheless, will still have to be won through analyses which are fully phenomenological – in a sense which distinguishes phenomenology from any empirical discipline.

If such a programme already seems difficult in connection with the constitution of the Ego, these difficulties are augmented in the Fifth Meditation when he turns to the constitution of the other subject. For surely the transcendental Ego is by its very nature *solus ipse*? Worse, if the attempt to concretize the Ego with reference to what Husserl calls a 'mundanizing apperception' leads to a conception of the Ego which entitles it to the name 'monadic' then surely the transition to a 'genetic' phenomenology will make the problem of intersubjectivity even more acute? For did Leibniz not call his monads 'windowless souls' – and with good reason?

Again, in *Presence and Coincidence* I have given my reasons for thinking that a phenomenological constitution of the other subject is a contradictory project. All that I wish to do here is briefly to run through the steps which Husserl takes in the direction of a theory of monadological intersubjectivity.[10]

Husserl begins by introducing a second concept of the reduction, second in the sense that it comes after, and so presupposes, the phenomenological reduction, properly so called. This second reduction he calls the 'primordial' or 'primordinal' reduction. The phenomenological reduction reduces the world to its being for me. But included in such a world are entities which imply a reference to other subjects – cultural objects but also instrumental objects, even animate bodies. The primordinal reduction rules out any reference to something other which might have the mode of being of a subject and for the reason that the other subject cannot be reduced to its being for me. In this way Husserl arrives at a notion of 'pure nature' (*bloße Natur*) which exists only for me.

The new and quite distinctive sphere of immanence which emerges as a result of the primordial reduction is called the 'ownness sphere'. At the centre of the ownness sphere, I find a body given to me as what is peculiarly my own. It is the one and only body in which I 'rule and govern directly', the only body to which I can ascribe 'fields of sensation'. Surrounding my body I also find a natural world reduced to its simple being for me. This surrounding world (*Umwelt*) is my own in the sense that in it I find no reference to a subjectivity other than my own. In other words, the own world can now be regarded as belonging within a newly defined (and in a certain sense extended) sense of the sphere of immanence and which accordingly points beyond itself to a corresponding sense of the transcendent – namely, that which refers to a subjectivity other than my own. By redrawing the boundaries of the immanent–transcendent distinction in this way Husserl has effectively radicalized the solipsistic tendency inherent in transcendental phenomenology, but in such a way that the aggravation of the problem will lead, of its own accord, or so he thinks, to the solution.[11]

Let us suppose that, within the ownness sphere, there now appears something like a human being. Note that all that can be assumed at this point is the 'being for me' of a physical body of a certain type – that of a 'featherless biped', to employ an early definition of Man. Although I am given to myself primordially as an animate body I am, Husserl thinks, still capable of observing the physical form assumed by that body in which I 'rule and govern directly', for example, by looking at myself in a mirror. Consequently, I am capable of noticing the similarity which prevails between my physical body and the physical body of the other. Noticing this physical similarity motivates what Husserl calls an 'analogizing apperception', that is, a transfer over to the other of that very meaning (of being a body) which is fundamental to my sense of being a self. For me, what is fundamental is that I animate this (own) body. For the other, what is fundamental (for me) is the characteristic form and movements of a physical body. But, inasmuch as I notice a physical resemblance between my physical body and the physical body of the other, I am motivated to effect a transfer over to the other of the meaning of being an animate body, that very meaning which is fundamental to my own sense of self.

The very use of the term 'apperception' in connection with the theory of intersubjectivity brings with it a special difficulty. For 'apperception' ordinarily means, for Husserl, a perceiving which goes beyond what is actually present but in such a way that it could always be made present. Thus, I only perceive one side of the object even though I do, so to speak, apperceive the other sides which are not seen, in the sense that it pertains to the very meaning of a physical object that I *could* always go over to that point of view from which the other sides *would* be seen. By analogy, it might be thought possible to move from the *perception* of the physical body of the other to the *apperception* of the ownness of the other body. But this analogy obviously does not work. For I can never make present to myself that animation (of the other body) which tells me that, for the other, its body is own (that is, animate the other body).

We shall not seek to go into the difficulties associated with this notion of an 'analogizing apperception' and the notion of 'pairing' which goes along with it. Suffice it to say that this step (from the other as physical body to the other as other own body) is the critical step. Once the other has been constituted as an other *own body*, all the rest follows. In virtue of the fact that I am capable of attributing psychic predicates to that (own) body as which I am given to be originally, I am capable of reading psychic predicates into the other, once the other has acquired the meaning 'other own body'. And in virtue of the fact that I am capable of recognizing, in my own case, the necessity of supposing a transcendental consciousness as the very condition of such a recognition of psychic predicates in myself, I am also capable of attributing a transcendental consciousness to the other as the condition of my recognizing psychic predicates as attributes characterizing the being of the other.

Just as important as the foregoing is the fact that my recognition of the other as another transcendental Ego makes it possible for me to carry through a complete revision of what might be meant by 'objectivity'. Husserl will never let go of the idea that a monadic (that is solipsistic) constitution of objectivity is indeed possible and that in certain areas, for instance those of formal thought, it enjoys a certain precedence over intersubjective objectivity. But he is now ready, and able, to supplement this initial conception of a solipsistically constituted objectivity with another concept of objectivity which not merely recognizes the existence of others but recognizes the co-constituting that necessarily takes place when the objective world is built up along intersubjective lines. I and the other can now be seen as *co-operating* in those very operations by which an objective world is brought into existence in the first place and

indeed, in a certain sense, *prior* to that transcendental constituting which takes as its starting point the already achieved
accomplishments of an original construction of the real, that
very construction which gets set up in the natural attitude.

HUSSERL'S GENETIC PHENOMENOLOGY

I shall have to keep my comments on the third period of
Husserl's 'genetic' phenomenology to the minimum, not only
because Husserl's philosophy is usually understood either as a
radical epistemology or as a transcendental philosophy and not
only because the format of this study calls for concision but also
because the texts upon which an understanding of his genetic
phenomenology would have to be based are largely unavailable
to English students. In fact, aside from *Cartesian Meditations* (to
which we have already referred), only *Crisis* and *Experience and
Judgment* have been available to the English speaking world for
over a decade.

The starting point for any understanding of this third period
in Husserl's development must be an awareness of the limitations of transcendental phenomenology. One way (and there
are others) to describe Husserl's entire intellectual enterprise
might be 'the quest for originality' (*Ursprünglichkeit*). Science and
common sense are naive in that they take for granted the
objectivity of the world and the various regions into which it
can be divided up for the purposes of theoretical investigation.
Transcendental phenomenology seeks to overcome this naivety
via a movement of return to a transcendental subjectivity
capable of explicating those very constitutive operations without which this objectivity would not itself be possible. But if
such a regression takes its start in the world of the natural
attitude then is it not guilty of an equally limiting naivety? For
consciousness does not arrive on the scene with an already
constructed world of objects given to it from the first (as
empiricist philosophy assumes). Rather, prior to the emergence
of the natural world (and as the condition of the possibility of
the latter) an entire constitutional process must be presumed
which cannot be reduced to the transcendental approach since
the latter follows upon rather than precedes the natural

attitude – indeed takes the latter as the starting point for its own theoretical investigations into ultimate foundations. To put it in other words, the (transcendental) regression from the natural attitude to the transcendentally modified attitude now has to be contrasted with an alternative regression the task of which it would be to go back *before* the starting point of a properly transcendental analysis and to consider how the world of the natural attitude arose in the first place. This new, and in a certain sense more original, regression (*Rückfrage*) can perhaps best be brought out in terms of a contrast between abstractness and concreteness. The direction of the transcendental regression is the *teleological* direction of accentuated abstractness. The direction of the other, more original (ontological) regression is the *archaeological* direction of accentuated concreteness.

That an entirely new way of doing phenomenology is foreshadowed here is indicated by the fact that the new turn did not so much lead to new themes as to a reworking of the old themes along new lines. Just as epistemological phenomenology has its formal studies (*Logical Investigations*) so genetic phenomenology also has its formal studies (*Formal and Transcendental Logic* and *Experience and Judgment*). Further, just as transcendental phenomenology has its own characteristic way of performing the reduction, the so-called 'direct' or 'Cartesian' way (direct because it goes straight back from the world to the Ego), so genetic phenomenology has its own characteristic way of performing the reduction, the so-called 'indirect' way, a way which passes by way of a phenomenological psychology.[12] Just as the transcendental reduction leads to a characteristically transcendental procedure of constitution, so the genetic reduction also leads to its own characteristic way of examining the coming into being of the objective world, a way whose key word is '*erstmaligkeit*' (being-for-the-first-time). Just as transcendental constitution has its own characteristically active synthesis (the explicit unification of a noetic manifold in a noematic identity), so genetic constitution has its own quite different, passive synthesis (the residual deposit of intentional activity in a *habitus*).

Rather than attempting an exposition of the relevant texts, I shall simply present this new beginning in terms of three interrelated topics; the self, the world and time. In each instance we shall be concerned with the transformation of an abstract, theoretically motivated, descriptive science into a concrete, practically motivated enquiry into the being of human being.

The concretization of the self can be understood along two converging lines, the line of a philosophy of embodiment and the line of a philosophy of action. Husserl's interest in the phenomenology of the body begins, as we have seen, in *Ideas II*. But it continues, for instance in his *Analysen zur passiven Synthesis*, with a detailed investigation of such themes as those of kinaesthesia, affection, feeling and the will. The new emphasis upon an originally embodied concept of the self requires Husserl to develop the notion of a self which is originally anything but a personal subject, namely, an 'anonymous' agent. In *Cartesian Meditations*, as we have seen, the concrecity of this original self is brought out with reference to the concept of habit and habitualities. But these habitualities are only the sedimented deposits of an activity which, in turn, calls for a transformation of the very conception of the reflexivity of the self. In place of the Cartesian 'I think', we now find an 'I do' (*Crisis*, p. 161) or, as Merleau-Ponty will call it, a *practical cogito*. But a critical question still remains: is the transcendental Ego operative from the very beginning? In *Crisis*, Husserl states quite unequivocally that the transcendental Ego is at work in the natural attitude. 'In truth, of course, I am a transcendental ego, but I am not conscious of this; being in a particular attitude, the natural attitude, I am completely given over to the object poles, completely bound by interests and tasks which are exclusively directed towards them' (p. 205). Or again a little later: 'I know through my phenomenological studies that I, the previously naive ego, was none other than the transcendental ego in the mode of naive hiddenness' (p. 210). The question is whether this naivety is supposed to cover both the properly objective natural attitude and the attitude which precedes the emergence of an objective reality and on the basis of which indeed such a reality gets built up in the first place. My suspicion is that, for Husserl, human being is most essentially a transcendental Ego and that, in consequence, the transcendental Ego has to be taken as something that is there from the very beginning but which only becomes fully manifest to itself in and through the reduction. If this suspicion is correct it leads straight over to the objection which forms the starting point of Heidegger's ontological critique of Husserl, that the attempt to characterize the being of human being in terms of its being a transcendental subject fails completely to come to terms with the primordial concrecity of the self.

With a view to supporting such a position let us turn to the second topic, the world. In the third period of his genetic phenomenology Husserl saw the need to replace his naturalistic concept of the world with a more genuinely primordial concept of the life-world (*Lebenswelt*). If the self is originally an embodied being whose life is therefore manifest in action, the relation to the surrounding world will inevitably assume the form of an interaction. The extensive analyses devoted to kinaesthesia, affection, reaction, feeling and so on attest to his new recognition of the need to develop an intentionality which is practical and interactive rather than theoretical and object oriented. Once again, there can be no doubt that, for Husserl, the life-world precedes and is prior to the world of the natural attitude: 'the universal *a priori* of the objective-logical level – that of the mathematical sciences and all others which are *a priori* in the usual sense – is grounded in a universal *a priori* which is in itself prior, precisely that of the pure life-world' (*Crisis*, p. 141). And yet we are left with the suspicion that it is the transcendental subject which, for Husserl, is at work already in the life-world. How else can we explain such questions as: 'How can we make it more concretely understandable that the reduction of mankind to the phenomenon "mankind" . . . makes it possible to recognize mankind as a self-objectification of transcendental subjectivity which is always functioning ultimately and is thus "absolute" ' (*Crisis*, p. 153)?

Notice the key term: self-objectification! It suggests that, for Husserl, embodiment is an objectification of the transcendental Ego rather than the opposite thesis (to which I would subscribe), namely, that the transcendental Ego is a 'subjectification' of embodied human being, indeed the ultimate subjectification, grounded in a constitutive *abstraction* of consciousness from the body.

Finally, time. From a more strictly topical standpoint, this third period in the development of Husserl's thinking leads in the direction of a concept of the 'living present' as an absolutely original flux in and through which all temporal differences initially arise. Rather than even attempting to present this fascinating notion let me recommend to the reader Klaus Held's excellent study *Lebendige Gegenwart*.

More important for our purposes is Husserl's new 'historical' perspective, a genetic historicality which replaces the typically ahistorical assumptions of his fully transcendental phenomenology. Just as his new-found interest in the concrecity of the subject leads in the direction of a growing awareness of the process of individual growth and development, so an analogous interest in the concrecity of the species leads in the direction of a growing awareness of the importance of that through which the species comes to terms with itself, its history, primarily, for Husserl, its cultural history. Hence the greater part of *Crisis* is taken up with an examination of the development of European science and philosophy as the cultural history which has been determinative for the development of mankind, at least over the past millennium.

It is easy to find fault with Husserl's predilections, his epistemological bias, his faith in scientific rationality, his inability to appreciate the spiritual greatness of ancient civilizations, the contradiction involved in his plea for a return to the wisdom of the Greeks – whereas his own philosophy is entirely dominated by the example set by modern philosophy from Descartes to Kant. But who can doubt the depth of his commitment to reason, to a reason founded in interiority, in inwardness, and therefore to a rationality which is, in essence, spiritual? In the words of a citation from Augustine's *De vera religione*, with which he closes the *Cartesian Meditations*: 'Noli foras ire; in te redi, in interiore homine habitat veritas.'

'Do not go out; go back into yourself. Truth dwells in the inner man.' What a world away from the configuration that defines contemporary philosophy and which, following the lead of Wittgenstein and Heidegger, seeks to jettison the bag and baggage of interiority, subjectivity and spirituality as a cultural anachronism! Indeed, if a single phrase were required as an epitaph for Husserl's thought, it might be this: *Truth dwells in the inner man*.

NOTES

1 For a detailed summary of Husserl's pre-transcendental phenomenology see: Marvin Faber, *The Foundation of Phenomenology* (State University of New York Press: Albany, NY, 1943).

2 G. Frege, *Zeitschrift für Philosophie und philosophische Kritik* 103 (1894), pp. 313–32.

3 Brentano's best known text is his *Psychologie vom empirischen Standpunkt* (*Psychology from an Empirical Standpoint*) (Leipzig, 1924).

4 For instance in his *Hume-Studien* (1882), *Phantasievorstellung und Phantasie* (1889), *Zur Psychologie der Relationen und Komplexionen* (1891).

5 See especially Meinong's *Gegenstandstheorie*.

6 See, for instance, Izchak Miller's *Husserl, Perception and Temporal Awareness*, (MIT Press: Cambridge, MA, 1984).

7 The definitive study of Husserl's theory of the Ego is to be found in E. Marbach, *Das Problem des Ich in der Phänomenologie Husserls*, Phaenomenologica 59, (Kluwer: Dordrecht, 1974).

8 Husserl's *Vorlesungen über Ethik und Wertlehre (1908–1914)* are being prepared for publication by Ullrich Melle in the Husserliana series. But an earlier (1960) study by A. Roth, *Edmund Husserls ethische Untersuchungen* in the Phaenomenologica series (no. 7) has already presented the substance of Husserl's ideas in the matter of value theory.

9 See E. Marbach, *Das Problem des Ich in der Phänomenologie Husserls*.

10 In addition to the relevant section of *Presence and Coincidence* the reader should also be referred to Michael Theunissen's excellent study of the theory of intersubjectivity, *Der Andere*, translated by me as *The Other* (MIT Press: Cambridge, MA, 1984).

11 For this, see Ricoeur's study 'Husserl's Fifth Cartesian Meditation', in *Husserl: an Analysis of his Phenomenology* (Northwestern University Press: Evanston, IL, 1967).

12 This distinction is explicitly referred to in the Amsterdam Lectures. See *Husserliana*, vol. IX (Martinus Nijhoff: The Hague, 1962), p. 347.

Chapter 2

Martin Heidegger

Martin Heidegger was born in 1889, in the village of Meßkirch, where his father was a minor clerical official. He was one of that small and select band of philosophers (the classical examples being Plato and Aristotle) who was able to develop his philosophical understanding under the tutelage of another great philosopher, in this case Edmund Husserl. He was associated with the rise of National Socialism in Germany in the 1920s; and in 1933 he briefly took over the Rectorship of the University of Freiburg as a candidate acceptable to the Nazi government, thereby creating the context for a debate about his political persuasions and their connection with his philosophy, a debate which still rages today.[1]

His major work is still reckoned to be *Being and Time*, which was originally planned as a programme also including a historical dimension (his Kant book, his interpretations of Aristotle), which, along with a number of subsidiary texts such as *Was ist Metaphysik?*, *Vom Wesen der Wahrheit* and *Vom Wesen des Grundes*, forms a body of thought which may be called his 'first philosophy'. Later on his thinking developed in other directions, indeed to the point that he eventually came to characterize his first philosophy as belonging to the very metaphysical tradition which, he thought, had to be overcome. In what follows, I shall concentrate my attention almost exclusively upon *Being and Time*.

BEING AND TIME

Being and Time was Heidegger's first major publication. It was originally published in 1927 in Husserl's *Jahrbuch für phänome-*

nologie und phänomenologische Forschung and appeared simultaneously in a separate printing. Rarely has a work of philosophy
(and more unusually still a *first* work) created such a stir upon
its appearance.

Being and Time is a carefully constructed and tightly woven
work which, moreover, was originally intended as but the
preliminary to a much larger programme much of which was
never carried out as intended. Before attempting to come to
terms with the details of this *Meisterwerk*, it will therefore be
necessary, first, to spell out the parameters of the entire
programme announced therein, and second, to seek to obtain
an overview of the basic structures which command the entire
book.

The first of these tasks can best be accomplished with
reference to the last section (§8) of the second part of the
Introduction, entitled 'Design of the Treatise'. We find Heidegger claiming, in the single page which makes up the contents of
this section, that the question of Being branches out into two
distinct tasks:

Part One: the Interpretation of Dasein in terms of temporality, and the explication of time as the transcendental horizon for the question of Being.
Part Two: basic features of a phenomenological destruction
of the history of ontology, with the problematic
of Temporality as our clue.

In other words, in this introduction, Heidegger says that he
plans to write an ontological philosophy and, in conjunction
therewith, an interpretation of the history of philosophy (or at
least of certain relevant figures) which will support and confirm the frame of reference established by the philosophy. With
the possible exception of Hegel, no philosopher has spent as
much time as Heidegger developing a conception of the history
of philosophy specifically intended to justify the positions
assumed in his philosophy. Neither part, however, was actually
worked out as originally planned.

To begin at the end, Part Two falls into three divisions. The
first is supposed to deal with Kant's doctrine of schematism and
time. Here we may say that Heidegger kept the spirit, though
not the letter, of his own law. Of the three books (volumes 3,
25 and 41 of the *Gesamtausgabe*) specifically devoted to Kant, the

first (the famous *Kantbuch*) does focus on the schematism (of which Heidegger says that 'these eleven pages of the *Critique of Pure Reason* form the heart of the whole work'[2]) though it also covers the rest of the *Critique* up to the Principles (which is more specifically addressed in *What is a Thing?*, *Gesamtausgabe*, vol. 41). The second division is supposed to address 'the ontological foundation of Descartes' "cogito sum" '. Though Heidegger does engage in an extensive debate with Descartes throughout his intellectual career,[3] it would be fair to say that the substance of this division is already incorporated into a well-known section of *Being and Time* (Section B of Chapter III) and so did not need to be separately addressed. Finally, the third division is supposed to address 'Aristotle's essay on time'. Again, it would be truer to say that his discussion of Aristotle far outreaches the limits of the essay on time and, indeed, centres mostly on questions of Truth and of Praxis.[4] Although in his author's preface to the seventh German edition Heidegger tells his readers that the present edition has eliminated the designation 'First Half' since 'after a quarter of a century, the second half could no longer be added unless the first were to be presented anew', it could still be said that Heidegger did address all the historical figures anticipated in the Introduction (though not perhaps in the manner originally envisaged).

With regard to Part One a more interesting anomaly arises. Division One (the Preparatory Fundamental Analysis of Dasein) corresponds to Part One of *Being and Time* and Division Two (Dasein and Temporality) to Part Two. But Division Three, Time and Being, only appeared in a form which was surely very far removed from the form anticipated in 1927. A text 'Time and Being', which started life as a lecture given on 31 January 1962, was published under that same title in 1968. But it does not so much represent a continuation of *Being and Time* as rather a reversal, the reversal enshrined in what has become known as the 'Kehre'. The merest glance at the style and manner of the latter will suffice to confirm that between *Being and Time* and *Time and Being* not only Heidegger's thinking but his *way* of thinking had undergone a profound change. To all intents and purposes, therefore, what is known as *Being and Time* consists of the first two divisions of Part One of the programme originally drawn up at the end of the Introduction.

As already indicated, *Being and Time* falls into two parts, a part devoted to the theme of Being (Preparatory Fundamental Analysis of Dasein) and a part devoted to the theme of Time (Dasein and Temporality). Let us postpone for the moment further consideration of the internal organization of Part Two to concentrate upon that of Part One. Part One is organized around a structure articulated in the hyphenated compound expression *being-in-the-world*. The being of Dasein, as we shall see in a moment, is characterized by the fundamental structure: being-in-the-world. From this fundamental structure Heidegger is able to derive three sub-structures which furnish the topics of Chapters III, IV and VI (Chapters I and II feature as a preliminary introduction to the first part and as a presentation and justification of the basic structure: Being-in-the-world). Chapter III takes the world as its theme, more specifically, the *worldhood* of the world. Chapter IV takes as its theme the one *who* is in the world, namely Dasein, and Dasein's relations with other beings of the same kind (that is, human beings). Chapter V takes as its theme the structure of *being-in* as such.

In an absolutely characteristic move (and one which is repeated in his Kant book and elsewhere), Heidegger then seeks to a find a unitary grounding structure which will express the intrinsic interconnection of those three aspects of the compound expression being-in-the-world which have just been separately analysed. This structure Heidegger calls 'Care'. And so Chapter VI is devoted to the analysis of 'Care as the Being of Dasein'. That the one term care expresses the primordial totality of the structural whole being-in-the-world serves to confirm that the latter is indeed a unitary structure, one which unites Dasein (apprehended as a unity) with the world (apprehended as a unity).

The Introduction

Before we turn to Part One, it is essential to come to terms with the lengthy Introduction in which, effectively, Heidegger sought to lay out the basic principles of his own (preliminary) conception of phenomenology and so to win his freedom from that conception of phenomenology laid down by the founding father of twentieth-century phenomenology, Edmund Husserl.

The Introduction falls into two divisions, the first entitled 'The Necessity, Structure and Priority of the Question of

Being' – which is basically ontological in character – and the second entitled 'The Twofold Task in Working out the Question of Being'. The two tasks in question are the task of undertaking a 'phenomenological destruction of the History of Ontology' and the task of working out a phenomenological ontology. Consequently, this second division might be regarded as the phenomenological complement of the first.[5] At any rate, the core of this second division is to be found in §7, entitled 'The Phenomenological Method of Investigation'. For this is the section in which Heidegger lays out his own, quite specific, conception of phenomenology, more specifically, of the phenomenological method which he proposes to employ in his own investigation into Being and Time.

Heidegger opens his Introduction with a quotation from Plato which serves to substantiate the general thesis that the question of the meaning of being has passed into oblivion, is no longer addressed, or worse, is addressed in such a way that it conceals rather than reveals the true import of the question. In a certain rough and ready sense, Heidegger argues, we all know what being means. But we no longer know how to address the question of the meaning of Being and this largely because we have lost sight of the correct mode of access to the question. The crucial question of the *correct mode of access* then gets answered in terms of the claim that Dasein is itself that very being whose mode of being must first be investigated if there is to be anything like a satisfactory approach to the meaning of being in general, and this because it is Dasein, and Dasein alone, which is capable of raising such a question. More strongly still, it pertains to the very being of Dasein that questions of this kind, ontological questions or questions concerning first philosophy, should always be raised, even though they may not always, or may indeed never, have been adequately answered. (One is reminded here of Kant's distinction between metaphysics as natural inclination and scientific metaphysics.[6])

If Dasein is the being whose mode of being must first be investigated if we are ever to be able to arrive at an answer to the question of the meaning of being in general, if, in this sense, a Dasein's analysis has priority over any other analysis, then we need to know in what the being of Dasein itself consists. The short answer to this question is: *existence*. Dasein *is* in such a way that it has its being to be. This distinguishes the way Dasein is from the way in which anything else is. Things do exist but they do not, indeed cannot, adopt a relation to, or an attitude towards, let alone take account of, that *as* which they exist. Hence, Heidegger's introductory definition of the key term existence: 'That kind of Being towards which Dasein can comport itself in one way or another, and always does comport itself somehow, we call "existence" ' (p. 32). It is because, for Heidegger, the mode of being characteristic of Dasein is discovered to be that of existence that Heidegger may be called an existential philosopher.[7]

A little later Heidegger takes his relational concept of existence a step further. 'Dasein always understands itself in terms of its existence – in terms of a possibility of itself: to be itself or not to be itself. Dasein has either chosen these possibilities itself, or got itself into them, or grown up in them already' (p. 33). At least two things should be noted here. First, the force of the distinction between Dasein being itself or not being itself – this will later be spelt out at length in terms of the distinction between authentic and inauthentic Dasein. In so far as Dasein is itself it is *authentic*, in so far as it fails to be itself, it is *inauthentic*. Rather than going into the complications that arise in relation to the latter distinction let us turn instead to the second part of the citation, which falls into three parts. Those possibilities which define Dasein's existence may be possibilities which Dasein has explicitly chosen for itself. This takes existence in the direction of authenticity, not necessarily or inevitably, but at least in principle. If the possibilities determinative of one's own existence are to be authentic possibilities one must, at the very least, have chosen them for oneself. But one may have simply got oneself into them. This is indicative of the kind of thoughtlessness which leads people to adopt one course of life rather than another for relatively incidental reasons, that is, reasons only indirectly, if at all, connected with the person that, in fact, they are. Worse still, Dasein may simply have grown up in such possibilities already. Here Dasein simply takes over, unthinkingly, whatever possibilities are handed down to it, for example, by its parents ('like father, like son').

Immediately succeeding the above citation, Heidegger advances to a distinction which is of the first importance for an understanding of the existential implications of his first philosophy. What kind of self-understanding may arise will, in each instance, be dependent upon the course of life of the being whose existence is in question. But existential investigations of this kind are not really existen*tial* investigations. They are existen*tiel* investigations. An existential investigation, properly so called, is concerned with a laying out of the general structures which underlie, and so ultimately account for, existence as such, quite irrespective of the peculiar form which it might assume under this or that set of particular circumstances. What may happen to me in the course of my life and what kind of self-understanding may arise therefrom is one (existentiel) matter. An existential analysis of those general structures which characterize human existence as such and which, in consequence, are already presupposed by any investigation of the former kind is another, and more genuinely philosophical, matter altogether.

The long answer to the question of the meaning of existence will assume the form of a careful consideration of so-called 'existentialia'. These existentialia, which are four in number and which will be examined later under the several heads of Understanding, State-of-mind, Falling and Discourse, represent sub-structures whose individual elucidation and systematic interconnection will make up the topic of an existential investigation.

More important for the time being is a further distinction which goes hand in hand with the existentiel–existential distinction and which, so to speak, forms the broader horizon within which the latter takes up residence. This broader distinction is the distinction between an ontic and an ontological level of analysis. The simplest way to come to terms with what Heidegger might have meant by an ontical investigation is with reference to Husserl's concept of regional ontology. As we saw earlier, regional ontology means, for Husserl, the phenomenological investigation of regions of being already marked out, by science and common sense, in their distinction and independence each from the other. Thus the three sciences physics, chemistry and biology mark out three regions of being which can then be subject to phenomenological investigation (Husserl in fact only concerns himself with *Materie*, the region presupposed by physics, and *Leib*, the region presupposed by biology). Similarly, the common-sense distinction between the real and the imaginary can serve as the basis for a corresponding phenomenological investigation into real and imaginary objects. For Heidegger, regional ontology of this kind is inadequately fundamental. For it fails to concern itself with the Being of those very beings whose mode of being is, in a sense, already taken for granted by the very assumption of the regional demarcations in question. Moreover, the fact that there are indefinitely many such regions attests to the 'superficiality' of the phenomenological investigation in question since it never addresses the question of the *unitary* being of all these various regions, that in virtue of which they may all be said to belong to, or participate in, Being.

But perhaps the best way to bring out the distinction in question is with reference to one of the very few passages in which Heidegger takes up his distance with regard to Husserl by giving a specifically Husserlian term (the reduction) an entirely new meaning. In §5 of *The Basic Problems of Phenomenology*, an early text originally delivered as lectures given at Marburg in the summer of 1927, Heidegger presents his movement back to an understanding of the being of beings as the inverse of that effected by Husserl's reduction.[8] In place of the Husserlian procedure which moves from the world of the natural attitude *up to* a higher, transcendental plane with a view to bringing to light the transcendental structures constitutive of the objectivity of the entities encountered in the natural attitude, we find an alternative procedure which moves from the ontic level *down to* a deeper, ontological plane with a view to bringing to light the ontological structures constitutive of the being of the entities in question. The *fundamentality* of Husserl's phenomenological analyses lies in the fact that it traces the meaning of different regions of being back to those structures of transcendental consciousness in and through which the regions in question get constituted with the objectivity which belongs to them. The *profundity* of Heidegger's phenomenological analyses lies in the fact that he traces the taken for granted meaning which attaches to the being of the various entities encountered in day to day life back to that unitary structure of Being from which they all originally emerged.

We are now in a position to understand the paragraph (p. 34) in which Heidegger discusses the various kinds of priority which pertain to his existential analytic of Dasein. The first priority is ontical – because Dasein is one of those beings which does, as a matter of fact, exist and perhaps also because, as a matter of fact, Dasein is given to raising a question with regard to the meaning of existence. The second priority is ontological – because the being of Dasein can only be understood as a function of its 'having its being to be', that is, existence. The third priority is ontico-ontological – because it is only on the basis of an understanding of its own being that Dasein can come to an understanding of beings whose mode of being is *not* that of Dasein itself.

It only remains to conclude our presentation of the first division of Heidegger's Introduction with a further complication. In addition to the distinction between the ontical and the ontological Heidegger introduces a further distinction between the ontological and the pre-ontological. Heidegger introduces this further distinction in a somewhat murky passage: 'So whenever an ontology takes for its theme entities whose character of Being is other than that of Dasein, it has its own foundation and motivation in Dasein's own ontical structure, in which a pre-ontological understanding of Being is comprised as a definite characteristic' (p. 33). To be human is, in some sense, already to understand what is meant by being – by virtue of simply existing. This pre-ontological understanding is, by and large, wholly inadequate and indeed, for the most part, gets expressed in judgments which conceal rather than reveal the meaning of what is in question (for reasons which we shall take account of later). However, such a pre-ontological understanding can serve as a starting point (and we have to start somewhere) for a deeper, ontological investigation and indeed, without such a starting point, ontology would not know where to begin. Thus ontology, of the Heideggerian variety, can be seen as the explication (the explicit working out) of what is already, and from the first, implicit, namely a pre-ontological understanding of being.

As an explication of what has already, and from the first, been implicitly understood, an ontological investigation might seem to, and indeed in a certain sense does, move in a circle. The question is whether this circle is a vicious circle, one which therefore vitiates the validity of the analysis in question. Surely, we have already presupposed what we are seeking to prove if our proof only enables us to arrive at an understanding which has already been assumed as the very condition without which the investigation could not get started? Heidegger's answer does more than merely dismiss such a possible objection to his procedure. Rather it serves to define the very nature of the procedure in question. To do ontology is precisely to make explicit an understanding which was implicit, and only implicit, from the very start. Self-understanding of a certain naive kind is definitive of the kind of beings which we are. But, for the most part, we are so close to that very being which we are that our (implicit) self-understanding never gets a chance to develop into an explicit understanding of self, least of all an explicit understanding of the basic structures constitutive of the being of any and every self, inasmuch as it is a self. Worse, in the course of obtaining that distance from ourselves which will make something like a self-understanding possible, we are, in the first instance, driven even further away from anything like an authentic self-understanding. For what we tend to do is understand ourselves in terms of entities whose mode of being is not that of a self, but, rather, that of a thing. Thus it is that we come to understand ourselves as objects, or quasi-objects, something thing-like. And so the very first task of a properly ontological investigation of the self is to de-construct this misconstruction as a necessary preliminary to the reconstruction of a more authentic understanding of self, one which takes up a distance only in order to be able to understand the proximity of the relation of the self to itself. The understanding of that which is nearest (in the order of being) requires the most laborious detour and is, in this sense, farthest (in the order of analysis). That which is farthest from us, on the other hand, things or, more generally, whatever does not have the mode of being of a self, is what it is easiest for us to understand. It is for this reason that ontology is nothing but the making explicit of a pre-ontological understanding of being and of the self.

Thus an ontological investigation necessarily moves in a circle. And what is important is therefore not to try to get out of the circle but to get into it and, one might add, go round it in the right away. 'What is decisive is not to get out of the circle but to come into it in the right way' (p. 195). Indeed, so fundamental did the circularity of an ontological investigation

become for Heidegger that, with reference to the methodological procedure which he incorporated into his analyses (the
procedure of interpretation), he called it the 'hermeneutical
circle'. Rather than anticipating this issue of understanding as
interpretation, let us turn instead to the second division of the
Introduction, that devoted to the twofold task.

Having already alluded to the task of destroying the history
of ontology in the context of Heidegger's projected Part Two of
the overall programme (§8), we shall spend no more time on §6
and move straight on to §7, the critical section in which
Heidegger outlines his own conception of phenomenology.
Aside from a few introductory paragraphs, it falls into three
distinct parts, following the clue offered by the term 'phenomenology'. Phenomenology means an investigation of the 'logos'
of the 'phenomenon'. Hence Section A is devoted to the
Concept of the Phenomenon, Section B to the Concept of the
Logos, while Section C brings the two together in the Preliminary Conception of Phenomenology.

Critical to Heidegger's strategy in Section A is his specification, on the one hand, of an absolutely fundamental (Greek)
concept of the phenomenon – which he does not hesitate to
spell out in Greek: *phaenomen* – and, on the other, his derivation
therefrom of three (German) concepts of appearance or the
appearing: *Schein, Erscheinung* and *bloße Erscheinung*. The fundamental (Greek) concept of the phenomenon signifies: *'that
which shows itself in itself*, the manifest' (p. 51). This first positive
and primordial concept of the phenomenon as the manifest is
structurally connected with a second sense of phenomenon
which readily translates over into the German concept *Schein*.
For an entity can always show itself as something which in
itself it is *not*. This privative sense of the manifest is picked up in
the German concept *Schein*, which is rather poorly translated by
the English term 'semblance'. 'This kind of showing-itself is
what we call "seeming" ' (*Scheinen*). But even if something only
seems to be what it is (where by this 'seeming' it is implied that
it really is not as it seems), such a seeming appearance still
requires a manifestation of some kind.

Once Heidegger has marked out the privative concept of
Schein, he is able to obtain therefrom two derivative concepts,
based upon the latter, which permit him to enter into a critical
discussion of the concept of the phenomenon as it has entered

into the German phenomenological tradition from Leibniz, through Kant and Hegel, to Husserl. The derivation of *Erscheinung* from *Schein* is already indicated by the etymology of the terms in question. But Heidegger must also have had Hegel's *Logic* in mind here. For in the *Logic*, the move from a doctrine of being to a doctrine of the essence moves by way of a shift from the concept of *Schein* to that of *Erscheinung*. *Erscheinung* signifies the appearance of something which does not itself make its appearance but, so to speak, appears by way of its representative. Thus, in Locke's substance ontology, sensible ideas are presented as the appearances of a substance which, as an unknowable substratum, does not itself make its appearance. Heidegger uses the more commonplace model of the 'symptoms of a disease' to make his point. Symptoms are not themselves the disease; they are that by means of which the disease announces itself.

The final derivation of *bloße Erscheinung* or mere appearance is carried through with reference to Kant and with reference to a distinction between that which *does not*, as a matter of fact, show itself and that which *cannot* show itself. The Kantian thing-in-itself is an entity which not merely *does* not show itself; it is not the kind of thing which *could* ever show itself since it is located in an intelligible (noumenal) realm over and beyond that (the phenomenal) of sensible appearance.

The point of these derivations is to indicate where 'phenomenological' philosophy went wrong in the past. By relying upon the epistemological concept of *Erscheinung* (or even worse *bloße Erscheinung*) phenomenological philosophy failed to come to terms with the primordial root concept of *Schein* (itself intimately interconnected with that of the phenomenon). To be sure, the privative aspect of *Schein* must have deterred philosophers in the past. But not merely does all appearing have to be, in the final analysis, referred back to a seeming which may not present the entity in question as it really is. This immediate apprehension of the thing just as it gives itself without any critical queries as to whether it might appear differently to others or on other occasions is Heidegger's way of reclaiming for himself (and against Husserl) the famous Husserlian slogan: 'To the Things Themselves!' More important still, as we shall see later, the ambivalence inherent in the more primordial concept of *Schein* gets enshrined in a methodological principle which might be expressed as the necessarily complementary character of revealing and concealing, covering over and uncovering, closing off and dis-closing.

The strategy of Section B is quite similar to that of Section A. Here too Heidegger is concerned to bring out the derivative character of what is ordinarily meant by the *logos* with a view to getting back to the more primordial root meaning. Once the *logos* is taken to mean discourse and, still worse, once discourse is taken to mean what gets expressed and communicated in judgments of the subject–predicate form, all is lost. More fundamentally, the *logos* means making manifest what one is talking about, either for oneself or for those with whom one wishes to communicate, and this 'making manifest' occurs before anything gets said and as the very condition without which it could not be said. In this sense, the *logos* means the intelligibility of what manifests itself in so far as this intelligibility makes it possible to express what has been made manifest. Heidegger quite deliberately adopts the (Husserlian) language of 'seeing' to express the intelligibility of what manifests itself. 'The λογος lets something be seen (φαινεσθαι), namely, what the discourse is about;' Discourse 'lets something be seen' ἀπο . . .: that is, it lets us see something from the very thing which the discourse is about' (p. 56). In this sense 'letting be seen' comes before speaking and features as the condition of the latter. Because the *logos* lets something be seen in its intrinsic intelligibility and in such a way that what is seen can be pointed out and so expressed in discourse, the *logos* possesses the structural form of a synthesis. Here again Heidegger chooses to go back to the Greek term in order precisely to refuse that concept of synthesis which had held sway in German phenomenology hitherto – the binding and linking together of representations. Rather, for him synthesis has the signification of letting something be seen *as* something, where by this little word 'as' Heidegger means to bring out (as we shall see later) the interpretive element in any and every apprehension of something.

Heidegger ends this section with a brief anticipation of his later theory of truth. If the *logos* is to be taken as the primordial locus of truth then the truth cannot mean adequation, or agreement, or correspondence (of a judgment with a state of affairs). This substitution of a derivative concept of the *logos*, as

inscribed in judgment, goes along, of course, with the derivative concept of the phenomenon as appearance. In so far as
they both go together, they must both be discarded together.
For truth, as located in the *logos*, means the bringing of
something out of that hiddenness in which it cannot be seen
and into the light of intelligibility. But any such uncovering, in
one sense, is also and equivalently a covering over, in another.
'*Wieviel Schein jedoch, soviel "Sein"*.' This nice play on words brings
out the sense in which, for Heidegger, there is only as much ✓
being as there is seeming. And, one might add, where there is
seeming there is also non-being. Hence, from the above,
Heidegger will draw the epistemologically alarming conclusion
that being in the truth is equivalently being in the untruth.

The preceding analysis leads Heidegger straight on to a
conclusion which follows directly from the way he has chosen
to define the two concepts of the 'phenomenon' and the 'logos'.
'Thus "phenomenology" means ἀποφαινεσθαι τα φαινομενα – to
let that which shows itself be seen from itself in the very way in
which it shows itself from itself' (p. 58). The self-showing
proceeds, as it were, from Being, the seeing from Dasein. But
Being cannot *show itself* in the absence of a being to which it can
make itself known. And Dasein cannot *see* what shows itself
save in so far as Being lets itself be seen. Thus the 'self-
showing' (manifestation) and the 'letting be seen'
(intelligibility) belong together, thereby making up the integral
unity of thinking and being expressed in the original Greek
concept of the *logos*.

By the same token, this conjuncture of showing and seeing
also points to the juncture of phenomenology and ontology.
'Only as phenomenology, is ontology possible' (p. 60), – to
which Heidegger might have added: and only as ontology, is
phenomenology possible. For phenomenology is a methodological concept. It deals with the 'how' of what is to be analysed.
But phenomenology can only provide a correct 'way of access' if
that to which such access is sought exists. On the other hand,
Being (the existing) can only be seen in so far as it shows itself.
But the self-manifestation of Being would be meaningless were
it not for the fact that that very being for which Being is an
issue is itself capable of a seeing which renders intelligible the
self-manifestation of Being.

Division One: Preparatory Fundamental Analysis of Dasein

The first division opens with a specification of two essential characteristics of Dasein and a decision with regard to the method to be adopted with a view to undertaking an analytic of Dasein.

1 *The 'essence' of Dasein lies in its existence.*

This specification which comes near the beginning of §9 affirms, strictly speaking, not the priority of existence over essence (as Heidegger will himself suggest a few lines later when he complains about the priority accorded to 'existentia' over essentia⁹) but the equi-primordiality or the equivalence of the two. The essence of Dasein consists in its existence because Dasein does not simply exist but has its being to be. This is important in view of the fact that later, in 'Existentialism and Humanism', Sartre will make of the priority of existence over essence a fashionable slogan and so prompt Heidegger in his 'Letter on Humanism' to criticize Sartre for wrongly interpreting *Being and Time* as advocating the priority of existence over essence.[10]

2 *That Being which is an* issue *for this entity in its very Being, is in each case mine.*

Here we find Heidegger undertaking a delicate manoeuvre the aim of which is to avoid ascribing 'I'hood to Dasein while still recognizing its being as a self. I cannot remain indifferent or impartial with regard to that being as which I am but not because I am an 'I' but because this being is *mine*, my own. The use made here of the possessive form of the first person pronoun is intended specifically to accomplish this task. Having my being to be means having to take up an attitude towards that very being which is my own – which need not, however, be an authentic attitude. For, just because Dasein's being is an issue for it, Dasein can either seek to come to terms with its self or try to avoid coming to terms with its self, which latter attitude only means that it *is itself* inauthentically rather than authentically.

But how is one to go about investigating the being of Dasein? Can one plunge straight into that ontological analysis which is the aim of this first part? Or is it not rather the case that the very closeness of Dasein to itself stands in the way of any such direct access to the being of Dasein? If, as Heidegger claims, 'that which is ontically closest and well known, is ontologically the farthest and not known at all' (p. 69), then a detour will be necessary if the required ontological analysis is to be put into effect, a detour which will proceed from what is *familiar* and therefore only *superficially* understood to that which is unfamiliar and which therefore requires to be understood in depth. In other words, the starting point for the analytic of Dasein will be average everydayness – Dasein as it is manifests itself on a day-to-day basis in that taken-for-granted manner which leads us to believe, naively, that we all know who we are. This starting point on the ontic plane, however, will only be the preliminary to a move back to the ontological plane, the only plane upon which a genuinely philosophical understanding of Dasein will become possible. From the very beginning therefore Heidegger announces his intention to adopt an analytical strategy which can be spelt out in three steps. First, a place-ment of the analysis upon the ontic plane, the plane upon which the 'facts of the matter', the phenomena in question, manifest themselves in the most seemingly evident and incontrovertible manner. This first step, however, will only prove to be the preliminary to a regressive move, a move back to a more fundamental, ontological level of analysis. Finally, this ontological regression will in turn make it possible to show how ontic structures are grounded in ontological structures and so to effect a return to that from which the analysis took its start.

In passing, it is worth noting that Heidegger takes time out (§§10–11) to refuse any conception of a Dasein's analysis which would rely upon the findings of anthropology, psychology or biology or which would seek to support its conclusions with evidence drawn from primitive Dasein (presumably also from children). In my view, it is one of the limitations of *Being and Time* that it specifically disqualifies any attempt to support the philosophical investigation of human reality with data or theor-ies drawn from other branches of the human sciences. This did not deter philosophers, like Merleau-Ponty and Sartre, theo-logians like Bultmann and Tillich, psychologists like Medard Boss or Binswanger, and so on, from seeking to make the very connections Heidegger refused.

We are now ready to undertake the analysis in question. The analysis of Dasein is conducted in the context of a threefold differentiation of the compound expression being-in-the-world into its constitutive parts, thereby yielding an investigation which focuses upon the World, upon Dasein and upon the relation of Being-in – as has already been pointed out.

Our ordinary, familiar way of thinking about the world (as the place in which we live and move and have our being) is to think it as a totality of objects which are simply there, given in advance, existing independently of the self, with whatever properties the self may discover them to possess and so on and so forth. Even if the world is envisaged not as a 'common' objective world but as 'my' world, the only world which exists as a subjective correlate of my consciousness (thereby unleashing the philosophically unanswerable question how I am to justify the move from the world, as it exists for me, to the world as it exists in itself), still, according to Heidegger, we have not yet managed to hit upon a properly *ontological* concept of the world – hence the distinction between the ontic concept of 'world' and the more properly ontological conception of the 'worldhood of the world', the conception which guides the whole of the third chapter.

Ontically speaking, the world signifies the totality of objects which are simply assumed to exist and which, in their manifold interrelations, furnish a spatial framework with reference to which I can determine where in the world I am. Even if I shift my ground from a realist to an idealist position and think of the world as a correlate of consciousness (Husserl) or think of space as a form in the mind (Kant), I still have not yet begun to come to terms with the worldhood of the world. Whereas for Kant, or even for Husserl, the 'world' is in some sense 'in me', for Heidegger, it is Dasein which is 'in' the world. But even though Dasein is 'in' the world, 'ontologically, "world" is not a way of characterizing those entities which Dasein essentially is *not*; it is rather a characteristic of Dasein itself' (p. 68).

In order to bring out the distinctive sense of his own concept of 'world' or of the 'worldhood of the world', Heidegger now resorts to a distinction between two ways of being of entities encountered in the world. The first he calls the present-at-hand and the second, the ready-to-hand.[11]

Entities encountered in the world as present-at-hand are what we would ordinarily call 'objects'. Heidegger strenuously resists such a term as 'object', since it drags in with it its correlate 'subject', which implies a way of understanding Dasein (qua subject) which it is Heidegger's whole intention to avoid. Such entities are ordinarily taken to be what manifests itself, directly and immediately, in the world. But the present-at-hand way of envisaging what manifests itself is in fact the product of a complex *theoretical* construction whose philosophical antecedents can be traced back to Descartes. According to Heidegger, entities simply are not there, first and foremost, for theoretical inspection and examination. Rather, we do things with them, pick them up, discard them, manipulate them, put them to use.

This is the point at which Heidegger's critical reversal of the respective role of theory and praxis takes hold. Historically, philosophers have often thought of *praxis* as the application of a knowledge first developed in the course of a theoretical inspection and examination of things (and it is this concept of *praxis* which is fundamental to that activity which goes by the name of technology, a *praxis* which embodies the theoretical discoveries made by science). In fact, the very reverse is found to be the case. *Praxis* necessarily precedes, and provides the motive for, any merely theoretical enquiry into the being of entities. Here we find Heidegger appealing to Aristotle, whom he acknowledges as one of the first to recognize, and to explicitly articulate in concepts, the primacy of *praxis* over *theoria*.[12]

In order to carry through his analysis of the priority of the 'practical' ready-to-hand way of dealing with things over the 'theoretical' present-at-hand way of envisaging things, Heidegger makes use of a concept 'Zeug' for which, again, there is no direct English equivalent. Though Macquarrie usually translates this term as 'equipment', he admits that it also has the connotations of tool or instrument. Much more important than the term itself is the referential assignment which Heidegger locates in the term. Equipment exists 'in order to' (*um-zu*). I pick up a pen 'in order to' write a letter. Equally, the notepaper exists 'in order to' be written on, the envelope to contain the completed letter, the stamp to frank the letter, the letter box to receive the franked letter, the postal service to deliver the letter and so on. In other words, the referential assignment 'in-order-to' means that one thing is referred to another which in turn refers to others and so on, so that, strictly speaking, there is no such thing as *a* piece of equipment. Rather, any given piece of equipment implies a reference to an equipmental totality and these manifold assignments *vis-à-vis* an equipmental totality require a way of envisaging entities ready-to-hand which permits them to be discovered in their belonging together in one unitary frame of reference. This way of envisaging the ready-to-hand, Heidegger calls circumspection (*Umsicht*).

And now we have all the necessary ingredients to enable us to understand the world in its genuinely ontological character as the worldhood of the world. In so far as the ready-to-hand is there to be used, it brings with it an involvement character. And in so far as the involvement with any given piece of equipment leads to a *circumspection* which implies a manifold of references, it brings to light the *surrounding* character of the world (*Um-welt*). The world is that in which Dasein gets itself involved and which surrounds Dasein on every side. But since involvement and circumspection only arise on account of Dasein's dealing with things, 'world', in the ontological sense of the 'worldhood of the world', turns out to be a characteristic of Dasein. The world is not there for Dasein to exist *in*; rather, the world *is* only because Dasein *exists*.

But if the world is there for Dasein, first and foremost, as an environmental totality how is it that the theoretical attitude ever comes to take hold and, moreover, to so transform our very conception of entities encountered within the world that we come to think of them as objects? This is the point at which the regressive move back from the ontic to the ontological plane turns around into an investigation into the derivation of the secondary from the primary. It is absolutely characteristic of Heidegger's grounding tactic at this point that it should proceed by way of a disclosure of 'deficient' (that is, negative) characteristics. If the ready-to-hand is the primary and the fundamental attitude then the present-at-hand can only come into being by way of a loss or a deprivation, not by way of a gain or a supplementation.

In §16, Heidegger undertakes this derivation in terms of three deficient characteristics, 'conspicuousness' (*Auffälligkeit*), 'obtrusiveness' (*Aufdringlichkeit*) and 'obstinacy' (*Aufsässigkeit*). As is so often the case, the English fails to capture the etymological interconnection of the three German concepts (particularly the 'Auf' which introduces them all).[13] However, it is not difficult to figure out what is meant. A piece of equipment turns out to be unusable. Had we simply taken hold of it with a view to using it, we would hardly have noticed it as such. Our attention would have been directed not at the instrument itself but at the *work* which the instrument was intended to perform. Now, however, and precisely because it *cannot* be used for the purpose intended, the instrument itself becomes *conspicuous* in its very *unusability*.

Moreover, in our concernful dealings we also 'find' things which are missing, things which, so far from being ready-to-hand, are precisely *not* ready-to-hand. Had these things been there, readily available for the uses to which we intended to put them, we would hardly have noticed them. Now, however, we are obliged to search around to see if we can find them. This searching is guided by a conception of what it is we are looking for. And this sought for thing is all the more obtrusive for being absent rather than present. Precisely because it itself is *absent*, the presence of the thing in question now becomes *obtrusive*.

Finally, our ability to make use of equipment ready-to-hand may be impeded by something else which, as it were, stands in the way. Had the thing in question *not* stood in the way, it would hardly have been noticed. But because it stands in the way of our using the piece of equipment in the manner intended, we are obliged to take note of it. Thus the presence of what stands in the way becomes *obtrusive* by virtue of the fact that it *obstructs* our instrumental dealings.

But it is not just *what* has become conspicuous, obtrusive and obstructive which now presents itself to us; more, the very referential assignment which, if it could have been readily assumed would have remained hidden from view, now also gets disclosed. The 'in-order-to' which would ordinarily have simply regulated our manipulative activity now gets converted into an explicit theoretical reference, the reference of Dasein to things and things to the world. Indeed, it now becomes clear that the worldhood of the world consists in just such a system of referential assignments. More specifically, certain pieces of equipment can be seen to exist precisely in order to carry out this referring function. Such pieces of equipment are called 'signs'. Thus the preceding (§16) analysis of the derivation of the present-at-hand from the ready-to-hand leads naturally on (§17) to an investigation of the being of references and signs, which in turn leads on to an investigation of involvement and significance (§18).

Sections 17 and 18 should be read together since they both connect the analysis of the ready-to-hand with signification in the most general sense. But before we get to the details of the analysis, two preliminary considerations need to be borne in mind. The aim of these sections is to refuse any understanding of Dasein (and of the world in which it finds itself), which takes as its starting point either things or relations and then tries to understand what Heidegger takes to be more primordial, namely equipment and reference, through a strategy of supplementation. An instrument is not to be regarded as a thing present-at-hand, first and foremost, and which, on this basis, can *then* be used in various ways, its use value, so to speak, entering in as a supplementary property to be added to those which make up its being as a thing.

By the same token, Dasein's relation to the world is not to be thought of, first and foremost, as a 'formal' relation between one thing (Dasein) and another (that with which Dasein concerns itself). Nor is the world in which it finds itself to be thought of as a 'system of such formal relations' – as Leibniz or Kant had supposed. Rather, it is Dasein's own involvement in a world which first makes reference and assignment possible. Through such concrete assignments (which include and are founded in what might be called a self-assignment), the sign comes into being, and through the sign, the linguistic symbol. In turn, the coming into being of the linguistic symbol has the effect of transforming our understanding of being-in-the-world into a system of relations, to the point that it is no longer possible to see the world as that in which Dasein has its being. Thus although Heidegger's starting point here is reminiscent of the starting point of Husserl's *Logical Researches*, with its distinction, within signs, between indications (*Anzeichen*) and expressions (*Ausdruck*), his own analysis, unlike Husserl's, does not go very far in the direction of a comprehension of the phenomenon of language. Signification, for Heidegger, is something more primordial (and more general) than language – indeed, so much so that if one takes one's start in language one loses the meaning of signification in so far as it is the latter which brings out the ontological character of being-in-the-world.

In short, the movement of these two sections proceeds from equipment to things, from references to relations, from signification to signs, from world to language, in a word, from the ontological to the ontic. And the failure to understand the ontological structure of Dasein and of Dasein's being-in-the-world is attributed to the very attempt to proceed in the reverse direction and so to conceive of the more primordial in terms of the derivative – with, of course, the necessary supplementary qualifications.

The topic of §17 is reference and signs. Heidegger begins by identifying signs as pieces of equipment which, as such, already possess the structure of assignment (the 'in-order-to'). But whereas equipment, in the more basic sense of something which is there to be used, is not so constituted that its referential assignment is apparent, a sign is so constituted that this reference *does* become explicit and indeed in a threefold way. First, the 'in-order-to' of serviceability becomes a 'towards-which'. Heidegger takes the example of a car indicator (going back to the days when cars were fitted not with indicator lights but with pointers). The pointer is a piece of equipment which the driver makes use of. But the driver does not make use of it in any obvious or direct way, that is, take hold of it, apply it, use it to do something with. Rather, when the driver causes the indicator to stand out he intends thereby to let the other drivers on that road know of his intention to turn (to the right). But second, this reference cannot be isolated from the context in which it occurs. In other words, a sign belongs to a totality of equipment and to a context of referential assignments. The indicator is part of the driver's car which is itself a piece of equipment. It points in the direction of a road (on the right) which is there to be driven along. It warns other drivers of the intention to turn and these other drivers are themselves driving cars, and so on. And third, the sign is not just ready-to-hand with other equipment. Rather, through the system of references that are thereby brought to light, the environment is itself brought to light as just such a system of references.

References connect, but the connections in question have nothing to do with causal determination. The turning is not something which is causally determined by the rising of the indicator. The indicator does not mean a right turn as clouds may mean rain. Rather, the indicator is an advance warning signal making it possible for the other drivers to make whatever adjustments are necessary. 'Making whatever adjustments are necessary' means taking the whole environmental context into consideration, the road into which the driver is expected to turn, the distance between one's own car and that of the indicating driver, the relative speeds of the vehicles in question, the laws of the road, and so on. In short, referential assignments of this kind (embodied in signs like an indicator) bring out the environmental orientation of equipment ready-to-hand and do so explicitly, that is, in such a way that the referential assignments implicit in equipment get seen as such.

The 'abstract' character of referential (as opposed to equipmental) assignment prepares the way for an investigation of signification. But it is absolutely typical of Heidegger's ontological strategy in §18 that he does not take his analysis in the direction of an investigation into meaning, let alone language (even though the introduction of the loaded term 'understanding' already points the way to Heidegger's own conception of meaning as interpretation). Rather, he uses the disclosure of the structure of significance (in the 'abstract') to reinforce and confirm the 'involvement-character' of being-in-the-world. More particularly, he now brings together a number of *distinct* referential assignments. The 'towards-which' or 'for-which' (the explicit thematization of the 'in-order-to') is brought into relation with the 'with-which' (the instrument itself) and the 'in-which' (the world). When Dasein uses equipment in such a way that it refers, the equipment is itself that 'with which' such a referring gets done and the world is the context 'in which' such a referring takes place.

Most important of all, however, these references do not constitute an endless and 'outward' oriented series – the hammer, in order to hit the nail, in order to nail the plank, in order to construct the wall, in order to build the house. As long as the system of references proceeds 'outwards', from Dasein to entities whose mode of being is not that of Dasein (even when these entities are other human beings with whose reactions Dasein must reckon), the system must be endless and, as such, cannot, properly speaking, constitute a system. The ultimate 'towards-which' is, however, a 'for-the-sake-of-which' which brings the entire system of references to an end. For the house is built *for the sake of* that very Dasein who employs the hammer to hit the nail, to fix the plank etc. Inasmuch as the series of references 'outward' ultimately refers back 'inward' to Dasein itself as that very being whose being is in question in all such referential assignments, the system is, as it were, 'closed', or brought to a close.

'Involvement' is the word Heidegger employs to characterize the unity of all these referential assignments (implicit in the ready-to-hand way of dealing with things) in so far as this unity is made possible by an ultimate reference back to that *for the sake of which* the entire system of references arises in the first place.

The best way to bring out the fundamental character of involvement and the way in which it confirms the ontological significance of being-in-the-world is with reference to three concepts or conceptions of the 'world'. The first, and merely ontic, conception of the world is that of an aggregate of things present-at-hand. The second and, one might say, ontico-ontological conception of the world is that of an environmental context of references which is brought to light through a consideration of that specific equipment which has the character of a sign. The third, and properly ontological, conception of the 'worldhood of the world' emerges as that underlying structure which renders intelligible the very possibility of the latter and which can itself only be brought to light in so far as the referential character of assignment has become conspicuous through the investigation of signs and signification in general.

In order to bring out the novelty of his own conception of the worldhood of the world, Heidegger goes on in §19 to present his own conception in explicit opposition to that of Descartes, the founder of the present-at-hand way of envisaging both Dasein and Dasein's being in the world. Implicit in this critique is a critique of Husserl's transcendental phenomenology and its continuing allegiance to the Cartesian world view. In so far as Descartes failed to account for the being of the *cogito* (that very being which is implied in the *sum*), the strictly epistemological concerns of indubitability and cognitive assurance take the place of a more properly ontological investigation. And this 'falsification' is heightened by Husserl's own absolutization of the *cogito*. If Descartes unthinkingly assumes the substantial being of the *cogito*, Husserl goes further still by appealing to an absoluteness for which there can be no warrant. By misunderstanding the being of human being in terms of its being a thinking being (*res cogitans*) and then trying to underpin the latter either with reference to an outmoded concept of substance or by way of an unjustifiable appeal to the absolute, both Descartes and Husserl obscured the meaning of the being of Dasein and so the meaning of being in general in so far as the latter is only intelligible out of, and on the basis of, a preliminary understanding of that being for which alone the meaning of being in general can be an issue.[14]

Sections 22–4 resume Heidegger's own investigations into the being of the world or rather bring these investigations to a close with an examination of the *spatiality* that belongs to being-in-the-world. Once again Heidegger employs his familiar two-fold grounding strategy. He begins with a consideration of our ordinary taken-for-granted way of envisaging the spatiality of the world (§22) but only in order to press the analysis back into a more primordial dimension, where the properly ontological structures can first be brought to light (§23). Once these properly ontological structures have been brought to light, it then becomes possible to show how the present-at-hand (objective) way of envisaging space arises (§24) through *deficient characteristics*. Inasmuch as the ontic plane arises twice (once at the beginning and once at the end of the analysis) it could be said that Heidegger considers separately two components (science and common sense) which, in Husserl's analyses, are summarily clumped together in the notion of the 'natural attitude'. For if common sense (that with which we are familiar in ordinary day-to-day living) can be said to furnish the point of departure for a regressive movement back to the ground, science constitutes the end point of a complementary progressive movement.

The spatiality of being-in-the-world is brought out with reference to two structures which it is almost impossible to translate effectively. Broken up etymologically into its constituents, *Ent-fernung* means, literally, abolishing (Ent) the distance (fern), or bringing the distance to a close. It is quite typical of Heidegger's procedure that a positive structure (approaching something) should be rendered by a double negative (removing the distance). Though difficult to translate, the concept is easy to understand. Whenever Dasein seeks to make use of something (in the manner characteristic of the ready-to-hand), it has first to bring that thing to hand. Bringing to hand means going over from where I am now to where I see the thing in question to be. In so doing, I bring to light the spatiality of the world in which both I myself and the thing in question are to be found. Macquarrie translates *Entfernung* as de-severance or de-severing. In my own ontology I have used the term 'ap-proximation' in order to get nearer to familiar English. But there is no doubt that a double negative serves the purpose better than any positive term – even though the end result is a word which means almost the opposite of the ordinary German term *Entfernung* (roughly, distance). The important point to note is that, primordially, distances are never posited as simple relations (either as concrete relations between two things or between myself and something or as an abstract system of relations independent of anything which might occupy a position in such a system). Distances are measured by my dealings with things whose closeness or remoteness is in turn the index of their availability. Thus closeness has priority over remoteness. Since my basic intention is to 'make use of', distance has to be transformed into closeness by a closing of the distance – though, of course, flight from something feared would also lead to a corresponding attempt to increase the distance.

Just as important as the axial relation 'to' and 'from' is another relation to which Heidegger gives the name '*Ausrichtung*'. The thing which I wish to bring close always stands in a certain orientation *vis-à-vis* myself and the direction in which I myself might be going or might be facing. It is to my left or to my right, before me or behind me, above me or below me. The English term 'directionality' captures quite adequately this environmental characteristic. De-severance and directionality are then the two structures in terms of which Heidegger brings out his novel conception of primordial spatiality. The originality of Heidegger's conception of space is perhaps best brought out in a quote in which a critique of traditional conceptions is implied. 'Space is not to be found in the subject nor does the subject observe the world "as if" that world were in a space; but the "subject" (Dasein), if well understood ontologically, is spatial' (p. 146).

To put it crudely, directionality gives me two dimensions while de-severance gives me the so-called third, or depth, dimension. The crudity of these ways of talking about the three dimensions of space becomes obvious when we recognize, first, that they abstract from my being 'in' the world, from my involvement with things, and second, that they abstract from the environmental character of the world, its standing around the self. However, to press such crude descriptions to their logical conclusion, we might say that, in his later thinking, Heidegger sought to think the fourth dimension, the unification of time and space in a structure he called Zeit–Raum (time–space), though it should also be said that his presentation of time–space has little to do with the unification of space and time (space–time) in relativity physics or quantum mechanics.[15]

The term Heidegger introduces to characterize the way in which space manifests itself originally is 'region'. 'This "whither", which makes it possible for equipment to belong somewhere, and which we circumspectively keep in view ahead of us in our concernful dealings, we call the "region" ' (p. 136). I would like to recommend a term to bring out the difference between this primordial spatiality and objective space: the term 'place'. Along lines which correspond to Heidegger's analysis of the transformation of the ready-to-hand into the present-at-hand, we may therefore ask: how is it that an original spatiality of *place* gets transformed into the derivative concept of *space*? Heidegger answers as follows: 'When space is discovered non-circumspectively by just looking at it, the environmental regions get neutralized to pure dimensions. Places . . . get reduced to a multiplicity of positions for random things' (p. 147). Heidegger insists that it would not be difficult to describe in detail the stages involved in this reduction of a heterogeneous place to a homogeneous space (Bergson offers an extended description of this process both in *Time and Free Will* and in *Matter and Memory*) though he chooses not to do so since his concern here is simply to bring to light what has been missed in post-Cartesian analyses of space – the primordial character of an original space of place.[16]

Chapter IV brings us to the second of the three components implied in the structural whole being-in-the-world – Dasein as the one *who* is in the world. With a characteristic twist, Heidegger turns the Cartesian tradition back against itself when he suggests that the 'I' as which every Dasein thinks of itself as being testifies not to the being itself of Dasein but to Dasein's failing to be itself. Inasmuch as every self thinks of itself as an 'I' (subject), the term 'I' cannot provide a basis on which to distinguish any one subject from another. Thinking of myself as an 'I' is of course the personal equivalent of the present-at-hand way of thinking about things in general. When I make myself present to myself in this way I therefore take up a distance with regard to myself and to others, that very distance which makes it impossible for me to be myself in the sense implied by the Heideggerian term 'mineness'. Merleau-Ponty will talk, along rather similar lines, of the 'anonymity' of the primordial self, an anonymity which characterizes the self before it has become an 'I' and is still, so to speak, an 'it' (Id?) or a 'one'. Thus the shift from the ready-to-hand to the present-at-hand here takes on the character of a shift from a primordial being-one's-self to a derivative becoming an 'I' or a subject.

Primordially, the being of Dasein is characterized by being-with (*Mit-sein*). This means, among other things, that the entire issue of philosophical solipsism is ruled out from the start. It is pointless asking how I, on the basis of that subjectivity as which I take myself to be, can know that there are other subjects in the world since, in effect, 'I' am not, first and foremost, a subject but precisely a Dasein for whom being-in-the-world implies, as an equi-primordial structure, being-with others. More specifically there are two terms Heidegger employs to characterize the being-with others of Dasein: being-with (*Mit-sein*) and Dasein-with (*Mit-Dasein*). Being-with is the correlate of being-in-the-world and means that the world in which Dasein is is encountered as a world in which others are, or at least always can be, there too. The being there too with Dasein of others is called *Dasein-mit*. As a with-world, the world is already, and from the first, that in which others are there along with me and even if, as a matter of fact, they may for the moment be absent.

'Care' (*Sorge*) is the most general term employed by Heidegger to characterize the being-in-the-world of Dasein (and for this reason its detailed analysis is left to Chapter VI). Care brings with it two distinct ways of being, depending on whether the entities with which Dasein is preoccupied are entities whose mode of being *is*, or *is not*, that of Dasein itself. In the second case (that of the utilization of instruments), Heidegger prefers to talk of concern (*Besorgen*), reserving for the first the more 'personal' term solicitude (*Fürsorge*). To complicate matters still further, there are two modes of solicitude. The distinction in German between a solicitude which *leaps in for (einspringen)* and one which *leaps ahead of (vorausspringt)* is so difficult to translate effectively into English that it seems preferable to play a Heideggerian game with the English language. If my solicitude is such that I *stand in for* the other, I effectively take away from the other the need to 'care' for himself. On the other hand, my solicitude may be of such a kind that I *stand up for* the other, not by taking his/her 'care' away from him/her but by giving it back to him/her authentically – so that (s)he has to take responsibility for him/herself, rather than depend on me.

The last section (§27) of Chapter IV is devoted to the famous analysis of the 'They' – again an untranslatable rendering of the expression 'das Man', which, in German, sounds the same as both the English noun 'man' (*Mann*) and the personal pronoun 'one' (*man*). 'Das Man' refers to human being when it has so lost sight of what it is to be itself that it is capable of doing and thinking only what 'they' do or think or what 'one' does or thinks. It is the term used to describe the self in so far as it has effectively lost its selfhood, has ceased to be itself and has become what others want it to be. It might seem as though this analysis runs parallel to that devoted to the transition from the ready-to-hand to the present-at-hand. But there is a crucial twist which leads Heidegger straight on to the category of *Falling* but which, at the same time, seems to lead his investigation of Dasein towards a fundamental contradiction.

Hitherto, involvement in or with has gone along with what might be called an 'authentic' (because genuinely primordial) description both of Dasein and of the world in which Dasein finds itself. Now we shall find that it is the primordial structure of being-with which condemns Dasein to the inauthenticity of the 'They', of being no more than what others want it to be. Precisely because Dasein is proximally and for the most part 'with' others, Dasein is, from the first, integrated in a 'with-world' which takes it away from itself. Nowhere is this contradiction more blatantly expressed than when Heidegger uses the term 'distantiality' to characterize being with others. 'But this distantiality which belongs to Being-with is such that Dasein, as everyday being-with-one-another, stands in subjection to Others. It itself is not, its Being has been taken away from it by the Others' (p. 164). In the context of the earlier analyses, the primordial structure of the ready-to-hand brought with it involvement. Only with the transition to the derivative present-at-hand attitude does the proximity of the ready-to-hand give way to the distance of theoretical reflection. Now distantiality has become a characteristic of the primordial structure of being-with. By virtue of being-with (and the Dasein-with to which it leads), Dasein is taken away from itself, is removed from itself, from that very being which it is as being-there. It is for this reason, as we shall see later, that the theory of authenticity cannot mean the recuperation of a being-self as which Dasein was originally. To be sure, authentic Dasein will have to individualize itself, that is, struggle to win its freedom from the all-pervasive domination of the 'They'. But the coming back to self of authentic Dasein cannot mean a coming back to that very self as which it was originally, but only a going away from a 'They' which has already taken Dasein away from its self.

Being-with as integration 'in' or 'under' the 'They' is not only characterized by distantiality but also by averageness, levelling down, publicness, ir-responsibility and so on. As a member of the 'They' in everyday life, Dasein is not only taken away from itself but is levelled down by the others with which it now finds itself, whose attitudes and opinions it now reproduces as its own, and in such a way that it is no longer capable of determining *who* it is and so becomes incapable of taking responsibility for itself, for that very self *as* which it is given to be. However dubious the structural foundations of Heidegger's conception of the 'They' as a primordial existential structure (p. 167) might be, his descriptions offer a marvellously acute and perceptive investigation of the way in which human beings cease to be themselves, lose themselves, get absorbed into a social sphere which levels them down and neutralizes whatever might be distinctive about them.

Chapter V brings us to the third of the three components of the structural whole being-in-the-world, the one which, as it were, links them all together, being-in as such; that is, the specification of structures in which Dasein and World are already implied. These structures are four in number: Understanding, State-of-mind, Discourse and Falling.

A possible way to see these four *existentialia* (as Heidegger will call them) is in terms of an implicit critique of the history of philosophy. Kant, for example, worked out of a sense–understanding dichotomy. Since one of these terms (understanding) is common to both projects (note that Heidegger's *Verstehen* does not correspond even terminologically to Kant's *Verstand*), one might be disposed to conclude that 'State-of-mind' is Heidegger's way of introducing the sensible component. This would be misleading, however. For, so far from *presupposing* a dichotomy of mind and body, each of these terms is precisely introduced to *refuse* just such a (Kantian) dichotomy. As we shall see, Understanding, as interpretation, links Dasein with a world which is always apprehended interpretively, that is, in terms of Dasein's very own being. This concept of understanding was one which was already available to Heidegger from the work of Dilthey (where it features as one of a pair of terms, understanding–explanation, designed to account for the very different kind of intelligibility operative in the human and the natural sciences). Like Understanding, State-of-mind is also derived from the 'da' – the there. It refers to that mood in which Dasein always finds itself. Even the seemingly neutral and impartial State-of-mind that goes along with objective theorizing has its mood and this mood is a way in which Dasein stands in relation to what it is thinking about.

Of the two remaining *existentialia*, the first, Discourse, is relatively unproblematic. But again, it is important that this structure, which represents Heidegger's principal concession to the thematic of language in *Being and Time*, does not presuppose the dichotomy of language and reality but again precisely refuses such a dichotomy. Hence Discourse means the spoken rather than the written word, 'speech acts' (to use an analytic term) rather than propositional judgments. It is the fourth of these existential structures, Falling, which is, to my mind, the most problematic. And its problematic character is indicated in the very manner in which it is introduced. For Falling would seem to go along with Understanding and State-of-mind as belonging to the plane of being rather than that of the articulation of being in language. And yet it is introduced last, and indeed relies upon inauthentic forms of discourse (idle talk, curiosity) for its substantiation. But before we attempt to tackle this difficulty in detail it would be better to characterize each of the existential structures first.

Both State-of-mind and Understanding are explicitly developed out of the 'there' which is constitutive of Dasein's being. Heidegger is playing here on the fact that the German word 'there' (da) figures as an etymological component of Dasein (literally, being-there). With this emphasis on the 'there' Heidegger means to draw attention to the fact that all cognition is perspectival in character, that there can be no free-floating apprehension or comprehension of the world or of entities located in the world. For at all times the self brings its 'there', its perspective or its situation, along with it and in such a way that the 'there' determines in advance how the self apprehends and comprehends what is there for it.

Two subsidiary concepts help to confirm the existential character of State-of-mind. 'Thrownness' is indicative of the fact that, in the final analysis, I never choose my situation but always already find myself in a situation which furnishes the context for all choosing and deciding. Even if I successfully choose to assume a different situation it is always out of some already given situation that such a choice first becomes possible. And the very first of the entire chain of situations which regressively constitutes the already given contexts for all choosing and deciding can itself never be chosen or decided about – birth. Along with 'thrownness' we find the characteristic of 'facticity'. 'The expression "thrownness" is meant to suggest the *facticity of its (Dasein's) being delivered over*' (p. 174). In his own discussion of this interesting notion, Sartre uses the phrase 'necessary contingency' to bring out the paradoxical character of facticity. I cannot but be who I am (pure necessity) and yet it is a complete accident *that* I am at all, let alone that I am *this particular man* (sheer contingency).

Curiously, Heidegger chooses to illustrate the concept of State-of-mind with an analysis of fear, with a view to bringing out three structures: that in the face of which we fear, the fearing as such and that which fear fears about – Dasein. I say 'curiously' because later fear will be contrasted with anxiety (§40) and demoted to an existentially secondary status. For whereas fear, as the fearing of some threatening entity located in the world, offers the possibility of evading (flight) or defeating (fight) the fearsome, and so removing the danger, anxiety, as anxiety over self and over one's ownmost possibilities of being, is unavoidable and not to be evaded (I can neither run away from myself nor defeat myself). This is picked up in the third characteristic of fear (that which fear fears about – Dasein). But the full and complete development of this reflexive implication will have to await the later (and absolutely crucial) investigation of anxiety.

The analysis of Understanding proceeds by way of three characteristics: *possibility*, *projection* and *interpretation*. The characteristic of possibility is introduced first by way of a fascinating critique of the history of philosophy. For traditionally, possibility has been presented as one of three modal concepts and in such a way that what is merely possible is what is not yet actual and what can never be necessary. In the Kantian philosophy, for example (and something similar would hold of Husserl and even Leibniz), it figures as the junior partner, subordinated to necessity (necessary conditions of the possibility of) and actuality (what is actual). Heidegger reinstates possibility as the senior partner and does so on an *existential* basis. Dasein exists for such possibilities of being as are not yet actual and which therefore refer to a 'for-the-sake-of-which' without which life would be literally meaningless. '*Understanding is the existential Being of Dasein's own potentiality for Being and it is so in such a way that this Being discloses in itself what its Being is capable of*' (p. 184).

Understanding always presses forward towards possibilities of being which it is 'not yet' because, inherent in Understanding, is the existential structure of 'projection'. Projection does not mean that Dasein has some plan or design which it has thought out in advance and which it hopes to carry through in one way or another – though this may result from projection. Rather, projection means that Dasein has always already projected possibilities of being on the basis of its self and the kind of situation in which it finds itself. Dasein does not first find itself in a situation and then project ways of improving its situation. As thrown being-in-the-world Dasein always is already projecting possibilities of being whether or not it is ever aware of doing so. This is why Heidegger will introduce the concept of 'sight' (*Sicht*) to characterize the projective nature of Understanding. Sight has nothing to do with sensible seeing, still less with any supersensible seeing. It designates the kind of insight into entities (including the self) which is always at work just as long as Dasein *is* its possibilities.

This preliminary concept of 'sight' is further developed in the following section (§32) on 'Understanding and Interpretation' as one of three so-called fore-structures which between them make up the 'in advance' of interpretive Understanding. Once again Heidegger has a historical model in mind (Kant's *a priori*) to which he gives an entirely new twist. In any encounter with entities, Dasein has such entities there before it in the world. But, 'before' this before, there is already a *having* which determines in advance how things are there for me. If I need to get to town in a hurry, my car is there for me to be used for this purpose. Moreover this having 'in advance' is complemented by a seeing in advance. It is worth recalling that 'seeing' is the term Heidegger has already employed (in conjunction with 'showing') to describe the logos of the phenomenon – that which makes it possible for me to *render intelligible* what manifests itself. As such it has little to do with sensible seeing and more to do with what we mean in English when we talk of foresight (the German *Vorsicht* also carries the connotations of caution or prudence which again link with the English careful). The availability of my car is predicated upon my *knowing how* to drive, knowing the traffic code, and so on. Finally, the duality of fore-having and fore-sight is united in a third structure – fore-conception. The German *Vorgriff* links both with the basic verb *greifen* (seize or handle, appropriate therefore for the ready-to-hand) and with *Begriff*, the German word for concept, and so brings out the sense in which concepts themselves take hold of, bring reality to hand, within our reach. In advance, I know what kind of a thing a car is, how it works, what to do if it doesn't work and so on.

In virtue of this triple structure of interpretation, all understanding is always an understanding of something 'as', where by this 'as' structure it is implied that the entity in question could be interpreted in ways other than that which is presently operative. In one or two fascinating asides, Heidegger does talk of interpretation as operative both at the basic level of an understanding of the world and at the more developed level of an understanding of texts, texts which may already presuppose a certain understanding of the world, for example philosophical texts. And in view of the later importance of hermeneutics, or the science of interpretation, one would have wished for something more along these lines. Instead, in an absolutely characteristic move, he turns away from a characterization of understanding to an explanation of the grounds on which primordial Understanding, as interpretation, gets levelled down and transformed into something derivative and derivatively deficient, the subject–predicate conception of language as a procedure by which what is there is *identified* (pointed out), *characterized* (given a definite character) and *communicated* to others. This analysis parallels, on the plane of language, the analysis already carried through, on the plane of being, with regard to the transformation of the ready-to-hand into the present-at-hand.

Section B of this chapter (V) leads in to Falling in a way that has already been prepared by the immediately preceding study of language, more specifically, the derivation of (propositional) assertion from Discourse. Heidegger simply shifts from the theorizing attitude to that of common sense, average everyday-ness, where we encounter a quite different perversion of language, that in which discourse is 'on holiday', so to speak, where we thoughtlessly say whatever comes to mind and so engage in trivial chit-chat. This analysis confirms what was said earlier about the 'They'. But it also prepares the way for the introduction of Falling, the fourth of the four principal existential structures.

The rationale behind the structure of Falling is quite straightforward. Dasein is its 'there' as thrownness into a world. This means that so far from being reflexively (let alone reflectively) concerned with itself it is, in the first instance, 'absorbed in' the world. But the world is made up, for the most part, of entities whose mode of being is *not* that of Dasein. And even when those with whom Dasein enters into relation are themselves beings whose mode of being *is* that of Dasein itself, still the 'average everydayness' in which such being-with ordinarily takes place means that Dasein is, as it were, taken over by the 'They', the commonality of Man. Although I am a self from the very beginning, I have no sense of what it is to be a self initially. Indeed, in so far as it is from others that I first learn what it is to be a self, my own sense of self is, in the first instance, something I inherit from my being with others, my absorption in the 'They'. 'This "absorption in . . ." ', Heidegger tells us, 'has mostly the character of Being-lost in the public-ness of the "they" ' (p. 220).

Heidegger goes on to assure his readers that Falling does not mean a (biblical?) fall from some higher, primal status and does not even carry negative connotations (corruption of human nature) but simply serves to define the situation in which Dasein finds itself in the first instance. And yet it is this Falling Being-in-the-world which is described as *tempting*, as *tranquillizing* and even as *alienating* (Dasein from itself). To be sure, Heidegger will insist that nothing is decided about authenticity or inauthenticity by Falling. And yet, if Falling is fallenness into the 'They'; and if the 'They' is what levels Dasein down, takes Dasein away from itself, then 'inauthenticity' would appear to be the inevitable result of being-in. Worse, if Dasein is taken away from itself from the very first, then what sense does it make to talk of Dasein being brought back to itself again – as is required later by the theory of authenticity. Who is it that Dasein comes back to when it comes back to itself if there is no Being-self which pertains to Dasein, *prior to Falling*?

The category of Falling represents, in my estimate, the most serious structural defect to be found in *Being and Time*, a defect so serious that it cannot be patched up by any external tinkering but requires a rethinking of the entire work. If by the existential character of Falling Heidegger meant that an original ontological or pre-ontological mode of being has to give way to ontic modes of being and thinking then he would simply be acknowledging the *necessity* of the transition from the originary to the derivative – which is indeed a salient feature of my own, genetic ontology. But then there would be a mode of being of Dasein *prior* to Falling, a mode of being in which Dasein *was* (or at least *could be*) itself, a mode of being *from* which Dasein therefore falls away and *to* which therefore Dasein could be restored. This would make much better sense of the conversion implied in individualization and authenticity. But then Falling could no longer be posited as *being on a par with* (projective) Understanding and (disclosive) mood, since the latter are (presumably) operative from the beginning and since Falling is that which makes it be that they cease to operate in their original, ontologically distinctive, manner. But Heidegger is quite clear about the primordial status of Falling. 'Falling is a definite existential characteristic of Dasein itself' (p. 220). Or again: 'Falling reveals an *essential* ontological structure of Dasein itself' (p. 224). Rather than pressing this matter further, we shall simply conclude our presentation of the first part of *Being and Time* with an analysis of the meaning of 'Care'.[17]

Nowhere is Heidegger's insistence upon preventing the splitting of the phenomenon (see *Being and Time*, p. 170, where he refuses the Buberian concept of the 'between' as a legitimate strategy) more apparent than in his presentation of the ontological significance of Care. It might seem to have been enough to complement the analysis of the two terms world and Dasein with an analysis of that structure (of being-in) which links the two. Effectively, however, Heidegger undertakes this linking function a second time over when he hits upon the structure of Care, a structure which has already been etymologically prepared by the preceding analyses. For *besorgen* refers to the kind of *concern* which characterizes Dasein's involvement with entities ready-to-hand, while *Fürsorge* refers to that kind of concernful *solitude* which Dasein entertains in its relations with other human beings. Care (*Sorge*) is then that unitary phenomenon in terms of which it now becomes possible to grasp the unity of the structural whole of being-in-the-world, that whole which has just been analysed out in terms of the threefold configuration: World, Dasein, Being-in as such.

In order to provide a phenomenal basis for the structure of Care, Heidegger turns to anxiety as a quite peculiar State-of-mind which he now takes care to distinguish from fear. Unlike fear which is sponsored by the existence in the world of something fearsome, anxiety is and can only be prompted by the self. But in order to bring out the ontological significance of anxiety Heidegger connects this phenomenon with that of Falling. Falling is that ontological-existential structure which explains why Dasein is for the most part not concerned with itself but 'absorbed in' . . . 'distracted by' the world in which it finds itself. This absorption is not accidental but is founded in a distinctive way of being of everyday Dasein. How is the directedness towards self, characteristic of anxiety, to be reconciled with the directedness away from self, characteristic of Falling? Heidegger's answer must surely have been rooted in his reading of Kierkegaard, especially, *Sickness unto Death*, the text in which Kierkegaard grapples with the problem of anxiety and the efforts of unregenerate Man to avoid coming to terms with himself. Absorption in the world of the 'they' is grounded not so much in an attraction which accounts for the distraction of the self (from its self). Rather the contrary, the self lets itself be absorbed in the world in order precisely *not* to have to come to terms with itself. And understandably so. For if, as Kierkegaard insisted, the directedness of the self towards itself brings with it anxiety, then 'absorption in the world' relieves the self of the anxiety it would otherwise experience. The attraction of the world is motivated by a distraction which is itself attractive in so far as it makes it possible for Dasein *not* to have to come to terms with itself. As Heidegger puts it, Dasein's Falling is a 'fleeing' in the face of itself. That in the face of which Dasein shrinks and which has consequently taken on the character of the threatening is nothing other than Dasein itself. But it is worse than this. For the being of the self from which Dasein flees (into the world) is itself defined in terms of being-in-the-world. In other words, Dasein flees from itself in order not to have to take account of the fact that it has its being to be *in the world in which it finds itself*. In so far as Dasein lets itself be taken over by the 'They', it can let them determine *who* it is and *what* it is important for Dasein to become.

With a beautiful critical twist Heidegger both underlines the connection between anxiety and individualization and gives an entirely new meaning to the 'solus ipse'. Individualization does make of human being a 'solus ipse' but not in the traditional sense of a being who speculates emptily about the possibility of there not being any other subjects in the world but in the quite concrete, and for this reason also 'positive', sense of a being who is forced to come to terms with itself against the prevailing conceptions of itself which it inherits from the 'They'. Thus individualization becomes the necessary counterpart to Falling, that which reverses the decline and drives Dasein back up the slippery slope of its own authentic Being-self. Becoming oneself means giving up the tranquil familiarity of a world in which one is integrated as just *one among others*. It means coming to terms with the fact that, in a real sense, I am *the only one*, the only one who can determine what it is for me to be a self and how it is that I am to become what I have it in me to be.

Though the phenomenon of anxiety, as a distinctive State-of-mind, provides all the phenomenal clues needed for an understanding of Care, the formal definition of Care requires a more exact conception of the interrelation between the relevant existential structures. 'Thus the entire phenomenon of anxiety shows Dasein as factically existing Being-in-the-world. The fundamental ontological characteristics of this entity are existentiality, facticity, and Being-fallen' (p. 235). Typically, Heidegger characterizes each of these components in terms of a hyphenated phrase. Existentiality is *Being-ahead-of-itself*. With this definition Heidegger not only captures the movement of self-surpassing characteristic of existence, he does so in such a way as to offer a new conception of the traditional phenomenological problem of transcendence. As the *ahead-of-itself*, transcendence is no longer to be regarded as a self-surpassing 'towards other entities which it is *not*', but precisely a 'Being towards the potentiality-for-Being which it (Dasein) is itself' (p. 236). But that towards which Dasein surpasses itself (the world) is not something which is, as it were, brought into being by the very act of self-surpassing (transcendence) but is rather something which was *always already there*. Thus the *'ahead-of-itself'* is also an *'already-being-in'*, which latter is indicative of the *facticity* of Dasein. Finally, in *'being-ahead-of-itself'* (existentiality) as *'being-already-in'* (facticity), Dasein finds itself *'alongside'* those very entities which it finds attractive and through which it is distracted from itself. *'Being-alongside'* therefore corresponds to the moment of Falling. Hence a formal definition of Care now becomes possible: 'the Being of Dasein means ahead-of-itself-Being-already-in (the world) as Being-alongside (entities encountered within-the-world). This Being fills in the signification of the term "Care", which is used in a purely ontologico-existential manner' (p. 237).

The remainder of Chapter VI is devoted to a working out of the implications of the structure of Care for the traditional problematics of reality and truth. It shows the power of Heidegger's analyses when it comes to furnishing a solution (or resolution) of difficulties which have often bedevilled the discipline. From a strictly Cartesian standpoint, the problem of reality and the problem of truth go together. There is a problem with regard to the existence of an 'external' world because, on the one hand, the real is that which is supposed to exist distinct and independent of consciousness while, on the other, this same reality is supposed to exist *for* a subject locked up in an 'internal' world of its own ideas and representations. Hence the question: how is the being-in-itself of the world to be reconciled with the being-for-the-subject of this same world? For Heidegger there is no problem. The world is disclosed along with Dasein . 'World' is not a name for the totality of beings other than Dasein, nor is it a name for that 'in' which Dasein exists. Rather, world, or better still being-in-the-world, is a constitutive characteristic of Dasein's very own being. In a beautifully phrased sentence copied from Kant, Heidegger dismisses a long history (for example, Kant reacting to Hume) of problematic speculation about the existence of an external world. 'The "scandal of philosophy" is not that this proof has yet to be given, but that *such proofs are expected and attempted again and again*' (p. 249).

Along similar lines, there is a problem with regard to truth because truth has been located in judgment and because an *objective* judgment has been regarded as the product of a *subjective* act of judging. Thus I am supposed to have judged rightly (truthfully) when my judgment is in accord with (corresponds to) the facts, wrongly (untruthfully) when my judgment is not in accord with (does not correspond to) the facts. But while the judgment (or the meaning expressed in the judgment) is something purely *ideal*, the facts of the matter are supposed to be something *real*. How can something *ideal* accord with (correspond to) something *real*? Are we to presuppose some real psychic process (Husserl's *reelle Erlebnisse*) which makes the connection in a subject who thereby holds together what is real (*reell*) and what is ideal (*ideell*)? But then how does this duality, within the subject (*reell–ideell*), make contact with something absolutely different from itself, the objectively real (*Real*)? For Heidegger there is no such problem, because the being-uncovering of the entity itself (p. 261) is ontologically possible only on the basis of being-in-the-world and only because being-in-the-world has been shown to be a constitutive characteristic of Dasein's very own being.

From the foregoing, Heidegger draws the seemingly straightforward conclusion: 'Dasein is "in the truth".' But this conclusion is much more paradoxical than it appears. Because if Dasein is in the truth, it is also and equivalently 'in untruth'. Because entities get disclosed through Being-uncovering, the latter is also, and equivalently, a covering-over. All bringing to light (revealing), in one respect, is also a concealing, in another respect. This follows, of course, from the initial connection made between the phenomenon and the primary concept of appearing (*Schein*), with its dual aspect of letting what is *appear* and thereby enabling it to *seem* to be (what in reality it is not). And so it also follows that the more epistemologically appropriate concept of appearance (*Erscheinung*) can be accounted for by way of a deficient derivation of the latter from the former (appearance from semblance). Truth, in the derivative sense of the correspondence theory, is derived from Truth, in the primordial sense of disclosedness, by way of a *suppression* of the polarity   (truth–untruth/revealing–concealing/uncovering-covering) inherent in the primordial conception of being-in-the-truth.[18]

Division Two: Time

The second division of *Being and Time* is, as the name indicates, devoted to time. Despite the fact that he edited Husserl's manuscripts on the phenomenology of internal time consciousness, Heidegger always disclaimed any Husserlian influence on his theory of time. This disclaimer, however, should be taken with a grain of salt. For however disparate their theories might appear to be, they do at least share this one common characteristic that, for both, the structure of time and the analysis of this structure cannot be disconnected from the self; in the one case, the analysis of transcendental consciousness; in the other, the analysis of Dasein. The critical difference lies in the fact that, for Heidegger, time cannot be isolated as a specific region of being and so analysed *in isolation*, and this because time and existence are integrally interrelated.

Strictly speaking, Heidegger's existential theory of time is located in a number of sections spread over three chapters, notably Section 65 from Chapter III, Section 68 from Chapter IV and Sections 80 and 81 from Chapter V. The first of these three chapters deals with time as a function of the structure of Care, the second with the disclosure of a specifically ontological time, while the third offers an account of the derivation of the ordinary non-ontological conceptions of time. But these chapters, and their especially relevant sections, are embedded in an extended presentation which also takes in the problematic of death, of conscience and resoluteness and of historicality. Before we look at the theory of time, it will therefore be necessary to consider Heidegger's theory of being-towards-death and of resoluteness. The later chapter on historicality is more pertinent to Heidegger's attempt to develop a theory of the history of philosophy in conjunction with his ontological project and therefore will not be taken into consideration.

The first chapter of the second division celebrates the return of the philosophical theme of mortality – and after a long absence. But Heidegger's concern here is just as much with the *wholeness* of Dasein as it is with the topic of death. Just as Care was introduced at the end of the first division to characterize the static (synchronic) wholeness of Dasein so now Death is employed to characterize the dynamic (diachronic) wholeness of Dasein. As long as Dasein exists it has *not yet* reached its end, since there is a 'not yet' which has still to come (in both French and German, the word for 'future' is literally the 'to come' – *a-venir*/*Zu-kunft*). Death, as the end of life, brings life to an end and so represents that point in life at which the whole of Dasein's existence can be investigated as such, that is, as a whole. But there is a problem. Not only do I not experience my own death (still less that review of my life which is made possible by a view from beyond the grave) but only the death of others; I am congenitally disposed to suppose that it is in every instance others who die, not myself. Thus I deliberately avoid consider-ing my own death and, in so doing, act as if I had all eternity to become what I have it in me to be. But death, as Heidegger puts it, has to be analysed in terms of three characteristics: it is an *ownmost possibility* (as *my* possibility of not existing), it is *non-relational* (no one else can die for me) and it is *unavoidable*.

Because I cannot actually experience my own death, this ownmost possibility which is non-relational and not to be avoided can only be confronted *ahead of the event* in an attitude which Heidegger calls being-towards-death. By being for my end in such a way that at any given time I recognize that I might die, I not only bring myself face to face with an eventuality which individualizes me and does so in that State-of-mind which has already been called 'anxiety', this taking over for my self of my own death reacts back upon my life and makes me realize the necessity of so conducting my life that, at all times, those possibilities of being upon which I fasten are, or can be regarded as, ownmost possibilities of becoming my self. In other words, the theory of being-towards-death opens the way to a concept of authenticity which is not only central to

Chapters II and III but remains an abiding consideration throughout the remainder of the book.

Chapter II introduces the theory of authenticity in connection with the concept of resoluteness. The concept of resoluteness can perhaps best be grasped as the complement of that of anxiety. Anxiety isolates; it shakes Dasein down to the very foundations of its existence and so shakes Dasein out of its complacent acceptance of life as interpreted by the 'They'. But being brought back to self out of lostness in the 'They' is, in the first instance, quite indefinite. If, prior to the onset of anxiety, Dasein failed to choose itself, and if anxiety brought home to Dasein this very failure, still Dasein has yet to choose and to learn how to choose. If, prior to anxiety, Dasein led its life in accordance with the 'They', and if anxiety brought home to Dasein the self-loss inherent in such lostness in the 'They', still Dasein has yet to decide how to lead its life. In short, if anxiety is realization in the sense of a 'coming to terms with' (the necessity of being-self), a further realization is still required, a realization in the sense of 'making real', of realizing one's ownmost potentiality for being-self – through concrete decisions and actions in accord with these decisions.

The phenomenon that builds a bridge between anxiety and resoluteness is the 'voice of conscience'. The theory of conscience (drawn from Lutheran sources) has a triple function. It features as a critique of traditional (theological) concepts of conscience, an elaboration of Heidegger's own very different (and radically secular) conception and a preparation for the theory of resoluteness and authentic being-self. As an existential structure, the call of conscience is a mode of Discourse and therefore attests to the existentiality of the analysis of conscience. Hence, the elaboration of the theory proceeds by way of an investigation of the nature of the call implied in the phrase 'call of conscience'.

Who calls? Answer: Dasein. With this answer Heidegger disqualifies any theological concept of conscience as the call of God or of some other external power, even an internalization of some external power (Freud's conscience as the internalization of paternal authority). To whom does conscience call? Answer: again Dasein. But how can Dasein call to itself in this way, more especially in the context of a theory which specifically refuses any reflective conception of the self? Answer:

Dasein is called *to* itself *by* itself back *out* of its lostness in the 'They'. In other words, it is only because that *as which* it had taken itself to be is *not* its own self (but a creation of the 'They') that Dasein can be called *back* to its self and *away* from the 'They'. Precisely because the call of conscience has this reflexive (not reflective) structure, it says *nothing*. It takes place in silence, calling Dasein back *from* the 'idle talk' characteristic of the They' and *into* the reticence of its ownmost potentiality for being.

The best way on from the theory of resoluteness to that of time is to remind ourselves first of what was accomplished at the end of the previous division. The unity of Care was disclosed there as the unity of existence, facticity and Falling. Furthermore, this triplicity was spelt out concretely in terms of three prepositional phrases designed to capture the dynamic of Dasein's being: *existence*, as being-ahead-of (itself); *facticity*, as being-already-in (the world); and *Falling*, as being-alongside (entities encountered in the world). This triplicity is reproduced at §64. 'Through the unity of the items which are constitutive for care – existentiality, facticity and fallenness – it has become possible to give the first ontological definition for the totality of Dasein's structural whole' (p. 364).

In §65 Heidegger goes on to enquire into the temporality of Care in the light of the theory of resoluteness and in terms of the prepositional phrases mentioned above. The 'ahead of itself' is grounded in the *future*. This is because the future and the future alone can give rise to possibilities of being upon which Dasein can take hold and through which it can come to be itself. But seizing upon possibilities of being is itself only possible out of the *past*, out of what Dasein has already become by virtue of having existed. Only in so far as Dasein assumes its facticity as the thrown basis for any authentic potentiality for being a whole can Dasein come to itself out of its 'having been'. 'The primary existential meaning of facticity lies in the character of "having been" ' (p. 376). Finally, in so far as Dasein projects 'ahead of itself' out of its 'having been', it finds itself 'alongside' entities encountered in the world – which thereby become present to it. 'Making present' is therefore the primary basis for Falling. Thus Heidegger is able to conclude: 'The primordial unity of the structure of care lies in temporality' (p. 375).

A number of supplementary points should be made here. First, for Heidegger, temporality is not; rather, time *temporalizes itself*. One cannot talk about or analyse time itself, but only the way in which Dasein temporalizes itself through existing. Second, temporality temporalizes itself primarily out of the future. Heidegger calls the dynamic implied by the prepositional phrases 'ahead of', 'being already in', as 'being alongside', *ekstases*. Ek-stasis means, literally, 'standing out', and refers to the fact that, in temporalizing itself, Dasein is always already 'beyond' itself in the world. But in promoting the futural ekstasis over the present Heidegger, by implication, is criticizing an entire philosophical tradition which has sought to construct the time series on the basis of the present. But third, in so far as Falling results in 'making present', Falling explains the predominance of the inauthentic conception of time. Authentic time, the time of existence, has to be won *against* this ontological tendency to cover over and conceal the commonplace conception of time. Finally, if the commonplace conception of time does arise through just such a covering over and concealing then it must be possible to show how the latter is derived from primordial time in a manner akin to that in which we were shown, earlier, how the present-at-hand was derived from the ready-to-hand.

Chapter IV carries the ontological analysis of time a step further forward which, characteristically enough, means a step further back in the direction of the recuperation of earlier phases of the investigation. We have just considered the temporal interconnection of the items constitutive of Care: existence, facticity and Falling. But care was itself brought to light as the structural unity of the 'there', which is already constitutive of the being of Dasein in so far as the latter is characterized by being-in as such. Moreover, an existential analysis of the disclosedness which belongs to the 'there' has already been carried through in terms of the four existentialia: Understanding, State-of-mind, Falling and Discourse. So Heidegger now proposes to go back to these four existentialia with a view to specifying their temporal character. In every instance, Heidegger will be concerned to do three things; first, to specify the time dimension which is *primary* with regard to the existential item in question; second, to articulate those *subsidiary* structures which make it possible for Understanding, State-of-mind and Falling to give expression to the three dimensions of time; and third, to offer two interpretations of the temporal character of each of the relevant existentialia, one authentic and the other inauthentic.

It is easy to see that pursuing a programme of this kind is going to lead to extreme 'complexification'. And in fact the whole schema is really only carried through in detail with regard to Understanding. But before we concentrate our attention on the latter let us first sketch out the entire scope of this chapter. Understanding is primarily aligned with the future, State-of-mind with the past and Falling with the present. But each is examined both with regard to its subsidiary structures and with regard to its authentic and inauthentic modes. Then (sub-section d) Discourse is introduced to articulate the disclosedness of Understanding, State-of-mind and Falling. Finally, in §69, §70 and §71 circumspective concern (the ready-to-hand and the present-at-hand), transcendence, spatiality and everydayness are all examined with a view to articulating the temporality which is operative therein.

'If the term "understanding" is taken in a way which is primordially existential, it means to be projecting towards a potentiality-for-Being for the sake of which any Dasein exists' (p. 385). And already we see the futural implication underlying Understanding. To confirm the futural orientation of Understanding, Heidegger borrows the term 'ahead-of-itself' (with obvious futural connotations) from his earlier analysis of Care and then introduces the term 'anticipation' (*Vorlaufen*) to characterize the authentic future. Understanding anticipates what is to come inasmuch as it is only in the future that Dasein can put itself into possibilities of being and make them its own. On the other hand, inauthentic Understanding is constantly projecting possibilities which are only 'for the sake of which' in the degenerate sense of self-interest. The term Heidegger coins to characterize such an inauthentic projection into the future is 'awaiting' (*Gewärtigens*).

Since the future is the time dimension which is primary with regard to an existential interpretation of time, Heidegger extends his presentation of Understanding to show how both present and past are, as it were, contained in time future in a subsidiary manner. Expecting (*Erwarten*) is founded upon awaiting (the inauthentic projection into the future) and naturally leads on to what Heidegger terms 'Gegen-wart' – literally waiting 'towards' or 'over against'. Here we see Heidegger playing with the etymological roots of German words to make his point. For 'Gegenwart' is of course the German for present and so helps to bring home the sense in which Gegen-wart (the derivative of expecting) is not really a projecting into the future but a kind of 'making present' of the future. Thus the futural orientation of Understanding, together with its authentic and inauthentic modes, yields two corresponding modes of the present, the 'moment of vision' (*Augenblick*) when the present is as it were pregnant with futural possibilities and 'making present' (*Gegenwärtigen*) which is a kind of presentification of the future whereby the future is levelled down to a present yet to come. A similar kind of analysis is performed with regard to the subsidiary structure of pastness. There is an authentic recollection of the past which Heidegger terms 'repetition' (*Wiederholung*), and an inauthentic, which he terms 'forgetting' (*Vergessenheit*). Just as expecting is only possible on the basis of awaiting (as an inauthentic perversion of the former), so remembering is only possible on the basis of 'forgetting'. What Heidegger intends by this seemingly strange conjoining of forgetting and remembering is the insight that, when we 'remember' the past, in the typical mode of 'gone for ever', we are 'forgetting' that we *are* our past, that we are haunted by our past, that our past lives on in our present. *A la recherche du temps perdu* was written in the urgency of Proust's own anticipation of his death (Being-towards-death), which called upon him to recuperate his past in the only manner then available to him, in a work which would constitute a 'repetition' of the past worked out in a present whose urgency was derived from the anticipation of an imminent future in which there would be no further possibilities of being.

Just as Understanding is oriented primarily towards the future, so State-of-mind is oriented *primarily* towards the *past*. The mood I am in at any given time is indicative of my thrownness and there can be no such thing as a moodless existence. Even the seemingly moodless State-of-mind of neutral or impartial indifference is itself a mood. The two moods 'fear' and 'anxiety' are now reintroduced to illustrate the two ways (inauthentic and authentic) in which the past can be there for Dasein. Fear is always fear in the face of one's thrown being in a world which contains entities experienced as threatening. But the fear so disorients one's sense of self that one forgets that it is one's very own being which is in question in one's harried efforts to deal with what threatens (for instance, by one of the two mechanisms of fight or flight). Anxiety, on the other hand, is anxious not about any particular thing encountered in the world but about one's being-in-the-world as such and about one's own potentiality for being as being-in. Hence anxiety, as a mood, brings one face to face with one's past and therefore with the possibility of a resolute projection of one's self into the future on the basis of that past – that is, repetition.

Finally, the temporality of Falling is exhibited as oriented *primarily* towards the *present*. Here the two modes are 'moment of vision' and 'making-present'. Heidegger's principal concern is with the inauthentic mode of 'making-present' which he illustrates with an example derived from the earlier analysis of idle talk, curiosity and ambiguity, concentrating this time upon the temporal character of curiosity. Curiosity is novelty for the sake of its newness. The orientation is nominally futural (the latest fashion which renders obsolete what is presently available). But this future is no sooner seized upon than it loses its interest. The 'new' is only new so long as it is not yet 'now', but as soon as it is 'made present' it ceases to be new and so provokes the restless quest for a new novelty. Written in the 1930s, this analysis of curiosity is profoundly prophetic and anticipates an age in which obsolescence no longer just happens but is actually planned.

Discourse does not add a further temporal ekstasis to the three already considered but rather serves to *articulate* the three ekstases already under examination. 'Thus we can see that *in every ekstasis, temporality temporalizes itself as a whole; and this means that in the ekstatical unity with which temporality has fully temporalized itself currently, is grounded the totality of the structural whole of existence, facticity, and falling – that is, the unity of the care-structure*' (Heidegger's italics) (p. 401).

Implied in everything that has been said on the subject of time hitherto there lurks a sweeping critique of conventional conceptions of time. According to Heidegger, however various they may appear to be, such traditional conceptions of time share one thing in common: they privilege the present rather than the future and so conceive of time as a series of instants whose character, as an instant, is founded in the present.

Fundamental to such a perversion of the meaning of time (as Bergson showed in *Time and Free Will*) is the interpretation of time in terms of space. Sections 69 and 70 are devoted to destroying this prejudice in favour of space and to emphasizing the primacy of time. The spatiality of being-in-the-world is itself a spatiality which must be temporalized and which cannot be conceived in abstraction from just such a temporalization.

But if existential time is primordial time, how then does Dasein come to develop the ordinary conception of time, that very conception of time with which we reckon in our day-to-day dealings when we tell the time, make time for, take time off and so on? This is the question Heidegger addresses in the final chapter of *Being and Time*. The key to an understanding of this degeneration in our conception of time is the transfer of primacy from the future to the present. And the key to the understanding of such a transfer is, of course, Falling, the existentialia whose temporal interpretation (in its inauthentic mode) assumes the form of 'making present'. 'Making present' not only makes the present present as the 'now', it also makes present every moment which is 'not-now', characteristically in the two modes of the 'before' which is 'no longer now' and the 'after' which is 'not yet now'. But in so far as both the 'before' and the 'after' are characterized as 'no longer' and 'not yet' *now*, all of time is, in principle, absorbed into the present as a series of 'nows' based upon the present and standing in one relation or another to the present. Thus, for example, it becomes possible to talk of the period between the present 'now' and some future 'now' as a duration and, moreover, to compare this duration with other durations of differing 'lengths'.

In so far as some such concept of the 'time series' has already been developed, it then becomes possible to reckon with time in the sense of making time measurable. For this, reliable regularities are needed. The first and most obvious source of such reliable regularities is the sun, whose passage across the sky not only marks out the day but also dawn, dusk, midday. Sun clocks can be built which utilize the passage of the shadow thrown by the sun across the dial. Water and sand clocks have the further advantage that they stand in no need of a climatic condition such as the sun shining. And from here it is only a step to clockwork and the other instrumentalities designed to reproduce regular durations of time. These regularities, however, are reproduced across space. The time one tells is told by considering the relative spatial relations of two hands on a dial. And it is only because time is transmuted into spatial terms that it becomes possible to measure time, to count the intervals and so on. And nothing makes it clearer that primordial time has been levelled down to the mere presence of a sequence of presents than the commonplace conception of time as 'infinite', time as a line which can be extended *ad infinitum* in both directions.

But even when time is levelled down in this way, the primordial conception of time still gleams through, as it were, in the ordinary conception of time as 'irreversible'. From a strictly spatio-mathematical standpoint there is no intrinsic reason why time should not move backwards as well as, or even rather than, forwards. That time is seen to move irreversibly forward is simply due to the fact that Dasein has to live its time as the condition of possessing any conception of time whatsoever, whether authentic or inauthentic, worldly or primordial.

And then the 'Aufwiedersehen' (as inconclusive as it is conclusive), which brings *Being and Time* to its conclusion – §83 entitled 'The Existential Analytic of Dasein and the Question of Fundamental Ontology as to the Meaning of Being in General'. The entire work began with a quote from Plato which hints at the oblivion into which the question of Being has fallen. The very first section of the Introduction is entitled 'The Necessity for Explicitly Restating the *Question of Being'*. The second chapter of the Introduction talks of laying bare the horizon for an interpretation of the meaning of *Being in General* and ends with a statement to the effect that the only way to arrive at a concept of *Being in General* is by way of a preliminary analytic of that being, namely Dasein, for whom something like an understanding of Being necessarily arises. But has Heidegger actually given us anything like an examination of the meaning of *Being in General*, even a preliminary opening of the way towards such an understanding? Or has this question not already been converted (or perverted) into another question altogether, the question of the being-in-the-world of human being?

Joseph Kockelmans, an excellent interpreter of Heidegger, makes this point in the following way: 'In *Being and Time*, the question concerning the meaning of Being is raised but not explicitly treated as such. Heidegger states there that it is the function of ontology to concern itself with this question, whereas fundamental ontology must focus on the mode of Being of Dasein. Because the book was published in an incomplete form, the being question itself was never explicitly discussed in *Being and Time* . . . . That suggests that in his early works (*Being and Time* and the Kant book) Heidegger was of the opinion that "Being" and "world" to some degree are equivalent. For in these works Heidegger constantly maintains that Being is that which in the final analysis makes the comprehension of beings possible while, on the other hand, it is argued that beings become understood as what they are to the degree that they are projected upon the horizon of the world. World is that toward which Dasein transcends beings; thus world is the concrete form in which every being encounters Being.'[19]

Does this failure (to address the question of the meaning of Being in General) explain the series of questions with which Heidegger closes his *Meisterwerk*? 'How is the mode of the temporalizing of temporality to be Interpreted? Is there a way which leads from primordial *time* to the meaning of *Being*? Does *time* itself manifest itself as the horizon of *Being*?' To these questions, readers might well be moved to add their own. Are these questions actually answerable in the context of the fundamental ontology laid out by *Being and Time*? Is it his failure to answer these very questions to his own satisfaction which (in part) explains the *Kehre*? Does Heidegger abandon the perspective opened up with *Being and Time* in his later thinking or does the latter constitute a prolongation of the former in another mode?

It lies altogether outside the scope of this work to attempt a presentation of Heidegger's later philosophy. However, a few final remarks on the motives which might have impelled him to resist the conclusions to which he had been led by *Being and Time* are perhaps in order.

The 'objective regression' put into effect by *Being and Time* led Heidegger to put *praxis* before *theoria* and, moreover, to define the former in terms of such technologically biased practices as building houses, driving cars, operating machinery etc. Such ready-to-hand operations as these were supposed to 'save' thought from its derivative degeneration into theory. As he watched technology taken over by the Nazi party for its own party political purposes and as he witnessed the appalling destruction which the mis-application of technological practice brought with it, the 'saving grace' must have taken on something of the proportions of the 'devil incarnate'. When the 'saving grace' becomes the 'devil incarnate', then clearly a radical conversion is called for. But since, having already turned his back on Husserl, he could no longer appeal to disinterested rationality as the philosophical corrective, only one way out remained: to characterize his own 'first philosophy' as belonging to the same 'metaphysical' tradition as that to which Husserl's phenomenology had already been relegated – and then to disqualify the former along with the latter. The result was an interpretation of the history of Western philosophy which claimed to disclose a logic leading from Plato to Birkenau, from Aristotle to Auschwitz, and from which Heidegger's later thinking was exempt in so far as he had brought this tradition to an end and embarked upon a 'task of thinking' which was not contaminated by the tradition.[20]

The process of rethinking is inaugurated in the 1930s with the *Beiträge*, Heidegger's secret work, called by some his second *Meisterwerk*,[21] but which was never published until it was incorporated into his posthumous *Gesamtausgabe* as volume 65. Human being is no longer the one who takes over and controls (his thought, his art, his world, his death, his destiny) but becomes the one who is taken over, or rather, who is given over to being. Human being is no longer the one who calls but the one who is called – by being.

Thus we seem to see a movement in a Hegelian direction – with the priority accorded to being over human being. But appearances are deceptive. For instead of a *logic* of being, what Heidegger has to offer is a *poetics* of the being-in-being of human being. The groundedness in the being of human being is never entirely given up but is resumed in a new way which confers the initiative upon being. In the end, how human being is to think the 'mystery of being' is up to being, is left to being to decide. It is not even a matter of Man proposing and God (Being?) disposing. For so far from Man being able to propose, Man can only respond to what is exposed, to what gives itself for thought – the 'there is (being)' which is expressed in

German as an 'it gives' (*es gibt*), an 'it gives' which comes to signify, for the Heidegger of the *Kehre*, the gift of being.[22]

NOTES

1   A great part of the fourth volume of *Martin Heidegger: Critical Assessments* (Routledge: London, 1992) is given over to an examination of this issue. I would recommend, in particular, the papers by Dominique Janicaud (on the intellectual aspect of the issue) and Tom Rockmore (on the impact of the debate in French intellectual circles).

2   Martin Heidegger, *Kant and the Problem of Metaphysics*, trans. J. Churchill (Indiana University Press: Bloomington, IN, 1962), p. 94.

3   See Jean-Luc Marion's paper in *Heidegger: Critical Assessments*, vol. II.

4   See Franco Volpi's paper in *Heidegger: Critical Assessments*, vol. II.

5   Deconstructivists who legitimize their procedure with reference to Heidegger's much vaunted 'destruction' should note that, in *Grundprobleme der Phänomenologie*, Heidegger explicitly presents 'destruction' as one term in a trilogy, the other two terms of which are 'reduction' and 'construction', thereby affirming his belief that 'destruction' cannot be separated from its complement, 'construction'. Such is the dearth of constructive thinking today that this point cannot be too persistently emphasized. See *Gesamtausgabe*, vol. 24, p.31.

6   Metaphysics, Kant argues, will always be with us since human beings are so constituted as to be condemned to raising metaphysical questions. But whether such questions have ever been, or indeed are even of themselves, susceptible to a scientific answer is the question to which the *Critique of Pure Reason* represents a sustained response. See especially section VI of the B Introduction to the *Critique*.

7   Cf. Kierkegaard's existential definition of the self at the start of *Sickness Unto Death*, trans. Walter Lowrie (Princeton University Press: Princeton, NJ, 1941): 'The self is a relation which relates itself to itself.'

8   Heidegger, *Gesamtausgabe*, vol. 24, p. 29.

9   Heidegger, *Being and Time*, p. 68 (H. 43).

10 Heidegger, *Wegmarken, Gesamtausgabe*, vol. 9, p. 326.

11 These are the English terms employed by Macquarrie to translate the almost untranslatable distinction between 'Vorhandenheit' and 'Zuhandenheit'. The fact that 'hand' forms the etymological root of both expressions helps to bring out the practical (handy) context in which this whole analysis is conducted. But the German 'Vorhandenheit' is a fairly common expression used to signify what is there, that is, present. Even the less familiar expression 'Zuhandenheit' also serves to indicate what is there in the sense of readily available.

12 For a superb and exhaustive treatment of this issue, see the article by F. Volpi in *Heidegger: Critical Assessments*, vol. II.

13 Macquarrie translates Auffälligkeit as 'conspicuousness'. Translating as 'obvious' would keep the common stem 'ob' – even though it might bring with it other disadvantages.

14 For a full and complete presentation of Heidegger's relation to Descartes and through Descartes to Husserl see Jean-Luc Marion, 'Heidegger and Descartes', in *Heidegger: Critical Assessments*, vol. II.

15 For an excellent discussion of Heidegger's concept of space see the paper by Maria Villela-Petit in *Heidegger: Critical Assessments*, vol. I.

16 The limitations of Heidegger's conception of primordial spatiality are brought out in the massive ten-volume work by Hermann Schmitz entitled *System der Philosophie* (Bouvier: Bonn, 1964–80), no less than five volumes of which are devoted to space.

17 For a full discussion of the problem connected with the ontological character of Falling and its consequences for the theory of authenticity, see my paper 'Who is Dasein?', in *Heidegger: Critical Assessments*, vol. IV, as also the paper by Christina Schües: 'Heidegger and Merleau-Ponty', vol. II.

18 Ernst Tugendhat has brought out the limitations of Heidegger's concept of truth in his paper 'Heidegger's Idea of Truth', *Heidegger: Critical Assessments*, vol. III.

19 Joseph Kockelmans, *On the Truth of Being*, Indiana University Press: Bloomington, IN, 1984), p. 47.

20 For an extremely subtle examination of some of the absurdities to which this position is capable of leading, see the paper by Jean-Pierre Faye, 'Heidegger and the Thing', *Heidegger: Critical Assessments*, vol. IV.

21 See, for example, the paper by Friedrich-Wilhelm von Herrmann, the editor of the *Gesamtausgabe*, in *Heidegger: Critical Assessments*, vol. I.

22 The elements of this new way of thinking are to be found in the lecture *On Time and Being*, whose very title is already indicative of a *Kehre*. However, in my estimate, the reader who seeks in *Time and Being* an answer to the unresolved issues raised in *Being and Time* is doomed to disappointment.

Chapter 3

Jean-Paul Sartre

Jean-Paul Sartre was born in 1905. Having lost his father early on, the formative influence upon his intellectual development was his grandfather on his mother's side, a member of the Schweitzer family, later to gain world-wide recognition through the Nobel prize winner Albert Schweitzer. Sartre obtained admission to the prestigious Ecole Normale Supérieure in Paris where he met Simone de Beauvoir, with whom he remained in contact throughout his life.

Perhaps the most remarkable feature of Sartre's literary life was that it was, in the fullest sense of that word, a *literary* life. Sartre belongs to a very small band of *literati* (almost all of French provenance) whose writing covers virtually the entire spectrum of literary genres from plays, short stories and novels, through biographies, autobiographies and critical works of one kind or another, to original pieces of philosophical thinking. But the manifoldness of Sartre's accomplishments had little to do with any ostentatious display of literary versatility but was integrally bound up with the central concern of his life – to convey, by all available means, his own unique (and tragically qualified) vision of life and of the human condition.

The course of his specifically *philosophical* career can be traced in four main works. There is first of all his beginning essay, *The Transcendence of the Ego*,[1] in which he acknowledges his affiliation with phenomenological philosophy while refusing the transcendental assumptions of Husserl's own philosophy. Next we find *The Psychology of Imagination*,[2] a treatise in phenomenological psychology deliberately oriented towards a theme dear to Sartre's literary heart. To some extent, and particularly with reference to the nothingness of imaginative presentation, this study anticipates his best known work. But in a very real sense, *Being and Nothingness* was an entirely new departure, a complete and fully worked out existential philosophy, born, in part at least, of his experience with the French resistance. The excessively individualistic implications of his existential philosophy, together with his increasing commitment to the cause of socialism, led him later to write a new work, *The Critique of Dialectical Reason*, in which he sought to integrate existential phenomenology with Marxism.

In my estimate, however, *Being and Nothingness* remains by far the most important of Sartre's contributions to philosophy and it is to this work alone that the rest of our presentation will be devoted.[3]

BEING AND NOTHINGNESS

Being and Nothingness falls into four parts. The first part opens with a difficult but important Introduction which plays the same role with regard to this work as Heidegger's Introduction plays with regard to *Being and Time*. That is, in this Introduction Sartre sets out to explain, in general terms, what he means by 'phenomenological ontology' (the work is subtitled 'An Essay in Phenomenological Ontology'). This Introduction is then followed by two chapters devoted to a theory of consciousness developed under the auspices of the category of Nothingness. Part Two shifts the focus of attention from consciousness to the self, more specifically, to the category of the For-itself. The analysis of the For-itself, however, is accomplished in connection with its complement, the In-itself, and in such a way that the two Hegelian categories of the For-itself and the In-itself now take over the commanding role of that ontological duality originally laid out under the heading of Nothingness and Being. Part Three shifts the focus once again, this time to human relations, or Being-for-others. The duality in question at this point is that of the For-itself and the For-others. Since the body is that by means of which I stand in relation to others, the body is integrated into the structure of the self in the context of this third section.

Finally, there is a fourth part devoted to the topics Having, Doing and Being. The addition of this part appears strangely incoherent, since it calls for nothing less than the substitution of a new set of ontological categories for those in terms of which the entire analysis has been conducted thus far. I cannot help feeling that the addition of this fourth part might have had something to do with a reading of the influential (though by no means academically structured) text by Gabriel Marcel, *Etre et Avoir*,[4] as a result of which Sartre was no doubt brought to recognize the supplementary value of the categories of Doing and Having.

The Introduction

If one were to sum up the substance of Sartre's existential philosophy in one phrase, one could do no better than to call it a 'dualist ontology', an ontology which, in this sense, moves against the spirit of Heideggerian ontology and harks back to Descartes. The dualisms shift their focus from part to part, moving from an initial dualism of *Being* and *Nothingness*, to that of *Being-for-itself* and *Being-in-itself*, to finish up with the dualism of *Being-for-itself* and *Being-for-others*. And yet the very first words of the Introduction talk about modern thought (more specifically, phenomenology) as having overcome 'a certain number of dualisms which have embarrassed philosophy' and having replaced these dualisms with 'the monism of the phenomenon'. Through the new notion of the phenomenon, the dualism of interior and exterior is eliminated, together with that of being and appearance, potency and the act, appearance and the essence. But, Sartre asks, is it not rather the case that all of these subsidiary dualisms have simply been swallowed by a new, all-embracing dualism, the dualism of the finite and the infinite? As we shall see, from the spark of this new duality of the finite and the infinite, Sartre is able to rekindle the flame of dualism.

From the (Husserlian) standpoint of the duality of the finite and the infinite, the essence regulates a series of appearances which are, in principle, inexhaustible. Being no longer features as an 'over and beyond' of what appears but as that infinite multiplicity of appearances which, together, go to make up the reality of the object – the object seen from all possible points of view. In other words, being and the appearing now appear to be one and the same – and yet not altogether so.

There is an appearing of being, called 'the phenomenon of being'. The question is whether the 'phenomenon of being' is identical with the 'being of the phenomenon' – in which case ontology would be reducible to phenomenology. Sartre thinks not. And the key concept in terms of which he explores the non-identity of the 'phenomenon of being' with the 'being of the phenomenon' is that of the *transphenomenal*. 'The "phenomenon of being" requires the transphenomenality of being' (p. xxvi) – which means in the end that it will have to appeal to the being of the phenomenon. But he proceeds about his business in an interestingly devious manner – by first bringing to light a transphenomenality on the side of consciousness or the subject. It is this *subjective* transphenomenality which is then transferred over to the other side to yield the irreducibility of being to appearance or our consciousness of it.

No philosopher has gone further in the direction of a reduction of the 'being of the phenomenon' to the 'phenomenon of being' than Berkeley. And so it might seem strange that, at the beginning of Section III of the Introduction, Sartre should appeal to the Berkleian formula *'Esse est percipi'*, and, moreover, should link Berkeley quite explicitly with Husserl in this connection. Admittedly, if being is reducible to its being perceived, then, in the first instance at any rate, it becomes impossible to attribute a transphenomenality to being. Being just *is* its appearing. But what if we shift the focus of attention from the *percipi* to the *percipere*, from the perceived object to the perceiving subject? Even Berkeley will concede a being to the subject, to the perceiver, indeed will not permit substantial reality to be attributed to anything but mind or spirit, whether finite or infinite. And Husserl too will admit that the law of being of consciousness is to be consciousness 'of'. In so much as, for phenomenology, consciousness is already a consciousness 'of', it pertains to the very being of consciousness to transcend itself, to pass beyond itself 'towards'. But even if the positionality of consciousness is sufficient to confer a certain transphenomenality upon consciousness, does it indeed follow that a *being* can be conferred upon consciousness as self-transcending? And if so, what conclusions can be drawn therefrom for the 'being of the phenomenon'?

It is in order to answer these questions that Sartre introduces his famous notion of the *pre-reflective cogito*. For Sartre,

Descartes's *cogito* is essentially reflective; that is, it emerges in the course of an enquiry which throws consciousness back upon itself and upon its own ideas. Prior to the disclosure of such a *reflective cogito*, prior therefore to the methodological doubt through which such a disclosure is brought about, consciousness exists as simply positing its objects, taking for granted the reality of the objective world and the validity of the formal sciences. The question is whether inherent in, and featuring as the condition of the possibility of, just such a positional consciousness there might not be a *pre-reflective cogito*, a *cogito* which would indeed serve to bring to light the being of positional consciousness, the *sum* of the *cogito ergo sum*. On the face of it, a *pre-reflective cogito* would appear to be a contradiction in terms – a self-consciousness which precedes the very possibility of reflection, that is, self-consciousness in the ordinary sense of that word. By making a distinction between an implicit consciousness of self which is not yet however an explicit self-consciousness, this seeming contradiction can be resolved and in such a way as to confer a being upon consciousness.

All positional consciousness 'of' presupposes, and is founded upon, a consciousness of self as being the one who *is* that consciousness. When I see a table, I am implicitly conscious of myself as *not* being the table which I see. This consciousness of self cannot be anything like an explicit self-consciousness, for otherwise it would require a higher consciousness of self to make possible that positing of the self by itself which is implied in self-consciousness, and so on *ad infinitum*. In order to avoid such an infinite regress it is necessary to admit a non-positional consciousness of self as the condition of every positional consciousness of anything whatsoever, including the self itself. This *implicit* self-consciousness is not to be regarded as a new consciousness but as the only mode of existence which is possible for a consciousness of something. To be conscious 'of' is to exist oneself (in an absolutely immediate relation of oneself to oneself) as the one who is conscious.

But in according a *being* to consciousness (in the form of the *pre-reflective cogito*) it would seem that consciousness had become the absolute with reference to which what appears is merely relative. Being is not; it merely appears *to* a consciousness *for* which it is and *from* which it therefore derives whatever being it possesses, qua appearance. We have been able to confer a being upon the *percipiens* but only, it seems, at the expense of the *percipi*. Consciousness has acquired a being, but only at the expense of being in-itself which, in being reduced to what it is *for* consciousness, would seem to have been divested of its being. In other words, consciousness has being; but being has been reduced to nothing. This, the apparent conclusion to be drawn from the above, Sartre then neatly reverses to arrive at his own quite opposite, ontological conclusion: consciousness is nothing, but being is.

Sartre effects this reversal in Sections V and VI. If being were nothing, consciousness could not be conscious of it save by way of a pure and simple creation! But how would it then be possible even to accord a being to *consciousness*, since the being of consciousness has been accounted for in terms of a pre-reflective *cogito* which, so far from being operative *independently* of positional consciousness, is nothing but the mode in which this consciousness exists itself, and must exist itself, if it is to be conscious of something? But if non-being cannot be the foundation of being, could being not be the foundation of non-being, of non-being in the specific form, admittedly, of consciousness? This is the alternative for which Sartre now opts and in opting for which he effectively carries through a reversal of the absolutism which lies at the root of the Husserlian conception of consciousness.

The fact that consciousness exists itself as consciousness 'of' means that transcendence is a constitutive structure of consciousness. But the relation of consciousness to that which it is conscious 'of' could not be a relation of transcendence unless, in coming beyond itself, consciousness found itself confronted with a being which was not reducible to its appearing, to its being for consciousness, but rather possessed a mode of being of its own. This is what Sartre calls 'the ontological proof'. To be sure, the being of what appears is still nothing more than its transphenomenality. In other words, there is no in-itself (in the Kantian sense) over and beyond what appears. Still, that by means of which being appears, the phenomenon, is no longer to be regarded as identical with, or as reducible to, what it is for consciousness. Rather the contrary, consciousness could not be what it is unless it related itself to a being which, as distinct and independent of consciousness, stood in no need of consciousness – even though consciousness is entirely dependent upon it. The transphenomenality of being, a transphenomenality first conferred upon consciousness but then transferred back to being, means that being does not exhaust itself in its appearing, that 'the being of that which appears does not exist only in so far as it appears' (p. xxxviii).

The characteristics in terms of which Sartre finally sums up the transphenomenality of being are three in number: Being *is*; Being is *in-itself*; Being is *what it is*. The spirit of these three seemingly vacuous characterizations can perhaps be better captured in a more graphic portrait of Sartre's ontological stance. First, Sartre's position is that of a realist, in the following sense: Prior to, distinct from, and independent of consciousness, or of any being possessing consciousness, being, for Sartre, not only is but is more or less as it appears to be, a material plenitude utterly alien to consciousness. Moreover, for Sartre, it is as unremarkably correct to assign to science the task of investigating the exact nature of the material universe (being In-itself) as it would be for a positivist. Second, this reality which is simply there for us is that without which consciousness itself would be inconceivable, since consciousness is bound up in its being with the being of that of which it is conscious. Third, since the being of consciousness lies in its being conscious of being, a relation towards being is always and necessarily presupposed on the part of consciousness, a relation which divides being in general into two regions, and in this sense makes of Sartre's philosophy a dualist ontology. But, as we shall see in a moment, it is a dualism of a very special kind, more specifically, a dualism not of two substances or of two self-sustaining regions but of one essentially independent and one essentially dependent region, a dualism which, in a certain sense therefore, is even reducible to a materialist monism, more especially if consciousness (the dependent term) is itself regarded as a more or less superfluous accident – as adding nothing to being In-itself.

Part One: The Problem of Nothingness

From the beginning of Part One the terminology changes. More specifically, and for ontologically motivated reasons, the concept of Nothingness comes to take the place of the more familiar phenomenological concept of consciousness. It should be noted that Sartre is not particularly original here where he seems to be forging his own conceptual terminology. Heidegger's *Introduction to Metaphysics* takes its start in the concept of nothingness and already raises the question whether the concept of nothingness is the outcome of the negative judgment or whether, on the contrary, the logical concept of negation presupposes the ontological. More specifically, a question Heidegger raised in *Being and Time* might well be construed as an authorization of the kind of project in which Sartre later became engaged. 'Has anyone', Heidegger asks, 'ever made a problem of the ontological source of notness, or, prior to that, even sought the mere *conditions* on the basis of which the problem of the "not" and its notness and the possibility of that notness can be raised?'[5] The Problem of Nothingness is Sartre's attempt to answer this very question.

True to his literary approach, he offers us a real life example. 'I have an appointment with Pierre at four o'clock. I arrive at the café a quarter of an hour late. Pierre is always punctual. Will he have waited for me? I look at the room, the patrons, and I say, "He is not here." Is there an intuition of Pierre's absence, or does negation indeed enter in only with the judgment?' (p. 9) Sartre's extended analysis of this example shows first that there is an experience of nothingness, in the form of the absence of Pierre, and further that this experience suffices to organize all the elements of my experience in the sense that each element is thrust into the background by the dynamic compulsion of my quest. And finally, it is this experience of nothingness which is the condition upon which I build the negative judgment: 'Pierre is not here.'

An intermediary critique enables Sartre to dismiss both the Hegelian and the Heideggerian concept of nothingness before finally establishing his own alternative conception. According to Sartre, Hegel not only makes the mistake of conferring a being upon nothingness; both these terms function in a purely abstract way, whereas the concept of nothingness which interests Sartre finds its confirmation in concrete human experience. Sartre's critique of Heidegger is more relevant to his own position since they have more in common. Basically, for Heidegger, nothingness is brought to light in order to throw light upon being, that there is being, that being possesses these characteristics rather than others, that being possesses a unity, and so on. For Sartre, on the other hand, nothingness has little or nothing to do with being. Even Man's relation to being as a self-transcending relation fails to capture the significance of the 'not', unless and until this nothingness is traced back to consciousness itself as a constitutive characteristic. Nothingness is not. There is only a negation of being and the only being capable of introducing negativity into the plenitude of being is human being itself or, more generally, a conscious being.

Human being is the being by way of which nothingness arrives in the world. As such, human being must not only *be* that nothingness but be it in such a way that the nothingness of its being is always in question. 'The being by which Nothingness comes to the world must be its own Nothingness' (p. 23). And this by nihilating Nothingness in its being in connection with its own being. The question is whether these formal characterizations of Nothingness can be given concrete content, that is, can be brought to light with reference to specific experiences in which they are made manifest.

The two pillars on which Sartre relies for a substantiation of his theses with regard to the Nothingness of that being which human being essentially is are freedom and time. Strictly speaking, both of these structures are, and have to be, introduced here in a preliminary way, prior to their detailed examination later on (Freedom in Part Four and Time in Chapter Two of Part Two). The Nothingness of consciousness means that causality cannot get a hold on consciousness. For causality is only operative within the plenitude of being. One being can only cause or be caused by another. But Nothingness effects a withdrawal, a detachment of the self from being, and therefore a suspension of universal determinism. If the essence of consciousness is its nihilating capacity, it follows that human existence cannot be determined by anything like an essence or nature. Here we meet again a form of that formula: existence precedes essence which was already encountered in the Introduction (p. xxxii) and which will provide the sloganesque theme of Sartre's popular lecture: 'Existentialism and Humanism'. 'Human freedom precedes essence in man and makes it possible; the essence of the human being is suspended in his freedom' (p. 25). By the same token, the Nothingness of consciousness implies an abrogation of the objective concept of time as a series of instants, a series whose real continuity (the flux of being or even of consciousness itself) is taken to be the ontological condition for its analytical division into distinct moments. If consciousness is a Nothingness, then, at every instant, consciousness effects a break with the past and with the future and indeed makes time itself possible by just such an irruption of vacuity into the assumed plenitude of being. I am separated from my past (and from my future) – by nothing. But this Nothingness which intervenes between me and my past (or future) is anything but an ineffectual or vacuous nothingness. For it means that the past can have no hold upon me now, as also that my intentions (to realize this or that project) can have no hold upon the future. At every instant I am in question in my very being, both as *no longer* being the one who I was and as *not yet* being able to be the one who I hope to be or anticipate becoming.

But if the Nothingness of consciousness does indeed condemn me to freedom and to a conception of time in which I cannot count upon the past or the future, there should be some experience in which the nihilating force of consciousness makes itself known. This experience ought to be a more or less constant accompaniment of consciousness, or of my own awareness of being a self, that is, if the above mentioned analysis is not to prove illusory. Does such an experience exist?

Here Sartre follows Heidegger in following Kierkegaard. Anguish or anxiety is the phenomenon in question. Anguish has to be distinguished from fear since fear is ordinarily understood to be fear in the face of some *external* threat, therefore fear in the face of a threat which can be either conquered or evaded by means of the two basic strategies of fight or flight. But anguish is essentially the anguish of the self in the face of itself, therefore anguish in the face of that which can neither be overcome nor circumvented. Sartre begins by taking two examples which illustrate anguish in the face of the future and of the past. I am walking along the edge of a precipice. My fear of falling can be constrained by measures expressly designed to ensure that I remain on the path. But I may still be afflicted by an experience of anguish, the experience namely that nothing prevents me from throwing myself over the edge. This may be called anguish in the face of the future. Anguish in the face of the past is illustrated with the example of the gambler who has resolved not to gamble again. Faced with the gaming table, he recognizes that nothing prevents him from ignoring his prior resolution and from continuing along a course which he knows from experience will prove ruinous. In place of the term 'nothing', *freedom* can readily be substituted: 'For this freedom which reveals itself to us in anguish can be characterized by the existence of that nothing which insinuates itself between motives and act' (p. 34).

The existence of a nothingness between myself and my past, my self and my future and even, one might say, between myself and my self means that I live under the obligation of constantly remaking my Self. This book which I am engaged in writing will take me some considerable time to complete, so long indeed that it makes sense to say that I can define myself in terms of one project – to write this book. My intention is of long standing. I possess both the ability and the opportunity to write it. And yet *nothing* stands between me and my abandonment of this project, therefore between me and the abandonment of that conception of my self which will follow from my being the author of this book. It is therefore not just the project which is at every moment in question but the self which has committed itself to the project and which defines itself in terms of the project to which it has committed itself. Thus my anguish is aggravated by the recognition of my total, and totally unjustifiable, responsibility for myself.

So it is that freedom becomes a burden, but a burden which it is not too difficult for the subject to disburden itself of. The last part of The Origin of Negation is devoted to a characterization of just such patterns of flight from freedom. Essentially, there are three patterns. First, there is the pattern of psychological determinism. Here the excuse typically takes the form: 'I couldn't help myself.' I fall back upon a determinism which links me to my past or to a nature which condemns me to act in a certain way. I confront myself, but I explain my behaviour away as lying outside the province of my control. But second, instead of relying on theoretical hypotheses which link me to my past I can, as it were, overtake my own future, present my future possibilities to myself as though they were not mine, that is, as though they were already endowed with some self-realizing efficacy which would disarm them of that disquieting possibility of (possibly) not coming into being. I can think of the completion of my book as pre-ordained, as establishing with respect to myself a purely external relation, therefore one which can be discounted in so far as it no longer has to be sustained in being by me. In other words, through such a pattern of distraction, I deny my freedom *not* to complete the book and, in so doing, deny that very condition which makes the writing of the book one of my possibilities of being. Both of these ways of taking flight are reducible, in the end, to a third pattern which consists in conceiving of my self as an essence or nature. Freedom then becomes nothing but the means by which my actions are conformed to my nature, by which my existence is seen to flow from me as from an essence for which I do not have to be responsible because I did not choose to be this essence even though, in fact, it serves to define me as that very being which I am.

The question remains, however, whether I really can hide my freedom from myself in this way, whether I can successfully avoid the anguish of freedom by taking flight in reassuring reconstructions and, if so, what kind of explanation can be given for a possibility which consists, in effect, in the very denial of possibility, that is, in the reduction of existential possibilities of being either to irresistible necessities or to actualities for which I cannot be held responsible. Sartre's answer to this question is to be sought in his fascinating descriptions of one unique, and uniquely inauthentic, possibility – that of 'bad faith'.

Sartre's concept of 'Bad Faith' (Chapter Two) is sometimes treated as a psychological discovery and illustrated with examples such as obsession, resentment, irony, role playing, self-deception and so on. Such a psychological assessment, however, is liable to overlook the phenomenological 'logic' which underpins this discovery and which follows from the very definition of consciousness as a Nothingness. The law of being of the For-itself is to be what it is not and to not be what it is.

Sartre begins by identifying the specifically negative attitude he has in mind and distinguishing it from falsehood. An obvious analogy to bad faith would be that of the lie. The trouble with this analogy is that the liar is aware of the very truth which he conceals from those to whom he tells his lies. But bad faith involves lying to oneself: 'what changes everything is the fact that in bad faith it is from myself that I am hiding the truth' (p. 49). Since Sartre works within the Cartesian frame of the 'total translucency of consciousness', the very possibility of someone lying to himself becomes eminently problematic. How can I, the deceiver, deceive myself with regard to the very deception I am engaged in perpetrating?

A possible explanation which Sartre rejects provides a first insight into the grounds for his dismissal of Freudian psychoanalysis. For Freud, the self is divided into two incommunicable parts, the Ego and the Id. If the self is a duality rather than a unity then it might seem to make sense to say that one of these two parts deceives the other. Could it be the Ego which deceives the Id? But then this can only be because the Ego assumes the role of censor, repressing whatever contents it does not want to acknowledge. But then, in order to repress this content, the Ego must know what it is that it is repressing and why. Could it be the unconscious complex which deceives the Ego? But then, according to psychoanalytical theory, the unconscious is capable of being brought back within the sphere of consciousness. 'Where the unconscious was, there shall consciousness be.' Citing Steckel's famous work on the frigid woman, Sartre points out that in a certain sense the patients in question *want* to be frigid and adopt a number of tactics to conceive of themselves sexually in this way. If it is the destiny of the unconscious to become conscious and if this task is one which psychoanalytical theory devolves upon the therapist then it must be one which, in principle, can always be assumed by the patient himself.

To support this conclusion, Sartre adopts a method which has almost become the hallmark of his phenomenological procedure, the construction of familiar examples taken from life, which are then followed up with an appropriate analysis. There is the example of the woman who is out on a first date with a man of whose interest in her she is well aware but to whose advances she is not yet ready to respond. He takes her hand. What is she to do? If she removes her hand from his, she will have given offence unnecessarily. But if she leaves her hand in his she will, by default, have given her consent to an intimacy for which she is not yet ready. The Sartrian solution is well known and admirably exemplifies the attitude of bad faith.

She leaves her hand in his but *withdraws her consciousness* from her hand. The physical hand remains embraced in his but it no longer belongs to her and so does not compromise her emotionally. Then there is the example of the waiter playing a role. What is he doing? Playing at being a waiter. In what sense is this an instance of bad faith? Because it assumes that it is possible for a human being to identify with a role, to be what others define him as being, to deny that very negativity which is constitutive of his being, qua consciousness.

Such a denial is constitutive of the project of good faith. And indeed the logic of Sartre's position on bad faith is best brought out by considering the implications of its opposite, good faith. The ideal of sincerity is to be what one is. But can a man be what he is? The very impossibility of such a project is brought out by considering that being what it is is the defining characteristic of being-in-itself, that mode of being, namely, which characterizes things. But to be human is to be conscious, more, to be conscious of being human. And with consciousness comes negativity. This does not mean that a consciousness cannot *pretend* to be thing-like, put itself into the state of a quasi-thing, think of itself as a thing. But to do this is precisely what it means to be in bad faith. I am not sad in myself. I make myself be sad. And in making myself be sad I am effectively denying with respect to myself that I *am* this sadness which presently overwhelms me, or by which I have permitted myself to be overwhelmed. 'The condition of the possibility for bad faith is that human reality . . . must be what it is not and not be what it is' (p. 67).

And yet bad faith *is*, is indeed almost a defining characteristic of the majority of mankind, certainly a distinctive characteristic of that type for which Sartre experiences a deep-rooted loathing, the bourgeoisie. That bad faith can exert such a tenacious hold over human beings is due to its character as faith. Faith, like belief, falls short of knowledge and, in the case of bad faith, necessarily so. I believe Pierre is my friend. And I act on this belief. I believe it in good faith and can only so believe it, for there can be no self-evident intuition of Pierre's good intentions towards me. Similarly, my conviction that I am a certain kind of person is a faith and a faith to which I am prepared to hold tenaciously since, for the most part, it gives me back that image of myself which conforms to what I would have myself be or how I would have others take me.

And so what of the possibility of authenticity, undoubtedly the (Heideggerian) source from which Sartre draws the inspiration for his analyses? Clearly we are faced with a dilemma. I cannot *be* a homosexual in the sense in which I can be a body of such and such a weight or colour or sex. But if my inclinations are homosexual then, in denying that I am a homosexual, I am in bad faith. I am trying to conceal both from myself and from others what I am. But what if I admit my homosexual nature and choose to be it? Such a person will claim for himself the prerogative of sincerity and he asks of others only that they respect this self-avowed confession and accept him for what he is. But this is to suppose that it is possible for him to be something, a homosexual or a heterosexual. And once again we find ourselves in the presence of bad faith. This is the sense in which Sartre will concede that 'the goal of sincerity and the goal of bad faith are not so different' (p. 65). However, he does also provide us with alternative formulae which help both to distinguish these two phenomena and both these phenomena from the possibility of authenticity. Good faith is the attempt to be what one is not. 'Bad faith', on the other hand, 'seeks to flee the in-itself by means of the inner disintegration of my being. But it denies this very disintegration as it denies that it is itself bad faith' (p. 70). This means, according to Sartre, that bad faith can be presented in terms of the formula 'not-being-what-one-is-not'. Between the two formulae, 'being what one is not' (good faith) and 'not being what one is not' (bad faith), both of which turn out, ultimately, to be instances of bad faith and, in consequence, to exhibit a distinct tendency to slide into each other, a third alternative presents itself, namely, *being what one is not and not being what one is*. But what does this mean? Surely it can mean nothing more than the lucid recognition of the impossibility of good faith or sincerity.

The key word is 'lucidity' since it links up with the concept of anguish. For the lucidity in question here is the recognition, in anguish, of the impossibility of sincerity, of one's total and unqualified responsibility for that very being which one is, a being which one did not choose to be and which, moreover, one cannot even succeed in being. Can one argue that the formula 'making oneself be' saves the day, in the sense that I can always assume complete responsibility not for being who I am but for making myself be someone? Yes and no; yes, if by this is meant that I am free to make myself be; no, if by this is meant that, in making myself be, I have become something in my own right. For, in making myself be I have, at the same time, to recognize that my being is at all times in question. There is no essence which I am by nature (and from which my existence follows as the reactions of a chemical compound follow from the law of its being) nor even an essence which I can become by making myself be and then effecting a sort of retrospective recuperation of my own self creation.

Part Two: Being For-itself

It should perhaps be said at the start that the terms In-itself and For-itself, which Sartre takes over from Hegel, are used in a sense which is contrary to, and almost the opposite of, that in which they are used by Hegel. For Hegel the *In-itself* already contains the *For-itself* in itself, at least implicitly. The coming into being of the *For-itself* is the making explicit of this original inherence of consciousness in being. The *For-itself* makes being present to itself in the form of an 'over against' of consciousness and through a process of becoming. In turn, however, this duality, inherent in the *For-itself*, has itself to be overcome through the return of consciousness to itself out of its self-alienation in the objective universe. The consciousness for which being has become something alien in turn becomes a consciousness which is *In-and-For-itself*, a consciousness which has made the other own (to itself) and has made itself other (to itself). Thus the intermediary duality of being and consciousness is one which, in the Hegelian context, is both preceded and succeeded by unity, the unity of the *In-itself*, on the one hand, and the unity of the *In-and-For-itself*, on the other.

For Sartre, however, ontological duality is of the essence. For all that, it should also be said that the transition from a theory of consciousness to a theory of the self is accomplished through the concept of unity, in this case, the unity of the self. In turn, the concept of unity in question is one which can only be comprehended as a sort of intermediary between two alternatives, identity on the one hand and duality on the other.

Being-In-itself is characterized by identity. A thing is

identical with itself. If a concept of synthesis can be recuperated within the limits of such a coincidence (of being with itself) it can only be with reference to some such concept as that of 'density', 'plenitude' or 'compression'. Being-In-itself is itself so fully and completely that there can be nothing like a difference, even an ideal or incipient difference, between It and itself. As we have already seen, consciousness arises as a kind of *decompression* of this original density or plenitude of being and this is why it is called a nothingness, a hole or rift in being. In so far as, here and there, just such a decompression arises as a sort of absence, this absence in turn makes possible a certain presence, the presence of being to consciousness. Only through the nothingness of consciousness can being become present to itself as consciousness.

'The law of being of the For-itself, as the ontological foundation of consciousness', Sartre tells us, 'is to be itself in the form of presence to itself' (p. 77). Whereas nothingness implies an absence of foundation, a disengagement of being from itself, the For-itself, as that to which consciousness can be attributed, does possess the character of being. The For-itself is itself in the form of presence to itself. But what is meant here by 'presence'? Essentially, two very different characteristics which, however, belong together. On the one hand, presence refers to the presence of being to the self. In this sense the ontological foundation of presence is a duality, the duality of the For-itself and the In-itself. On the other hand, the For-itself is present to itself and must be so if it is to be a consciousness. The unity implied in the presence of the For-itself to itself is the unity of the self, a unity which can only be negatively clarified. For the unity in question here is not that of an identity. The For-itself cannot be identical with itself since self-identity is the law of being of the In-itself. On the other hand, the unity of the For-itself with itself cannot be comprehended as that of a self-conscious consciousness which makes of its own self an *object* of consciousness. To be sure, the self *can* always make itself an object of consciousness but only on the basis of that very unity of its self which is in question here and which must already have been presupposed. To account for this coincidence of the self with itself, a coincidence which neither is reducible to an identity nor yet can be opened up into an explicit duality, Sartre reverts to his concept of a *pre-reflective cogito*, which he now further elaborates in terms of an interesting structure of the dyad 'reflection–reflecting'.

Prior to, and as the necessary condition of, any positional consciousness 'of', there exists a pre-reflective self-consciousness,which can never, however, be clarified by way of any normal procedure of reflection. For as soon as I try to grasp the consciousness reflected on I am immediately referred to the reflecting consciousness, and as soon as I try to grasp the reflecting consciousness I am immediately referred back to the consciousness reflected on. It is this 'game of reflections' which characterizes the 'two in one' definitive of the unity of the For-itself. The For-itself is a unity. That is, there is in principle a difference between consciousness and itself, a difference which makes it legitimate to talk of the self as a synthesis. But the two terms of this synthesis can never be separately represented. For the attempt to represent either of these two terms refers consciousness to the other, and vice versa.

The first section of Part Two is devoted to the disengagement of a concept of the self. The rest of Part Two is devoted to a characterization of the selfhood of the For-itself. The critical terms 'facticity' and 'possibility' are taken from Heidegger. But they are employed in a new way. Facticity characterizes the For-itself in its very relation to itself. In addition to this relation of itself to itself the self also exists in a world, that is, relates itself to that which is *not* itself. However, as that nothingness which it is, the relation of the self to the world can only take the form of a projection of the nothingness of itself upon being. In projecting the nothingness of itself upon being, the self brings into being *values*, on the one hand, and *possibilities*, on the other. Value is not; it is made to be. Possibility is not; it is made to be. In other words, both the being of value and the being of possibility are traceable back to a self which cannot be the foundation of its own being though it can, and must, be the foundation of its own nothingness. As the foundation of its own nothingness, what the self brings into being by being-in-the-world, namely, value and possibility, is precisely what does not itself possess the mode of being of the In-itself.

The facticity of the For-itself is arrived at by way of two seemingly antithetical concepts, that of *contingency* and that of *foundation* or even self-foundation. The In-itself is, of course, entirely contingent. For this very reason it cannot found itself qua In-itself. But it can found itself in a secondary sense by giving itself the characteristics of the For-itself. However, the In-itself can only become the For-itself in so far as it loses itself as In-itself, negates itself qua In-itself in order to become a For-itself which denies with regard to itself that it is an In-itself. So being In-itself can neither found itself qua In-itself nor even found itself through the 'absolute event' or 'ontological act' by means of which it becomes a For-itself since, in the latter case, it has to lose itself as In-itself as the very condition of becoming a For-itself. Does this mean that the For-itself, unlike the In-itself, can found itself? Yes and no. For although it is through the For-itself that the idea of a self-foundation comes into being, this does not mean that the For-itself can found itself by furnishing itself with a being. Rather, the For-itself can only found itself by being the foundation not of its *being* but of its own *nothingness*. In so far as the For-itself is the foundation of its own nothingness, it is totally responsible for itself. In so far as being the foundation of its own nothingness means negating being, more specifically negating the In-itself which it is, the For-itself is totally unjustified.

If the For-itself were able to found itself, qua being, it would give itself whatever characteristics it wished; that is, it would cease to be a *contingent* and would become a *necessary* being. The For-itself is not a necessary being and yet it has to take responsibility for that very being as which it is. So facticity brings with it not merely the sheer contingency of being this very person who I am but also the anxiety of having to take full responsibility for myself – without ever having chosen the self for which I am, and have to be, responsible.

It is this facticity of the For-itself which makes it be that the For-itself is, exists. In other words, the nothingness of the For-itself does not imply a nihilation or suspension of existence. Rather, I am in every instance this one, born on such a date of such and such parents, in such and such a country, of a certain sex, colour, racial type etc. Thus, although at this point the descriptions retain a purely abstract and general character, the facticity in question may by implication be assumed to refer to at least two things: my being a body (which will be dealt with in Chapter Two of Part Three) and my being-in-situation (which will be dealt with in Chapter One of Part Four). To put it another way, just as the doctrine of presence sufficed to account for the *unity* of the For-itself, the principle of facticity suffices to account for the *concrecity* of the For-itself.

And yet the law of being of the For-itself is to be what it is not and to not be what it is. If the phenomenon of facticity concentrates primarily upon the 'not being what it is', 'being what it is not' is the primary focus of Sartre's analysis of value (Section III). It is for this reason that the analysis of value is introduced by way of a reference, first to the structure of *transcendence*, and then to the structure of *lack*. The self-transcending character of human being Sartre takes over from Heidegger. But the conception of human reality in terms of consciousness and the definition of consciousness as a Nothingness adds a new poignancy to the problematic of transcendence. For the For-itself is condemned to 'perpetually determining itself not to be the in-itself' (p. 85). Consciousness is born as a negation of that In-itself which it is not. For this very reason, it experiences the In-itself as that which it would have to be to be itself. Or rather, it experiences its own self-transcending relation to the In-itself as the attempt to accomplish a synthesis of the For-itself and the In-itself, a synthesis which, by the very nature of things, is impossible. Though the 'impossible synthesis' (Sartre's own expression) can never be achieved, the For-itself is not free *not* to project such a synthesis and to *seek* to attain it. For the being of consciousness as a Nothingness which stands in need of being is a mode of being which is experienced by the For-itself as lack. Lack is therefore not an additional characteristic which somehow supervenes. Rather the For-itself is constituted, in its being, by lack, by the lack of that which would if, *per impossibile*, it could ever be realized, enable it to *be itself*.

Sartre analyses the being of lack in terms of three mutually supporting structures: that which is lacking, that which lacks and the lacked. The lacked is precisely that impossible synthesis (of the For-itself with the In-itself) which motivates the movement of transcendence. That which lacks is the being which exists itself as not being what it is and being what it is not – human being. The lacking is what existing human being lacks in order to be the 'impossible synthesis' of the For-itself with the In-itself. Sartre uses the existence of desire to illustrate the nature of this ontological lack. Desire is existed as a lack which points beyond itself towards that which would (if it ever could be attained) make the For-itself be what it lacks, therefore cease to exist itself as lack. But in surpassing itself towards a being by which it would be completed, the For-itself would be converting itself into an In-itself and, in so doing, suppressing the very consciousness engaged in such a self-surpassing. Drink, drugs and other such anaesthetizing remedies do represent just such a project of self-annihilation, and the satisfaction which they may momentarily bring is the satisfaction of an artificial completion which, however, is not merely doomed to extinction but to an extinction destined to drag its proponent down into ever more abysmal depths.

And so to *value*. The being of the self, Sartre tells us, is value. And value, he goes on, is the being of that which does not have being. So far from either of these statements appearing either internally incoherent or inconsistent with its complement, the complementarity of the two claims should now be immediately apparent. For if the being of value is the being of that which does not have being, this can only be because that being by which alone value can be made to be and sustained in being is a being which itself does not possess being (in the sense of an In-itself) but has to make itself be and sustain itself in being, namely, the For-itself. Notice what this conception of the being of value implies. First, there are no transcendent values, no values 'in reality', whether this real being of value is sought along the lines of Platonic realism, theological dogmatism or utilitarian naturalism. But second, the being of value cannot even be conceived as an ideality, neither a Kantian prescriptive norm nor even a phenomenologically descriptive ideality in the Schelerian sense. All such attempts (to confer a being upon value) are doomed to failure. For they all assume that value *is* whereas, in reality, the being of value consists in *not being*.

As long as Sartre restricts his analyses to such phenomena as desire or feeling, the sheer relativism of the wanting implied thereby seems both relatively realistic and harmless. But as soon as the focus is shifted to the more properly moral realm of the will it becomes apparent that the Sartrian ontology not only makes the construction of a morality difficult (as does Heidegger's) but actively militates against the very possibility of such a morality. Sartre decides to postpone discussion of the moral implications of his conception of value until the examination of the For-others. But we know how seriously he must have viewed this impossibility not only from the last chapter of this book where it is addressed under the head of 'Ethical Implications' but from his obviously unsuccessful attempt to rectify this lacuna in the very inadequate lecture: 'Existentialism and Humanism'. No doubt one of the motives for his later Marxist conversion was his appreciation of the need for an ideology which would make it possible for an individual to struggle *against* injustice (therefore *for* the value of justice), *against* exploitation (therefore *for* the value of fairness). But the intellectual inadequacies of this later project (let alone its radical inconsistency with his first philosophy) only serve to highlight the unjustifiablity of value in the Sartrian philosophical universe, with all the consequences that follow therefrom. To borrow (and then to bend) a phrase from Dostoyevsky, if consciousness is a Nothingness (and if in consequence the being of value consists in its having no being), then anything is possible – as the history of this century has amply demonstrated.

In order to understand what Sartre means by the being of possibilities (Section IV), it is best to begin at the end with Sartre's own definition. 'The possible is the something which the For-itself lacks in order to be itself' (p. 102). From this it is clear that the being of possibility represents yet another attempt at the impossible synthesis (of the For-itself with the In-itself). As such it is just another expression of the structure of transcendence. The For-itself exists itself as a lack which, as such, stands in need of something in order to be itself, that is, to complete itself. One might say for purposes of convenience that with regard to this triple structure, For-itself–lack–world, facticity relates primarily to the self, value to the world, while possibility brings the two sides together in the unitary structure of lack. For possibility can only come into being through the For-itself. But the For-itself can only be the being through which possibilities arise in so far as it is not itself, that is, in so far as it fails to coincide with itself, transcends itself *towards* the world. Through this dynamic of transcendence, possibilities are projected by the self upon the world and, moreover, projected as the self's own possibilities of being.

We should not, however, be under any illusions about Sartre's originality. Though Sartre does give the concept of 'possibilities of being' a new twist, it is more or less straightforwardly taken over from Heidegger. We find here the same exclusion of logical possibility or of any concept of possibility which would make of it a thought, a mental representation. We find the same exclusion of the deficient concept of possibility as that whose imminent realization cannot be categorically affirmed. We also find a refusal of the Aristotelian concept of possibility as potentiality – in this case because it would imply a category of becoming which Sartre will never admit.

Chapter One concludes with a section (V) on the self which is deliberately foreshortened due to the fact that Sartre had already dealt with the central issue in some detail in his fascinating article: 'The Transcendence of the Ego'. Essentially, Sartre simply repeats here what he affirmed there, namely, that the self cannot be conceived as an Ego. Such a conception results from an attempt to objectify the self, to fix the For-itself in terms of categories which belong exclusively to the In-itself. Not-being-itself means that the For-itself can only be by continually transcending itself, surpassing itself towards a world which is other than itself but without which, nevertheless, it could not even conceive of itself as a For-itself, that is, as a lack, since the very concept of the lacking would be vacuous in the absence of something which could, possibly, make up the lack in the self.

Chapters Two and Three of Part Two belong together in the sense that they spell out the two co-ordinate dimensions of time (Chapter Two) and space (Chapter Three). This is not quite accurate. For the nomenclature 'transcendence' rather than space was no doubt deliberately adopted for Chapter Three to accommodate the disclosure of a worldly time, what Bergson would have called 'spatialized time'. Furthermore, Chapter Three focuses not so much upon space as upon knowledge, and the mode of appearance of the In-itself (quality and quantity) in so far as the latter is what I am not (determination as negation). With these qualifications, let us turn to Sartre's theory of time.

Once again, Sartre is deeply indebted to Heidegger, in this case for his concept of existential time. But the static, dualistic ontology to which Sartre now attempts to accord a specific and characteristic temporality is, in my opinion, so far removed from what is required to render intelligible a variant of

Heidegger's existential time that this section cannot but fail in its basic intention, which is to render intelligible the existential temporality of human being. To put it another way, Sartre is still so very much under the spell of Descartes that he finds himself more or less incapable of transcending that very instantaneity which he himself will criticize as the limiting factor in the Cartesian conception of time. But when a creative thinker makes life difficult for himself something interesting always results!

Sartre chooses to divide his analysis of temporality into three parts, a first part devoted to a so-called 'pre-ontological, phenomenological' description of the three dimensions of time, a second part devoted to an 'ontological' description of static and dynamic temporality and a third part devoted to reflection in connection with the relation of 'original' to 'psychic' temporality. It is difficult to justify these headings, particularly the distinction between an initial, phenomenological and a subsequent, ontological analysis. In a very real sense they are both ontological since they both bring out the connection between time and the ontological categories fundamental to *Being and Nothingness*.

The aim of the so-called phenomenological description is to offer an account of the three temporal dimensions, one which connects these dimensions, quite explicitly, with the mode of being of the For-itself and the In-itself. Sartre's first task is to dissociate his theory from any view which isolates Man on the 'instantaneous island' of the present. Since he accepts the premises of a philosophy of consciousness, premises which link him with Descartes and Husserl, among others, and which forbid him to conduct his analyses on the plane of an objectified conception of time (time as an order and connection inherent in being), he is able only to escape the charge of according primacy to the present in two ways. The first way is by stressing the transcendence of consciousness. The For-itself is not obliged to remain within the limits of an immanental analysis for which the truth of evidence is available only in the present. Indeed, it cannot remain so confined. For it pertains to the very being of the For-itself to transcend itself, to be for that which is other than itself. And second, the transcendence of consciousness in turn makes possible a reversal without which an adequate understanding of the relation of both past and future to the present would be impossible. I do not have to, and indeed cannot, ask how the past and the future stand in relation to the present. On the contrary, I have to take my stand in a present which is *my* present and then ask how this being which is myself (in its self-transcending relation to that which is not itself) comes to stand in relation to a past (which is not myself in the mode of the 'no longer') and a future (which is not myself in the mode of the 'not yet').

Fundamental to Sartre's analysis of the temporal dimension of the past (as also of the other temporal dimensions) is the insight that there is no such thing as a universal or objective past, a past which is quite independent of any consciousness to which it is present as past. There is a past only because there are beings whose mode of being is such that they cannot be who they are. I am, in the first instance, *my* past and I am it in the mode of not being able to be it (re-live it), as also in the mode of not being able to change it (I can reinterpret the meaning of my past but only on the basis of a factual reality which is given), and again, in the mode of not being able to be without a past (I cannot be who I am without having been already). 'This contingency of the for-itself, this weight surpassed and preserved in the very surpassing – this is facticity' (p. 118).

'In contrast to the Past which is in-itself, the Present', Sartre tells us, 'is for-itself' (p. 120). But does this not imply that, at least, I can *be* my present? Sartre's rejection of this possibility not only saves him from the instantaneity of a conception of time based on the present, but this conception is ruled out by the very way in which he conceives of the For-itself. For the For-itself is what it is not and is not what it is. What is present to the self in the present is being In-itself. And this is what the self cannot be. Again, that to which being In-itself is present is a For-itself. But the For-itself cannot even be itself. The structure of negation is to be found as deeply rooted in the present as in the past and it is for this reason that there can be no question of founding time on the present. The present is not and the internal negation which refuses the identification of the self with itself (or with being) at the same time forces the self beyond itself – primarily towards the future.

The future is what the For-itself can still be in the sense that it is a lack which needs the future to make up what it lacks. The future is the dimension of possibility, possibilities which I can project in advance and strive to realize. If the self could be the possibilities which it projects it would succeed in being itself in the fullest sense, where by being itself is meant being the foundation of its own being. But, of course, as each possibility is realized, it ceases to be a possibility and becomes a reality, a reality which, as such, now falls back into the In-itself. But I cannot be this fixed and reified possibility. For being my possibilities means being for ever beyond myself towards that which is not yet but still has to come.

But if the past, the present and the future are not, this does not mean that time is non-existent, unreal, or what have you. It only means that time is as unreal (or as real) as that very being whose structures it reproduces so exactly, namely, the For-itself. Time is as real (or as unreal) as the self, indeed is the self in so far as the structure of negation (constitutive of the self) can be articulated in such a way as to bring to light the being past, present and future of the self.

Section II dealing with the ontology of temporality is itself then further divided into two sections, the first devoted to a *structural* analysis of the relation 'before–after', the second to a *dynamic* examination of the way in which the 'before' becomes the 'after'. The key to Sartre's position is his insistence upon an *intrinsic* connection between the 'before' and the 'after', the kind of connection which only a consciousness is capable of establishing. Only a being which temporalizes itself is capable of engendering the negativity inherent in one instant not being the next – by simply existing. Is there such a being? Yes, the For-itself.

The negativity characteristic of the For-itself is a triple negativity: (1) to not-be what it is; (2) to be what it is not; (3) to be what it is not and to not-be what it is (p. 137). What one is (already) is what one was. So, to not-be what one is means to stand in relation to one's past. What one is not (yet) is what one will be. So, to be what one is not is to stand in relation to the future. Finally, that being which 'is what it is not and is not what it is' is the For-itself in that very relation of presence to itself which is constitutive of its being. The temporal dimension of presence is however – the present. Thus Sartre is able to get the three dimensions of the time-order out of the triple negativity of the For-itself. Even nominally, however, it is clear from this exposition that the present must be the privileged dimension since it includes both the other two within itself. Recognizing Heidegger's insistence upon the future and not wishing to be associated with Descartes and Husserl, Sartre plays down this primacy. But his qualification: 'No one of these dimensions has any ontological priority over the other. . . . Yet in spite of all this, it is best to put the accent on the present ekstasis and not on the future ekstasis as Heidegger does' (p. 142) gives the game away. Sartre's theory of time and of consciousness is still committed to the 'doctrine of presence', that very doctrine which Heidegger condemns as the prejudice of traditional metaphysics.

In Section II, devoted to the dynamic of temporality, Sartre's problems are compounded. If a static structural analysis of the order of time proved difficult enough, it becomes that much more difficult for Sartre's essentially static and structural conception of consciousness to come to terms with the passage of time (the kind of duration to which Bergson devoted so much attention). The difficulty can be presented in terms of a simple question: How can change be a characteristic of the For-itself if there is no place in Sartre's analyses for the category of becoming? And yet, the For-itself does temporalize itself, does drive the present back into the past by anticipating a future. His answer, that the For-itself is a spontaneity, a spontaneity which is obliged to refuse what it affirms and then seek to recuperate this very refusal, does perhaps give him a certain lee-way. But is a succession of negations (not this, not this, not this) really so different from a succession of instants (this, this, this)?

Much more interesting than the above is Section III which purports to be about the relation between an original temporality and a derived, psychic temporality but which really has much more to do with Sartre's account of two forms of reflection, an *impure* form which accounts for the reification of the self and the hypostatization of states and qualities (and which can be dismissed because it is a project in 'bad faith') and a *pure* form which accounts for the Husserlian project of a pure phenomenological reflection (and which can be dismissed as representing just another attempt to realize the impossible project – of being one's own foundation). Thus, this third section can be seen as an integral part of two critical intellectual battles constantly waged by Sartre against *psychology*, on the one hand, and *transcendental phenomenology*, on the other.

Though pure reflection turns out to be a failure it is, one might say, a glorious failure in that it succeeds in conducting its analyses upon a genuinely original plane. By contrast, impure reflection might be called an inglorious success. It accomplishes what it sets out to attain but only by losing sight of the original dynamic of consciousness and so substituting for the latter a pale, because reified, reflection. To cut a long story short, it is impure reflection which makes psychology possible as the study of a pseudo-object given in such a way that the Ego can be *in itself* what it is in reality only *for others*. The Ego, together with its psychic objects (states and qualities and acts), is not; it is made to be and made to be through impure reflection.

Thus far Part Two has been dominated by the investigation of the self and of consciousness – to the point that it might even be supposed that, following Husserl, Sartre too was committed to the absoluteness of consciousness *vis-à-vis* being. In fact the exact opposite is the case. For Sartre, it is being In-itself which is the absolute, with regard to which consciousness is a merely relative and dependent being. It is time therefore to give being its due, more specifically to investigate anew the original ontological bond between the For-itself and the In-itself. Sartre undertakes this investigation under the head 'Transcendence'.

'The for-itself is a being such that in its being, its being is in question in so far as this being is essentially a certain way of not being a being which it posits simultaneously as other than itself' (p. 174). This is how Sartre defines the original negation constitutive of the ontological bond which connects the For-itself with the In-itself, and from which a number of important conclusions can be drawn. First, it confirms the non-substantial character of Sartre's ontology, and so its supposed opposition to Cartesianism. This was always obvious on the side of consciousness since the very definition of consciousness as a Nothingness sufficed to establish this point. But Sartre will also refuse to accord the characteristic of substantiality to being In-itself. This becomes particularly clear in the identification of quality with being. 'Quality is nothing other than the being of the *this* when it is considered apart from all external relation with the world or with other thises' (p. 186). To be sure, being In-itself stands in need of nothing in order to be itself – and in this sense it possesses an independence which is denied to the For-itself. But even the permanence of the object is explained in terms of temporality and therefore in terms of the ontological relation between the In-itself and the For-itself (p. 193).

Second, as simply being what it is, being In-itself is not to be regarded as having been constituted or constructed by consciousness. In view of the fact that by being In-itself Sartre means more or less 'objective reality', we may discount his claim to the effect that, with the original upsurge of the For-itself, being already manifests itself as being In-itself. We know (from psychology and from anthropology) that being does not give itself originally as an objective reality and it was this limitation which Husserl sought to overcome with his constitutional analyses and which Heidegger, in his own very different way, sought to rectify with his regressive enquiry into a more primordial being-in-the-world of human being. Just as serious as this ontological deficiency (and indeed based upon it), is Sartre's epistemological failure to account for the relation of adequation (correspondence of knowledge and its object). Because Sartre simply assumes that being gives itself to consciousness *from the very first* as an objective reality he never seriously raises the question how knowledge (as knowledge of an objective reality) is itself possible. Instead, his ontological epistemology is restricted to a simple, and to this extent superfluous, insistence upon the being of knowledge.

The section (II) concerned with determination as negation is misleading. For it seems to address the famous statement of Spinoza '*Omnis determinatio est negatio*', a statement which forms the starting point for Hegel's dialectical treatment of negation. In fact, Sartre's fundamental dualism runs counter to ontological monism and to the progressive differentiation of reality (through negation) which such a position permits. So Sartre's own treatment of totalizing negation moves along completely different lines. The nihilating act by which the For-itself makes itself be what it is is also an act by which the For-itself totalizes itself, that is, grasps its self as a unity. But since this self totalization is only possible by way of a negation of that which it is not, namely, the In-itself, the act by which the For-itself totalizes itself is also an act by which it totalizes what is not itself. This does not mean that being is or ever can be given as a whole (whatever that might mean). But it does mean that any particular 'this' (item of experience) can only give itself as such against a ground. In this way, Sartre is able to bring the Heideggerian concept of 'world' into relation with the Gestalt psychological concept of the figure–ground relation and, at the same time, to clear the way for a more explicit investigation of spatiality.

Fundamental to Sartre's conception of space is his distinction between an internal and an external negation/relation. 'By an internal negation', Sartre tells us, 'we understand such a relation between two beings that the one which is denied to the other qualifies the other at the heart of its essence – by absence' (p. 175). The original ontological bond which brings the For-itself into being in its opposition to the In-itself is an (indeed the most basic) instance of an internal relation, based upon an internal negation. Through the totalizing function of that self which denies with respect to its self that it is the In-itself, the In-itself is itself totalized as a worldly ground. But this totalized ground may always collapse into a collection of distinct beings. And it does do so whenever the internal negation, constitutive of the world as ground, is superseded by an external relation (or system of such relations) obtaining between one this and another. As a purely indifferent relation between two or more beings, an external relation leaves the beings so related unaffected in their being by the relation which may be said to obtain between them. Quality is the being of the 'this' in so far as an *internal* relation relates the 'this' to a For-itself. Quantity characterizes the being of more than one 'this' in so far as an *external* relation distinguishes each from the other, an external relation which, in so far as it can only exist for a For-itself, is itself dependent upon the more primary internal relation (of the For-itself to the In-itself). Finally, the systematic formalization of this purely external relation between 'this and that' is space.

In addition to the difficulties and limitations we have already noted there is much that is either derivative or inadequate in this chapter. *Instrumentality* is undoubtedly introduced to accommodate Heidegger's ready-to-hand. But instead of tackling this extremely important theme the analysis wanders off into a further examination of the phenomenon of flight from self. As one of the very few philosophers to feature as an artist in his own right one might have expected more in the way of an aesthetics from Sartre. But the few paragraphs devoted to *beauty* do little more than bring out the connection between beauty and value. The extended investigation of a *time of the world* is again a concession to Heidegger and attempts to explain how universal, objective time arises on the basis of ontological temporality as a kind of pseudo-time explicable in terms of an inherent tendency (on the part of the For-itself) to reify itself, that is, confer upon its self the mode of being of an In-itself.

Part Three: Being-for-others

Part Three, entitled Being-for-others is, in my estimate, one of the most brilliant and intriguing sections of *Being and Nothingness*. Beginning with a strictly philosophical enquiry into the problem of the existence of others, it moves through a concerted attempt to integrate the body into the structure of the For-itself, to conclude with a fascinating account of concrete relations with others, an account which is amply and variously illustrated in Sartre's literary projects. In fact, the most famous line of his play *No Exit*, the oft quoted 'Hell is other people', is nothing but a literary comment upon the philosophical theme: 'conflict is the original meaning of being-for-others' (p. 364).

Part Three falls into three chapters, the first devoted to the existence of others, the second to the body and the third to concrete relations with others. The most important chapter is undoubtedly the third and conclusive chapter where the concrete implications of Sartre's theory of intersubjectivity are spelt out. In order to save time, I shall pass over the historical critique entitled 'Husserl, Hegel and Heidegger', even though I recommend this section wholeheartedly to the student interested in Sartre's own placement of his theory in relation to the tradition in which he situates his philosophy. Moreover, since I have grave doubts as to the legitimacy of Sartre's concept of the Body-for-itself I shall not engage in a detailed exposition of Chapter Two, more especially as the theme of this chapter, body consciousness, is much more adequately dealt with by Merleau-Ponty.

Perhaps the best way to begin is with a point Sartre makes at the end of the first chapter. Being-for-others is in fact the third of three so-called ekstases – a term taken from Heidegger but applied by Sartre in a distinctive way. Literally 'ekstasis' means standing out. Heidegger links 'ekstasis' primarily with his own conception of transcendence. For Sartre, on the other hand, it is linked primarily with the structure of negation. The *first ekstasis* in this trilogy is that whereby consciousness denies with regard to itself that it is the In-itself. The nihilation in question is therefore one whereby the self first comes into being as a consciousness which denies with respect to itself that it is the In-itself. The *second ekstasis* is one whereby the self nihilates its self with a view to founding itself as a Nothingness. The self which cannot be its own foundation but which can be the foundation of its own nothingness founds itself through a kind of reflective recuperation of its self, one which is constitutive of its self as that very nothingness which it is – and which it is in consequence aware of itself as being. The *third ekstasis* is one whereby the self constitutes itself as not being the Other, in which the self becomes aware of itself as taken away from itself by the Other which it is not. The third ekstasis is, in fact, the most radical of the three, since the Other is not just that being which the self is not but is itself a self in its own right, a self for which therefore the original self is itself an object. Hence the problem of solipsism.

With a view to representing the problem of solipsism (which Sartre's analyses endeavour to overcome in a new and original way), one could do no better than to present this problem in Sartre's own words. 'My body as a thing in the world and the Other's body are the necessary intermediaries between the Other's consciousness and mine. The Other's soul is therefore separated from mine by all the distance which separates first my soul from my body, then my body from the Other's body, and finally the Other's body from his soul' (p. 223). These distances are by no means identical. The distance which separates me from my own body will turn out to be an internal distance overcome by way of an internal relation – and the same goes for the distance which separates the Other from its body, which is the only way the Other can appear to me. On the other hand, the distance which separates the Other's body from mine is a purely external distance, one which can therefore only be surmounted by way of a purely external relation. However, an external relation cannot provide the foundation for an 'ontological bond' between self and other. Thus in the end this external distance will, as it were, have to be suspended, or at least subsumed beneath an internal relation (between my self and the Other) which will constitute the basis for an ontological bond without which the problem of solipsism will remain unsolved and unsolvable in principle. Thus it is that, in his critique of Husserl, Hegel and Heidegger, Sartre lays the primary stress on the error which consists in affirming that my fundamental connection with the Other is realized by knowledge (p. 233).

Sartre's solution to the problem of solipsism is given by the structure of what he calls 'the look'. As always, Sartre's starting point here is the *cogito*, a *cogito* which is as existential as it is epistemological in character. Due to the *cogito*, I can have no access to the subjectivity of the Other, who appears to me as a simple object of consciousness. That immediate access to my own being as a being which exists its consciousness 'of' is for ever denied me in connection with the Other. In so far as I look at the Other, I affirm myself as an existing consciousness for which the Other is an object. How then am I to become conscious of the Other *as* an Other, that is, as someone who has its own being to be in much the same way as I have to be myself? It is at this point that Sartre abandons the terrain occupied by traditional theories of intersubjectivity with a view to solving what has hitherto remained unsolvable.

I cannot see the consciousness of the Other or indeed enjoy any other mode of access to the consciousness of the Other for the simple reason that my very attempt is self-defeating. For in making the Other that which I am conscious 'of', I transform the Other into an object of consciousness. I cannot be conscious of the Other but I can be aware of the transformation which the consciousness of the Other effects in *me*. If my attempt to become conscious of the Other transforms the Other into an object for me (and so places the Other beyond my reach) then the only way to re-establish the link between myself and the Other is through an experience which the Other induces in me by his very presence – the experience of being transformed into an object by the Other.

The phenomenon of shame (extensively analysed by Scheler) is the one which Sartre selects to illustrate his theory of 'the look'. I am standing in a corridor looking through a key hole into a room. In so far as my whole being is engaged in the look I am not aware of myself as a physical presence located on this side of the door. Rather I have already transcended myself, am already beyond myself in the room in which my gaze is situated. But suddenly I hear the sound of footsteps descending to the corridor on which I am standing. The sound effects a transformation of my relation to myself. In so far as the implied presence of the Other makes me ashamed of my self, I cease to be a pure transcendence and become a 'transcendence transcended', a transcendence transcended by the implicit presence of the one who is looking at me looking through the key hole. I experience this transcending of my transcendence in shame. Shame makes me be what I am not for myself but for an Other for whom I am nothing but an object. Shame is therefore the experience of my own subjectivity being wrenched away from me, appropriated, even expropriated by the Other – for whom I am nothing but an object. I cannot experience the subjectivity of the Other. But I can experience the transformation effected in me by the subjectivity of the Other.

The beauty of this 'proof' (of the existence of Others) is that it seems to accomplish the impossible, to reach a demonstrative conclusion about the existence of an other consciousness from a standpoint (that of the *cogito*) which would seem to preclude just such a possibility. To be sure, I do not know that the Other whose presence I appear to have intuited is in fact another consciousness. The sound I hear may turn out to have been caused by the footsteps of a dog. But the very fact that my shame dissolves before the knowledge that the Other is only a dog is indicative of the fact that there *are* other consciousnesses, since otherwise I would not be susceptible to feelings such as shame, fear or pride. For feelings of this kind are only so many ways in which I appear to myself *in the face of* an Other.

But the Other is for me not just the one through whom I lose my subjectivity, the one who takes me away from myself, he is also the one who, in another sense, makes me be what I am. In so far as I become aware of my being for the Other, the Other becomes the one through whom I regain my objectness, through whom I acquire a kind of being. Moreover, unlike the quasi-being which I try to make myself be through self-objectification (and which is contradicted by the very nature of that as which I really am, namely, a consciousness), the being which I acquire through the Other is a real being. I really am an

In-itself for the other consciousness, and therefore I can be an In-itself for myself too, in so far as I am aware of myself as being for the Other. But this being (In-itself) which I acquire through the Other will turn out to be an 'unhappy consciousness'. For I can only become something for the Other in so far as I cease to be for myself what I really am, namely, a For-itself. In becoming something for the Other I am robbed of that which constitutes my autonomy and dignity as a For-itself. So far from representing a mutual confirmation of each by the Other, Sartre's theory of inter-personal relations will lead inexorably in the direction of a mutual and reciprocal struggle in which each will seek to negate the Other, will seek to affirm itself at the expense of the Other and will be able to affirm the existence of the Other only at the cost of a self-(ab)negation or subjection of its self to the Other.

But before we turn to Sartre's theory of concrete relations with the Other we need first to cast a glance at the theory of the Body-for-itself. Chapter Two on the Body-for-itself falls into three sections in accordance with a readily comprehensible structure: a first section devoted to the body for-itself, a second section devoted to the body for-others and a third section devoted to what might be called the body-for-others-for-me. In more neutral language, I am, first and foremost, my body. Second, it is as a body that the self appears to others. And finally, my sense of self is largely derived from the way others respond to that body as which I appear to them. The third section is therefore, in an obvious sense, a synthesis of the other two.

The body with which Sartre is concerned here is of course the body subject, what Merleau-Ponty will call 'corps propre' or own body. There can be no question that, for Sartre, the body is to be regarded as a structure of the For-itself. In connection with his definition of the body as the 'contingent form which is assumed by the necessity of my contingency' (p. 408; see also p. 432), Sartre says: 'The body is nothing other than the for-itself.' The question is whether Sartre is entitled to a concept of the Body-for-itself, given the general nature and structure of his ontology. While following Descartes in so many respects, Sartre chooses to depart from him radically on this subject. Whereas, for Descartes, the subject–object duality goes along with a mind–body duality, for Sartre, the equivalent of the subject–object duality (his being–nothingness duality) does not go along with the equivalent of the mind–body duality, the duality, namely, of consciousness (qua Nothingness) and the body (In-itself). Rather, the latter duality is supposedly overcome in the structure of the body For-itself.

But if my body is to be reducible to a structure of the For-itself then it must be subject to the law of being of the For-itself. The law of being of the For-itself is, as we have seen, to be what it is not and to not be what it is. But if the For-itself is itself only in so far as it effects such a double negation, then the incorporation of the body within the structure of the For-itself immediately poses a problem. For it now has to be possible to describe my being a body in terms of just such a double negation. To be sure, the external negation of what is not the self falls well within the scope of the Body-for-itself since it is simply indicative of the resistance of everything other to my action. But what of the internal negation? If it is as an In-itself that the For-itself negates its body then the body has obviously ceased to be a For-itself and become an In-itself instead. But how can the For-itself negate itself as a Body-for-itself without assuming a coincidence of itself with itself – the very coincidence which, for Sartre, would be the death of consciousness. As long as consciousness is not its body, it can always negate itself in the form of a negation of that body *as which* it is given to be but *with which* it cannot, nevertheless, be identified. But as soon as consciousness is supposed to *be* its body it can no longer assume with regard to itself that very distance from itself which makes of consciousness a nothingness. On the other hand, as soon as the For-itself takes up a distance with regard to itself, qua body, it ceases to *be* an embodied For-itself and becomes instead a pure consciousness which, at best, merely *has* a body.

We will not labour this point any further because, in a very different sense, we shall find Merleau-Ponty talking of a 'practical cogito' and, in accordance therewith, a body consciousness which is ontologically fundamental. It is not *what* Sartre attempts to do which is suspect but the *way* he attempts to do it. The very fact that he *first* defines the self in terms of consciousness and only *then* goes on to try to integrate the body into the structure of the self is already indicative of the basic incompatibility of his conception of consciousness with the conception of consciousness needed to make possible an analysis of what might be called body-consciousness. In fact, the Sartrian ontology is much more successful in explaining how it is that I *cease* to be my body than it is in explaining my original oneness with that body which is my own.

This becomes even more apparent in the final section on the Body-for-others. To be sure, the body is the way the other appears to me, and indeed the only way (s)he can so appear to me. But then, that is in large part because the other is *not* me. The seeming parallelism of the being for me of the other, qua body, and the being for the other of myself, qua body, is entirely deceptive. If the body is the way I appear to the other it is not, originally, the way in which I appear to myself, as Sartre himself concedes. If, originally, I am my body then it is through the other that, in a sense, I become aware of my body as that by means of which I appear to the other. The 'not-being-the-other' which defines my (internal) relation to the other becomes constitutive of my very being-self *only* in so far as I adopt towards myself the point of view of the other. Thus the alienation I experience in my relation to the other becomes constitutive of my own self-alienation in so far as I come to see my body as something alien to my self. Indeed, this self-alienation is already apparent in the original relation to my body in so far as the negativity of this relation serves to explain the genesis of the 'psychic body' – the body as it appears to me in so far as it is no longer identical with my self but has already become something alien.

Chapter Three on Concrete Relations with Others is surely one of the most interesting parts of the whole work. The inspiration is Hegelian in so far as Hegel too conceives of human relations in terms of conflict. But it is a Hegelianism with a difference. For instead of the op-position of one self and the other leading to a 'higher' synthesis in which this antinomy is overcome, the conflict leads downward, in the direction of ever more degenerate forms of relation. What is aimed at on one level can only be attained by a degeneration to another, lower level, which in turn collapses under its own weight and so has to be re-established at a yet lower level. It is for this reason that I shall call the logic of this chapter a 'dialectical degeneration'.

It could be said that the entire dialectical degeneration is motivated by the renewal of an old ambition, to be one's own foundation – the God-like ideal which haunts Sartre's conception of human reality. It has already been shown that, although I cannot be my own foundation, *qua being*, I can be the foundation of my own Nothingness. But the appearance of the Other seems to give me a new opportunity. For I am, for the Other, a body-for-itself, that is, something rather than nothing. Since it is through the Other's freedom that I am, for the Other, a being, if only I could appropriate the freedom of the Other, I should have appropriated that by means of which I am made to be what I am. Through the Other I can therefore aspire to being my own foundation, qua being, but only in so far as I can get hold of, appropriate, assimilate the Other's freedom, that freedom which is the consciousness of the Other in its self-transcending flight towards me. Can such an aspiration be projected? And, if projected, can it actually be realized?

The starting point for Sartre's analysis is his solution to the problem of solipsism – the look. There are two sides to the look (looking and looked at), and that is why there are two basic attitudes towards the Other, each of which starts its own sequence of degenerations. However, Sartre stresses that it is only for purposes of analytical convenience that these two attitudes are distinguished. In reality they belong to each other and are readily convertible each into the other.

If the Other looks at me, I experience the transformation of my self into an object for the Other. I become a transcendence transcended, a consciousness thrown back upon itself and forced to witness its own solidification under the gaze of the Other. But this transformation of the For-itself has its compensations. Through the Other, I can become something for myself. In so far as I can be that object in which the Other chooses to lose itself, the object through which the Other surrenders its freedom, I am founded in my being by an Other for whom I am an absolute end, the end in which the Other chooses to lose itself. This attitude is what Sartre calls 'love'. The degeneration of this attitude will eventually lead to 'masochism'. On the other hand, in order to save myself from the reification which comes from being looked at, I can look back at the one looking. In so far as I succeed in transcending the transcendence of the Other, the Other becomes for me an object. This attitude is what Sartre calls 'indifference'. The degeneration of this attitude will eventually lead to 'sadism'.

The very terms employed to describe the dialectical degeneration suggest what is in fact the case, that Sartre's theory of human relations is heavily weighted in the direction of *emotional* and even, one might say, explicitly or implicitly *erotic* relations. This is both its strength and its weakness. No philosopher has succeeded in capturing so effectively the logic underlying the 'battle of the sexes', a battle which, if Freud is to be believed, is fundamental to the very structure and dynamics of the psyche. And yet, obviously, more is involved in human relations than such unqualifiedly erotic ambitions.

The project of love is based upon the passive aim of being looked at. In allowing myself to be looked at, I experience my own possession by the other. The commonplace expression 'undressing someone with one's eyes' suffices to capture the force of this aim of being possessed by the look, even though, in so doing, it fails to recognize its compensations. For, in so far as the Other takes possession of me, I am founded in my being, as a concretely existing human being, by the Other. But this is to present the beloved in too passive a light. To be sure, the beloved wants to be possessed by the Other. But through this possession the beloved can also seek to possess the freedom of the Other by constituting herself as the end in which the Other consents to lose itself. The very freedom by which the beloved is transcended, transformed in its being into a sheer facticity, is the freedom which has to be ensnared and which, in being appropriated, makes of the beloved an absolute end for the lover. So far from being an unjustifiable contingency, the facticity of the loved one is now justified by the passion of the lover. *This* body, with all its *specific* characteristics, is what is loved and which, in being loved, founds the beloved in its very being.

But the project of being founded by the love of the Other is fragile. Though I do want to ensnare, I do not want to enslave the Other – and this is the difference of Sartre's analysis from Hegel. The Hegelian Master does not need or want the freedom of the Slave, who, for his part, experiences the freedom of the Master as a tyrannical imposition. But the beloved does not want to *suppress* the freedom of the lover. The beloved does not want the lover to be so infatuated that he cannot help himself.

Nor does he want the love of the Other through the kind of promise that is made in marriage and to which the lover will adhere only because he has so promised. The beloved wants to be chosen by her lover, that is, chosen by a freedom which is free to choose otherwise and which at every moment reaffirms its commitment to the beloved as a *free* commitment. Only so can the beloved attain what is really wanted, possession not of the body or the outward actions of the Other but of the Other's freedom.

In fact, the project of love is not merely fragile but inherently contradictory. The beloved wants to be loved by a freedom but wants this freedom to surrender itself in such a way that it is no longer free. In constituting myself as the absolute end for the Other, I want to be the one who cannot be transcended by the Other, the one who is everything for the Other and without whom therefore the Other could not continue to be. Worse, I want to capture the freedom of the Other not through my freedom (which would be a denial of the freedom of the Other) but through my own facticity. It is my body which is what the Other must want and yet the For-itself which now wants to be an unsurpassable facticity cannot be identified with its body since otherwise it would be an In-itself, incapable even of conceiving of the project of transcending the Other's transcendence.

The contradiction inherent in the project of love means that the *aim* of love can only be *attained* through a degenerate reduction of love to something else. Officially, Sartre calls this degeneration 'language', though, in my estimate, 'seduction' would have been a better title. It seems that at this point Sartre suddenly became aware of the fact that, hitherto, nothing had been said on the subject of language (one of the most hotly disputed fields of contemporary philosophy), and decided to make good this shortcoming at this point by identifying seduction with language. To be sure, there is such a thing as the 'language of seduction'. But the problem of language is so much larger than any that can be accommodated by expressions in which I make myself agreeable to the Other through words used to attain the objective of seduction that it is an absurdity to imply such an identification. Let us therefore call the 'fascinating language' with which Sartre is concerned here 'seduction'.

Seduction, one might say, is impure love. I am aware now that it is only through my body that I can ensnare the Other, and I deliberately risk assuming my object state in order to leave the Other free to be the one by whom I am appropriated – but only in order to be in a position to appropriate the freedom of the Other through my very object-ness. I wear clothes which make the most of my physical assets. I make myself up, thereby identifying myself with my body and letting it be known that I have consented to my status as desirable, therefore ready to be desired and possessed by the Other. But in so far as I succeed, I fail. For, if the Other is taken in by my seductive project, he gives up precisely what I want to possess – his freedom. If, on the other hand, he refuses to surrender his freedom, I cannot but be one among others for him, one whom he must be free to leave for someone else. But even if he commits himself, this very commitment is a contradiction. For, in 'loving' me, he is really asking to be 'loved' by me. But this demand is antithetical to the very condition of seduction – that I constitute myself as an object available for appropriation by him. And so, if I respond to this demand for love with 'love', the reawakening of my freedom will represent a threat to him, so dampening his ardour.

The failure of seduction motivates one more project, which consists in my freely denying my freedom. My freedom is engaged in the project of its own self-destruction in as much as I no longer even attempt to *use* my body to appropriate the Other's freedom but simply consent to *lose* my freedom through a total identification of myself with my body. This enterprise, Sartre tells us, will be expressed concretely by the masochistic attitude (p. 377). The difference from 'love' is simple. I no longer try to use my object-ness as a trap to ensnare the freedom of the Other. Rather I leave this freedom to be radically free, that is, so free that I myself am transcended by the freedom of the Other. I let the Other use and abuse me in any way (s)he pleases – and enjoy this alienation of myself by the Other.

But even masochism proves to be a failure. First, I must consent to my own object-ness, that is, freely deny my own freedom, which is a contradiction in itself. I do so in order to be nothing but an object. But I am only an object for an Other who is for ever out of reach. Worse, I can only enjoy my object-ness in so far as I am a subjectivity conscious of the reduction of itself to the status of an object – another contradiction. In the end, the pleasure which the masochist seeks can only be the pleasure of failure, the pleasure of knowing that the aim projected can never be attained.

The failure of the first basic attitude can be the occasion for assuming the second. Instead of allowing myself to be looked at, I look at the Other. In so doing I affirm myself as a pure unconditioned freedom confronting an Other who has been reduced to the status of an object. And right away my aim is in contradiction with itself. For if I have failed to attain love by letting myself be looked at then my attempt to apprehend the freedom of the Other through the look will cause the Other, qua subject, to slip through my fingers. As an Other transformed into an object by my look, the Other is a freedom transcended by my freedom, a freedom determined to be nothing but what it is. The peculiar blindness which follows from the reduction of the Other to the status of an object Sartre calls 'indifference'. And, in a graphically vivid phrase he comments: 'there are men who die without – save for brief and terrifying flashes of illumination – ever having suspected what the Other is' (p. 381).

But if indifference is the starting point of the second attitude, then what is to get the dialectical degeneration going? This is a serious question to which, in my opinion, Sartre has no real answer. Or rather, his answers seem contrived to enable him to escape from an untenable position. To be sure, if I install myself in an unequivocal affirmation of my subjectivity then the Other disappears as another subjectivity and I am left with my aloneness. But surely this aloneness will not suffice to generate the unease of loneliness, since loneliness presupposes that I still do recognize the existence of others with whom I *seek* to establish a relationship, a recognition which is at odds with the attitude of indifference. Again, it is all very well for Sartre to talk of 'my original attempt to get hold of the Other's free subjectivity through his objectivity-for-me' as 'sexual desire' (p. 382). But since, as Sartre admits, sexual desire does presuppose at least a minimal recognition of the subjectivity of the other, the basic conditions of the attitude of indifference have again been violated.

But one thing is certain, unless desire does intervene to

disrupt the complacent autonomy of indifference, the dialectical degeneration cannot get started. Allowing Sartre the upsurge of desire, let us now proceed to consider the way in which, for him, desire destroys the attitude of indifference. And this means determining, first and foremost, what desire is. First, desire is not desire for the satisfaction of desire. Here Sartre quite rightly objects to the absurdities of the Freudian analysis, which sees in ejaculation the objective of desire, since it represents the moment in which the tension of desire is released and so relieved. If desire is not desire for pleasure but for the Other through whom I am brought to my own pleasure, then it still remains to be determined how the Other is to be conceived. For second, desire is not desire for another body. Again, quite rightly, Sartre brings out the differences between sexual desire and hunger. Hunger is desire for food and has no other goal than consumption. Sexual desire, on the other hand, is desire for the other person as a For-itself made manifest in and through the body. In other words, sexual desire is, in the end, an attempt to appropriate the subjectivity of the Other as manifest through the body and, in this respect, resembles the appropriative activity of the first attitude.

But if I am presently installed in the attitude of pure self-affirming subjectivity then surely my appropriative project will cause the other to withdraw from the body leaving me with what, strictly speaking, I did not originally desire, the Other as pure and simple body. This is the point at which Sartre resorts to a brilliantly effective distinction between body and flesh. The body, for Sartre, is essentially the body in action, the body as the wilful manifestation of the subjectivity of the For-itself. But there is another way of being a body, being one with one's body – and that is the way of quiescence. In so far as I relax and let my consciousness permeate the body as a whole, I experience my body as consciousness or, if you prefer, my consciousness as body. More to the point, it is through the Other that I can be induced to consent to this quiescence in so far as it brings with it a certain pleasurable experience of myself as flesh. The name Sartre gives to the act by which one body-for-itself is able to establish that contact with another body-for-itself which will make it possible for the Other to enjoy its self as body made flesh is 'the caress'. But the condition of my being able to induce the Other to become flesh is that I should first have consented to my own incarnation as flesh.

We are now in possession of all the ingredients needed to explain how one body-for-itself seeks to take possession of another. Recognizing the futility of my own self-affirmation, I deliberately disguise my appropriative act, that is, present the act in the guise of a caress. By letting my consciousness be clogged by the body I reduce the threat represented by my appropriative activity and so induce the Other to allow its consciousness to be reciprocally incarnated as flesh. And the bribe with which I tempt the Other to consent to such a descent is precisely the pleasure that comes with just such a double reciprocal incarnation. I make myself be flesh in order that my desire succeed in eliciting an equivalent incarnation in the Other, an incarnation through which I am able to take possession of the other For-itself through its body.

But even this attempt to appropriate the Other through desire fails. First, and most obviously, sexual pleasure is the death of desire and a return to indifference. Worse, the desire I have aroused in the Other may be continued by the Other as the enjoyment by the Other of his or her own flesh – with no further reference to me. I, who have been the means by which the Other came to enjoy its flesh, now find myself faced with an enjoyment in which I no longer share. Confronted by a mass of writhing flesh locked into a self-contained enjoyment from which I have been expelled, desire turns to disgust. Worse, this desire turned disgust is a troubling desire, a desire which reminds me of the sacrifice (of my own autonomy) which I have had to make to arouse desire in the Other. But if I seek to re-establish my appropriative supremacy by becoming once again a pure unqualified subjectivity, I find that the Other can still respond to my withdrawal from the body by withdrawing herself from her body, leaving me to assuage my appetite upon a corpse from which the Other has already taken flight.

This is the point at which the seductive initiative turns to sadism. For although the Other may be free to refuse the temptation of *pleasure*, it is by no means so easy to remain oblivious to the pressure of *pain*. In order to appropriate the Other through the body, I need the Other to identify with his or her own body. The Other refuses to freely consent to her incarnation in the flesh? So be it! From bribing I can always turn to bullying, forcing upon the Other an incarnation (s)he is no longer willing to offer. To be sure, any residual element of affection has now turned to open hostility. But what of that? I can enjoy her inability to free herself from me and from the pain I have chosen to inflict upon her. I can experience her resistance as a resistance to be overcome and can enjoy the supplementary exertion required to subdue her.

Nevertheless, sadism too bears within itself the seeds of its own destruction. Sadism arose as the failure of desire. But desire returns to make sadism fail. Inasmuch as I begin to enjoy the pain I cause the other, this very pleasure undermines my determination to be an unrestricted freedom, a purely spontaneous consciousness unqualified by carnal components. Furthermore, I am forced to recognize that the freedom of the Other remains for ever beyond my grasp. To be sure, I can increase the pain step by step until the Other gives in. But then the Other has only been *forced* to give in, and therefore has not *consented* to the concession which has been wrung from it. What is done is belied by a consciousness which is now adamantly opposed to mine, which defines itself in abstraction from the actions forced from it and which preserves itself at an inaccessible distance from my For-itself. Even if my hatred for the Other reaches that point at which it demands the annihilation of the Other, still this very annihilation will prove self-defeating, since the death of the Other is the demise of the very freedom I had hoped to possess. The second line of descent (from indifference to sadism) proves as futile as the first (from love to masochism).

Brilliant as Sartre's descriptions of concrete relations with Others undoubtedly are, they remain radically flawed in certain obvious respects. First, they are restricted in such a way as to say little or nothing about either public relations or, even within the realm of the private, about friendship (that is, non-erotic personal relations). Second, even upon the plane which he selects as his terrain, Sartre refuses to concede the possibility of love or friendship in any but a pathologically destructive mode. Elsewhere, and later, Sartre did indeed admit that love and friendship might be an occasional reality. It is to his credit, however, that he did not qualify his analyses with such supplementary concessions. For the strength of his position lies precisely in the logic which he so astutely spells out, a

logic of dialectical degeneration which drives human relation-
ships on in a perverse direction. And surely, the experience of
this century has more than sufficed to confirm the *relative* truth
of Sartre's descriptions. Finally, and perhaps more seriously,
Sartre's own descriptions are open to serious objections. First,
the parallelism between the two starting points in love and
indifference seems strangely obscure. Worse, it is not at all
clear how the starting point in indifference is capable of giving
rise to a dialectic – as opposed to bringing such a dialectic to a
premature close.

Sartre's own attempt to broaden the basis of his analysis in
the little section entitled ' "Being-with" and the "We" ' must be
treated with reservations. Not only does Sartre himself treat
this concession to the Heideggerian thematic as derivative, he
concludes that the 'experience of the "We" and the "Us"
although real, is not of a nature to modify the results of our
prior investigations' (p. 429). In fact, the interest in this section
lies in its containing the germ of his later philosophy, the more
socially oriented philosophy of the *Critique of Dialectical Reason*.

Part Four: Having, Doing and Being

The first chapter of the fourth part on Having, Doing and
Being is devoted to the topic freedom, essentially an attempt to
make whatever qualifications are required to render plausible
his theory of an absolute unlimited freedom. If freedom is
linked to the Nothingness of consciousness, to the fact that
consciousness, qua Nothingness, is radically other than being
(wherein alone determinism can operate) then, in a certain
sense, we, qua conscious beings, are not only free but are
condemned to a freedom without limits. More, for Sartre,
every attempt to deny or to qualify this absolute and unrestricted freedom attests to a kind of moral fault, the 'bad faith' to
which he devotes such extensive analyses. And yet it would
seem that our lives are circumscribed by all sorts of obvious
limits – obstacles, resistances, frustrations, incapacities,
fatalities etc. An existential philosophy is obviously required to
address this apparent discrepancy. Sartre does so with reference to the complementary notion of facticity, which is itself
examined under a set of factors which are not supposed to alter
the character of freedom but merely to place it in perspective,

the perspective of a bodily existence lived out under certain contingent conditions. Essentially the factors in question fall under three heads: first, my being a body, with all that follows therefrom for a theory of action. But second, action can only be accomplished in a situation which may not have been chosen. My situation includes such factors as the accidents of birth and upbringing, my past as well as my environment. To these two dimensions of facticity which are not, or at least are not wholly, chosen Sartre adds another which responds to the Heideggerian thematic of resoluteness. The complement of an absolute, unlimited freedom is an equally absolute, unlimited responsibility for self and for what I make of myself. To be absolutely free, Sartre would have us believe, means to be absolutely responsible for oneself. To explain away one's behaviour in terms of hereditary and environmental factors, to make excuses for oneself, to appeal to any form of psychological or social determinism is to be in 'bad faith', to refuse to assume the burden of self-responsibility. If it is even possible to talk of a human or personal essence, it is so only in retrospect. I exist first, choose, make myself be. Only later is it possible for me to reflectively recuperate what I appear to have become by existing, and then only subject to the nihilating impact of a consciousness which can undo, or redo, everything it has made of itself previously.

This is the context in which the famous section on Existential Psychoanalysis occurs. Such is our familiarity (largely thanks to Sartre) with existential psychoanalysis today that it is difficult to appreciate how novel this concept was at the time Sartre wrote. Basically, this short section consists in a refusal of traditional psychology and the deterministic categories it employs to understand individuals. For any such theory will always be based on givens, on facts which are supposed to determine or control the life of the individual – his parental relations, his sexuality, his genes. For Sartre, such givens can operate in a variety of different ways, depending on the meaning ascribed to them by the individual. So, a man is born into a deeply religious family. This could explain his later religiosity, or his reaction to all things religious, or his indifference towards religion. In place of such meaningless givens, Sartre advises us to look for a fundamental *project of being* which is irreducible. We cannot explain why an individual adopts this rather than another attitude, only acknowledge that such a way of being has been adopted and understand the individual in terms of this project of being. To understand an individual means to put oneself in his or her position, to understand his or her life 'from within', in terms of the basic choices which have governed the life in question. It is for this reason that Sartre's psychoanalytical stance is heavily supported by biographies (Baudelaire, Genet, Flaubert) which, as much as anything else, represent an application of the categories of his philosophy to the lives of specific individuals.

The Conclusion is of interest mostly in what it fails to deliver. At the end of the Introduction Sartre asked: 'What is the meaning of that being which includes within itself these two radically separated regions of being?' (p. xliii). In the conclusion (metaphysical implications) Sartre confirms that this being in general which would include both the For-itself and the In-itself could only be the *ens causa sui* – the God of traditional parlance. This ultimate synthesis has been shown to be impossible, but its absence haunts the entire work – as a *Deus absconditus*.

Finally, just like Heidegger, Sartre too assures us that 'ontology cannot formulate ethical precepts' (p. 625). But even at the time of writing *Being and Nothingness*, and ever more thereafter, Sartre worried about the ethical neutrality, even the 'immorality', of existentialism. To save existentialism from the obvious charge of 'egoism', he appeals, in his lecture *Existentialism and Humanism*, to a universalizability principle (when I decide for myself, I decide for all mankind) which he takes over from Kant and to which his philosophy is simply not entitled. No doubt this was one of the reasons why he took refuge later in Marxism, thereby attempting an even more gratuitous synthesis of individualism and universalism – this time from the standpoint of socialism. Suffice it to say that the promise announced in the very last words of *Being and Nothingness* ('We shall devote to them [ethical questions] a future work') was never kept.

However exaggerated Sartre's overall position may be, one thing is certain; in its day it represented a real liberation. Sartre's readers were brought to recognize that their lives were more under their own control than they had ever suspected.

They were brought to recognize the paramount importance of taking responsibility for themselves and their situation, changing their lives if need be. Certainly, the 'bourgeois' morality against which Sartre waged a life-long battle has suffered very considerable reversals since the appearance of *Being and Nothingness* – though whether these reversals have augmented or diminished the quality of our lives is a matter which has yet to be decided.

To put Sartre's thinking in a more historical perspective, it should also be noted that his existentialism, if taken seriously, would have made impossible the thing which, in his day, undoubtedly represented the greatest danger – Nazism, the unthinking acceptance of a doctrinaire ideology, the submission of one's self, one's life, to a leader. A thinker cannot be expected to advance on several fronts simultaneously. It is enough that Sartre should have spoken up, and fought for – freedom.

NOTES

1 Jean-Paul Sartre, *The Transcendence of the Ego*, trans. F. Williams and R. Kirkpatrick (Farrar, Straus & Giroux: New York, 1957).
2 Jean-Paul Sartre, *The Psychology of Imagination*, trans. B. Frechtman (Washington Square Press: New York, 1966).
3 Jean-Paul Sartre, *Being and Nothingness*, trans. Hazel Barnes (Routledge & Kegan Paul: London, 1969).
4 Gabriel Marcel, *Etre et avoir* (Editions Montaigne: Paris, 1935).
5 Martin Heidegger, *Being and Time*, trans. J. Macquarrie and E. Robinson (Harper & Row: New York, 1962), p. 332 (H. 286).

Chapter 4

Maurice Merleau-Ponty

Maurice Merleau-Ponty was born in 1908. Like Sartre, he was a student at the Ecole Normale Supérieure and a school teacher before he became a university professor. Unlike Sartre, however, his professional career assumed a fairly orthodox course, culminating in his appointment to a chair at the most prestigious of France's academic institutions, the Collège de France. Merleau-Ponty's early death in 1961 cut short a life which surely had more to contribute to philosophy, in particular, the completion of his last work, *The Visible and the Invisible.*

Although Merleau-Ponty was a prolific author of articles and papers and although many of his lectures have been reproduced in published form, his reputation as a first rank philosopher rests on three books, two finished and published in his life time and one unfinished and published after his death. In many respects *The Structure of Behaviour* and *The Phenomenology of Perception* deal with the same themes in much the same ways – to the point that Merleau-Ponty has been accused of having written the same book twice. The institutional rationale for this apparent duplication was the requirement, at that time, that a Doctorat d'Etat be granted on the basis of two pieces of written work, respectively known as the 'thèse majeure' and the 'thèse mineure'. However, in his perceptive introduction to *La structure du comportement,*[1] Alphonse de Waelhens insists that the latter work, published three years before *La phénoménologie de la perception*, can be distinguished, in principle, from its successor on the grounds that it adopts the standpoint of a critique of scientific rather than of natural experience (p. xiii). Indeed it could be said that after a long detour through a critique of reflexology and Gestalt psychology, *The Structure of Behaviour* ends up, in Chapter Four, where *The Phenomenology of Perception* takes its start, in an examination of the relation of mind and body, or rather, in an overcoming of this very duality in favour of a more primary concept of the body subject or own body. A third principle of distinction should also be mentioned. *The Structure of Behaviour* is, first and foremost, a theory of the human organism and only secondarily a theory of perception while *The Phenomenology of Perception*, is, as its title implies, first and foremost, a theory of perception and only secondarily a theory of the human organism. Needless to say, however, for Merleau-Ponty these two sides of a more general conception of human reality are indissociably interwoven, perception being the primary function of the human organism and the human body constituting the only adequate foundation for a theory of perception.

While both *The Structure of Behaviour* and *The Phenomenology of Perception* rely for their conclusions upon a massive critical examination of prevailing psychological conceptions of human reality, *The Visible and the Invisible* marks a new departure in at least one very obvious sense; dispensing almost entirely with the findings of the human sciences, it sets about its task of reflexive interrogation directly, that is, as directly as is ever possible for a philosophy whose whole ambition it is to reflect upon the unreflected, to think the unthought, to name the unnameable, in a phrase, to adopt the laborious detour of language to express what, by its very nature, antecedes, and so provides a foundation for, language. But although it has become highly characteristic of the great philosophers of the middle of this century to traverse two distinct periods in their development, even to reverse, in the later, the basic intention and orientation of the earlier (one has only to think of Wittgenstein or Heidegger or Sartre), it would be more correct to say that *The Visible and the Invisible* represents a continuation or extension of earlier directives rather than a reversal. 'Being-in-the-world', the theme of themes in the earlier work, is now dealt with in terms of notions like the 'between', the 'chasm', the 'link', while embodiment is dealt with by way of an extensive investigation of the concept of 'flesh' or even of 'brute being' (*être sauvage*). But however intriguing it might be to consider the lines of development which Merleau-Ponty's thinking might have taken had he lived another ten years, for our purposes it makes good sense to restrict ourselves to *The Phenomenology of Perception*.

THE PHENOMENOLOGY OF PERCEPTION

The Phenomenology of Perception is divided into an Introduction and three subsequent parts, a first part devoted to the Body, a second part devoted to the World as Perceived and a third part devoted to Being For itself and Being-in-the-world. There is also a Preface which might more properly be called the 'Introduction' since the Introduction is itself devoted to a critique of 'Traditional Prejudices and the Return to Phenomena', in other words, to a preliminary clearing of the ground prior to the properly phenomenological study of the body and of the world as perceived from the point of view of the body. The core of the book is therefore made up of Parts One and Two. With these observations and reservations in mind let us turn to the Preface, the section in which Merleau-Ponty outlines his approach to phenomenology.

'What is phenomenology?' Merleau-Ponty asks, and stays for an answer, an answer which is admittedly somewhat contradictory. Phenomenology, he tells us, is *both* a philosophy of essences (Husserl) *and* a philosophy of existences (Heidegger), *both* a philosophy which starts with the reduction (Husserl) *and* a philosophy for which the world is always already there (Heidegger), *both* a 'rigorous science' (Husserl) *and* a description of the immediate structures of the life world (Husserl or Heidegger). Moreover, these contradictions, Merleau-Ponty insists, are not resolved by distinguishing between the transcendental phenomenology of Husserl and the ontological phenomenology of Heidegger because they recur in the development of Husserl's own thinking as he shifts from a transcendental mode of analysis to an investigation of the *'Lebenswelt'*.

It is this 'both–and' which defines Merleau-Ponty's own conception of phenomenology as he proceeds through the four themes which furnish the topic of his Introduction, the themes of description, the reduction, essences and intentionality. Phenomenology is a descriptive science and so has to be distinguished from any science which would seek to explain, that is, from science commonly so called, and this because phenomenology cannot take for granted the reality of the world which forms the starting point for any scientific investigation and so has to return to 'that world which precedes knowledge, of which knowledge always speaks, and in relation to which every scientific schematization is an abstract and derivative sign-language . . .' (p. ix). To be sure, as much as this is accomplished by analytical reflection – by which Merleau-Ponty mostly has Kant in mind – but in the wrong way. For the reflection which starts from our ordinary experience of the world and then moves back to account for this objectivity in terms of the synthesizing activities of a transcendental subject finishes up by locking itself into an interiority or immanence which loses the very world it seeks to reconstruct. But the reflective activity to which phenomenology appeals is one which reflects upon the unreflected, one for which therefore the world is not in man but man *in* the world.

The same 'va et vient' characterizes Merleau-Ponty's conception of the reduction. It would seem that the reduction takes me away from the common world and locks me into a private (phenomenologically reduced) world of my own. On the contrary, Merleau-Ponty insists, the reduction is precisely that through which I first become fully aware of my relation to the world and to the other subjects with which I share a world. 'Reflection does not withdraw from the world towards the unity of consciousness as the world's basis; it steps back to watch the forms of transcendence fly up like sparks from a fire; it slackens the intentional threads which attach us to the world and thus brings them to our notice' (p. xiii). It is for this reason that Merleau-Ponty is ready to go so far as to identify the reduction with the procedure of existential rather than transcendental phenomenology (p. xiv).

With regard to the theme of essences, Merleau-Ponty performs a very interesting double deconstruction to which more attention might have been paid. Merleau-Ponty begins by accusing Jean Wahl of having wrongly claimed that 'Husserl separates essences from existence'. On the contrary, he suggests, the separated essences are those of language' (p. xv). In other words, it is the expression of experience in language which first makes it possible to separate essences from the experiences in which they are originally situated. But transcendental reflection goes on to effect a second separation, taking the conceptual essences isolated and separated by language and making of them ideal meanings. In so doing, transcendental reflection actually frees essences from the rigid grid of a particular conceptual framework and so makes it possible for them to be re-situated in the experience out of which they originally arose, a pre-linguistic, pre-objective experience. Originally our existence is so 'tightly held in the world' that we are unable to recognize our involvement for what it is. Idealization offers us the lee-way to extract essences from existence but only in order that they should eventually be re-located in the very element from which they were originally abstracted.

Finally, Merleau-Ponty appeals to Husserl's distinction between an 'act' and an 'operative' intentionality in order to drive home, yet again, the basic theme of a return to things themselves, of a 'phenomenology of origins'. *Act intentionality* is the intentionality involved in judgments and in any analysis of experience which takes an already constructed world of objects as the starting point for its thematic investigations. *Operative intentionality* is the intentionality in and through which such a world is brought into existence in the first place. It is therefore a pre-predicative intentionality which not merely captures the original meaning of experience but does so in such a way that the life-world becomes the locus of feeling and desire as well as thought, of evaluation and projection as well as knowledge, indeed brings the former to light as the very root source of thought and knowledge.

Throughout this opening section, Merleau-Ponty makes frequent use of the concept of 'genesis'. But perhaps what is most evidently absent is anything approaching a 'logic' of the genesis of which he speaks. It seems that Merleau-Ponty sides with Heidegger against Husserl on the subject of the existential and ontological status of phenomenology. At the same time, he does not want to give up concepts and procedures such as 'reflection', 'subjectivity', 'consciousness', 'meaning' etc., concepts which have no place in Heidegger's existential phenomenology. In so doing, Merleau-Ponty appears to align himself with later Husserl, the Husserl of 'genetic' phenomenology, rather than with early Heidegger. And it is for this reason that Merleau-Ponty is not prepared to throw away the resources of transcendental phenomenology in favour of anything like an immediate situation of Dasein in a world. But if this aim (the return to origins) is not to be attained (as it is in early Heidegger) by a direct regression from the ontic straight back to the ontological, we need more information regarding the several steps and stages of the elaborate hermeneutical circle by way of which we are brought back to the place from which we originally started out. This information is not forthcoming. Instead we are offered paradoxical formulae such as the '*practical cogito*', a formula which combines in one expression the two extremes of (embodied) action and (disembodied) reflection. And the 'paradoxical' character of Merleau-Ponty's phenomenology is further confirmed by the deliberately ambiguous (not to mention metaphorical) language in which it is expressed, so that, in the end, the 'both–and' might just as well be formulated as a 'neither–nor'.

Be that as it may, the nature and character of Merleau-Ponty's phenomenology does at least make it clear that, in philosophy, the most difficult thing to understand is what is most obvious, that what is nearest (in being) is furthest away (in analysis) and, moreover, that the difficulties with which philosophical thinking is confronted, difficulties which can only be circumvented by the most elaborate circumlocutions, are not to be avoided since philosophy is, by its very nature, a questioning which cannot leave the questioner out of account. Hence phenomenology, for Merleau-Ponty, moves beyond the Hegelian concept of philosophy as 'thinking thinking itself' and precisely because, as this very kind of thinking, it is a thinking thinking about what is itself un-thought, even unthinkable, a thinking which thinks about what *must* happen, or rather, must *already have happened*, if there is to be any thinking at all.

The so-called Introduction (which forms the link between the earlier critique of scientific psychology and the phenomenological descriptions that begin with Part One) is nominally divided into four chapters which, however, can be seen to fall into three groups of analyses. The first two chapters on 'Sensation' and 'Association' are devoted to a critique of empiricism, the third chapter on 'Attention and Judgment' is devoted to a critique of intellectualism while the fourth chapter, devoted to 'The Phenomenal Field', is the one in which Merleau-Ponty

draws his own conclusions and which therefore paves the way
to Part One.

More important than any detailed presentation of Merleau-
Ponty's view in these introductory chapters is his naming of
protagonists who will conduct an on-going battle throughout
the entire work. The terms 'empiricism' and 'intellectualism'
are used so broadly as not merely to cross the frontiers of
philosophy and psychology but also to defy specification in
terms of any one philosopher (or school of philosophy) or
psychologist (or school of psychology). For example, Ratio-
nalists as well as Kant and Husserl will count as intellectualists
and Gestalt psychologists will also be classified as
intellectualists by comparison with their behavourist or exper-
imentalist counterparts. More important therefore than any
identification of the protagonists is the development of a
strategy whereby each successfully accomplishes not merely
the destruction of its opponent but its own self-destruction –
thereby creating an intellectual vacuum into which Merleau-
Ponty is able to move with his own alternative account of the
facts. It is this strategy which is operative throughout and
which confers force and conviction upon Merleau-Ponty's own
descriptions, since the latter are not simply presented as self-
evident and self-sustaining theses but as specifically required
by the manifest failure of alternative accounts to provide a
satisfactory explanation of the phenomena in question.

The starting point of Merleau-Ponty's critique of empiricism
is the doctrine of sensation. Sensations are supposed to be the
building blocks of experience, to furnish the atoms out of which
the composite whole of experience is constructed. As such,
sensations are supposed to be something absolutely originary,
the first elements out of which and from which experience is
built up. In fact, as Merleau-Ponty points out, there is nothing
original about the traditional notion of sensation. 'The notion
of sensation was not a concept born of reflection, but a late
product of thought directed towards objects, the last element in
the representation of the world, the furthest removed from its
original source, and therefore the most unclear' (p. 10; see also
p. 37). This reversal of last into first (and which carries with it
as an implication the translation of first into last) is based upon
a number of misconceptions. First, it presupposes the very
objective world which it is supposed to account for. It must do

so because the notion of sensation is only arrived at by abstracting qualities off from the objects in which they are ordinarily thought to inhere and, in this sense, represents a double derivation, an abstractive derivation superimposed upon a constructive derivation. But this is not the end of it; for the presupposed objective world, together with the function of abstraction required to lift qualities off from objects results in the isolation of data which are then projected back into consciousness as its subjective contents. Hence the absurdity of even attempting to reconstruct the objective world out of such subjective contents, since these same contents could in effect only be isolated in the first instance by presupposing not merely the objective world but such intellectual operations as 'abstraction'.

In fact, abstraction is not the only intellectual operation to which empiricism appeals when it sets about its reconstructive project. In response to the critical challenge represented by Gestalt psychology (which recognizes original wholes in experience), empiricism drags in its 'laws of association' which are supposed to establish the necessary connections between the parts in question. Thus, the several parts of a uniformly coloured extent are supposed to be related by the laws of resemblance and contiguity, laws which not merely explain the coherence of the sensational parts in one whole but, at the same time, account for the differentiation of this whole from a differently coloured background. And where present experience seems insufficient to account for the organization of the perceptual field, memory is also drawn in to lend the mind the support of past experience. But in order that memory should be of any assistance I must be able to recognize the present experience as one which can be referred back to a past experience which it resembles in certain respects. 'Thus the appeal to memory presupposes what it is supposed to explain: the patterning of data, the imposition of meaning on a chaos of sense data' (p. 19). More generally, Merleau-Ponty objects to all such mechanistic explanations of perceptual experience on the grounds that they represent 'blind processes' which take place in such a way that 'nobody sees', processes which, in leaving the perceiver out of account, prove incapable of accounting for the richness and variety of an experience invested with emotional as well as sensory qualities – the experience of the primitive as well as that of the citizen of advanced industrialized societies, the experience of the child as well as that of the adult.

The defeat of *empiricism* provides a rationale for *intellectualism*. But in standing opposed to empiricism and indeed seeking to overcome the explanatory limitations of the latter, intellectualism not only reveals its own quite distinct limitations but turns out to be little more than the reverse side of its opponent, in the sense that it can be seen to subscribe to the very same objectified world view as its intellectual adversary.

Merleau-Ponty introduces the concept of 'attention' as the first corrective device introduced by intellectualism to overcome the limitations of empiricism. Whereas empiricism seeks to arrive at a correct representation of the world without any advanced knowledge, intellectualism is in possession of the intelligible structure of the world from the first though, for the most part, only in principle rather than practice. Thus the 'light of attention' is needed to bring to light the truth of the objective world. But this seeming opposition conceals a deeprooted affinity. For both empiricism and intellectualism take the objective world for granted. 'Empiricism cannot see that we need to know what we are looking for, otherwise we would not be looking for it, and intellectualism fails to see that we need to be ignorant of what we are looking for, or equally again we should not be searching. They are in agreement in that neither can grasp consciousness in the act of learning, and that neither attaches due importance to that circumscribed ignorance, that still "empty" but already determinate intention which is attention itself' (p. 28). Merleau-Ponty's general strategy is beautifully exemplified in this quote. First, empiricism and intellectualism are presented as nominal adversaries. Then this nominal opposition is made to reveal a deeper agreement. This deeper agreement then finally brings to light a deficiency which both share and which now has to be overcome in turn.

A similar kind of critical analysis is applied to the notion of judgment. Judgment is introduced by analytical reflection to make up what is lacking in sensation and so thrives on the limitations of empiricism. Instead of remaining at the level of perception and seeking to trace the genesis of perceptual meaning in the contexts in which it is actually operative, intellectualism superimposes upon these sensible contexts a conceptual supplement, just that supplement, in effect, which is needed to correct the errors of sensibility. But then we are supposed to know what errors require correction and have therefore already presupposed the very world the genesis of which the theory is called in to explain. Empiricism assumes a world in itself to which consciousness has to be accommodated. But then intellectualism does nothing else when it corrects the deficiencies of empiricism with reference to a conceptual supplement which is exactly proportional to the deficiencies in question. Whereas in the first case the world in itself is supposed to produce in consciousness the corresponding presentations by way of a causal interaction with the subject, in the second, it is the subject which, through its own synthetic operations, is supposed to produce the relevant representations of the world in itself. In both cases, however, the world has already been presupposed – though possibly in the alternative modes of a substantial reality, in the one case (empiricism), and a noumenal reality, in the other (intellectualism).

If in the case both of empiricism and intellectualism the objective world has already been presupposed, then it becomes the primary task of a properly phenomenological reflection to conduct us back into a pre-objective realm. When empiricism and intellectualism are set against each other with a view to effecting a reciprocal demolition of each by the other, the role of a properly phenomenological reflection (not analytical reflection) is sometimes presented as a mediating role. In effect, however, it is the task of a phenomenology of perception not so much to mediate *between* empiricism and intellectualism but, on the ground of their mutual and reciprocal destruction, to enforce a departure from that which both take for granted, namely, the objective world, and so to inaugurate a new *regressive* questioning which carries the investigation *back* into the pre-objective realm. This is the theme of the concluding chapter on The Phenomenal Field.

Like the Preface, The Phenomenal Field is a methodological chapter, a chapter designed to familiarize the reader with the method of reflection the author proposes to employ. Merleau-Ponty begins by evoking the unholy alliance of science and perception, an alliance which sacrifices perception to the claims of knowledge. The world is polarized around the subject–object dichotomy. An exteriority without interiority confronts an interiority without exteriority, with the empirical self perched uncomfortably on the boundary, sometimes assimilated into the one, sometimes into the other system of explanation. But this world view is not original; it is derivative and so demands of us that we get back to the origin. Getting back to the origin means re-learning how to see, re-covering an immediacy which has been forgotten but which, as forgotten, can precisely be re-membered. The motive for such a recuperation is not just provided by philosophy but even by science itself. First physics, then biology and finally sociology have been forced to recognize the limits of their procedures and explanatory categories. More important still for Merleau-Ponty, psychology too has had to come to terms with its own inadequacies and, in so doing, has cleared the way for a new phenomenological psychology. The phenomenological investigation in question here is not mere-ly not to be identified with either empirical psychology, introspective psychology or Gestalt psychology; it cannot even be identified with transcendental phenomenology, if by the latter is meant a phenomenology which subscribes to the prejudices of universal reason, a phenomenology which leaves the phenomenologist out of account or ascribes to him a transcendental status which removes him from his being-in-the-world. In a word, the new phenomenology is to be 'genetic', 'that is, a study [which describes] the advent of being into consciousness instead of presuming its possibility as given in advance' (p. 61).

This new 'genetic' phenomenology seeks to retrace, in its descriptions, the 'immediacy' of an experience before it has been transformed by science and common sense. It is not, however, to be confused with anything like an unreflective confrontation, an 'inexpressible coincidence', even a Bergsonian intuitive identification with being – or rather with the flux of becoming. Rather, the most sophisticated reflection is required to undertake the task of reflecting upon the unreflected, re-directing the enquiry towards a 'lost world' which, precisely because it was once lived through in its authentic originality, must still be available for meaningful recuperation. Reflection upon the unreflected (the authentic reflection to which Merleau-Ponty's analyses calls the reader) is much more difficult than it might appear. For it not only requires that we reflect upon the pre-reflective, upon that 'lost world' which antecedes science and common sense. It also requires that we reflect upon the theoretical limitations of this same science and the practical prejudices of common sense. More still, it requires that we reflect upon that which transcendental phenomenology installs as an ultimately irreducible presupposition, the transcendental Ego itself, together with the entire apparatus of transcendental reflection. In other words, 'reflection upon the unreflected' includes within the scope of its task a reflection upon what still remained unreflected in the reflective extremity of transcendental reflection, the very reflection which claimed to have risen above all presuppositions, to have reduced all of life and experience, thought and action, to something reflected upon and which, in this very 'rising above' only gave rise to its own characteristically unreflected presuppositions. Furthermore, in going beyond the limits even of transcendental reflection, the properly phenomenological reflection to which Merleau-Ponty appeals demands from us a transformation in our very being. In learning how to *see*, we learn how to *be*, how to be something other than what we were when we remained blind to the new way of seeing that gives us access to the origin.

Part One

Perception is, first and foremost, perception of the world, not the self. And yet the focus of Part One is the body, that is, the incarnate form which the self assumes when it ceases to regard itself, first and foremost, as an Ego. Hence the need for an introductory chapter which will carry the analysis from the world to the incarnate subject. Merleau-Ponty's strategy is quite typical. The world is presented first of all as it exists for objective thought. From the standpoint of objective thought, not only does the distinction between object and horizon disappear, the object is defined as if it were seen from nowhere, as an infinity of possible perspectives – the object seen from here, from there, from everywhere. But an object seen from *everywhere* is an object seen from *nowhere*, an object conceived in abstraction from the very condition of its perceivability, namely, its relation to a perceiving subject. In fact, the world conceived as a totality of objects defined in this way is not a world at all but a universe (p. 71).

Since the coming into being of the objective universe presupposes a prior suspension of that very being whose existence brings the world into being and sustains it in being, the suspension of this suspension will reverse the process of objectification and so enable us to see how this objectification (which is itself a form of falsification) arises in the first place. The crucial moment in the objectification of the world is the objectification of the body. For 'since the genesis of the objective body is only a moment in the constitution of the object, the body, by withdrawing from the objective world, will carry with it the intentional threads linking it to its surroundings and finally reveal to us the perceiving subject as the perceived world' (p. 72).

Chapters 1 and 2 of Part One clear the way by first considering the prejudices of both physiology and psychology. Taking concrete examples like that of the phantom limb, Merleau-Ponty shows the inadequacy of physiological conceptions of the body as a reflex mechanism. In fact the physiological misconception is complemented by a psychological misconception, psychic factors being surreptitiously introduced to save appearances wherever the physiological explanation breaks down. By close examination of such exemplary cases, Merleau-Ponty shows not merely the limitations of objective thought but the impossibility of covering over these limitations by adopting a standpoint somewhere between the physical and the psychological or by shuffling to and fro between these two ways of thinking which, in the end, must be seen as belonging together. Moreover, by appealing to the more primordial concept of being-in-the-world, Merleau-Ponty is able to show how such a concept solves one of the most persistent problems of modern philosophy, the problem of the mind–body relation. 'It is because it is a preobjective view that being-in-the-world can be distinguished from every third person process, from every modality of the *res extensa*, as from every *cogitatio*, from every first person form of knowledge – and that it can effect the union of the "psychic" and the "physiological" ' (p. 80).

But the appeal to an existential integration of the organism in a pre-objective conception of the world brings with it implications which move beyond the conventional explanatory categories. In particular, in an uncharacteristic passage (uncharacteristic because, surprisingly, Merleau-Ponty makes very little use of psychoanalysis to substantiate his claim), Merleau-Ponty appeals to the psychoanalytical category of the unconscious to extend the scope of his own understanding and in such a way as to bring body, world, emotion and time together in one existential whole. Referring to the effect of an emotional trauma, he tells us: 'Time in its passage does not carry away with it these impossible projects . . . . One present among all presents thus acquires an exceptional value. . . . Impersonal time continues its course, but personal time is arrested' (p. 83).

This passage is of particular interest to us because we now know that there was once a young lady, Elisabeth Lacoin (a friend of Simone de Beauvoir), with whom Merleau-Ponty entertained a romantic interest but who was forbidden by her own family to continue seeing the young *normalien*, on the grounds that his family was not as wealthy as the Lacoins. De Beauvoir's *Mémoires d'une jeune fille rangée* are the story of a young girl who learnt to refuse, to revolt against her bourgeois background. Her friend, Elisabeth, was unable to countermand the orders of her parents. Merleau-Ponty, rejected by the Lacoin family, went his way and eventually married someone else. Elisabeth, *jeune fille bien rangée*, fell into a state of depression and died of a brain haemorrhage two weeks after the relationship had been broken off. Perhaps it was the appalling personal tragedy represented by this history which led Merleau-Ponty to characterize the pre-personal, anonymous, atemporal existence of the unconscious in so negative a light.

And yet these descriptions are strangely at variance with the general tenor of his treatise. If the aim is to break with the categories of objective thought, to recapture the wealth of meaning that resides in the sphere of a pre-objective existence and to do so not merely in order to learn how to think (that is, to overcome the evident inadequacies of objective thought) but in order to learn how to live, or rather to re-learn how to live, then surely the recuperation of a pre-objective dimension of existence (together with its mutually integrated parameters of time–world–body–feeling) deserves descriptions which do not simply point out the negative implications of that 'time past' from which we cannot free ourselves but which also point to the need to re-integrate this time past into our present, which point to the desirability not of repressing but of working through the past in order that the richness of such privileged moments be permitted, once again, to enrich our present.

The pre-objective realm is the realm in which animals lead out their lives instinctively. It is also the realm in which humans begin to exist and from which they have to separate themselves if there is to be any understanding of the world. This understanding, however, is in part a mis-understanding, a mis-understanding which it is the task of Merleau-Ponty's descriptions to correct, and to correct by precisely reviving that sense of the pre-objective which has been lost in the quest for (theoretical) explanations. This is why Merleau-Ponty's brand of reflection is, in principle, a reflection upon the unreflected, a reflection whose whole aim it is to bring back into the centre of our awareness that pre-objective, existentially primary realm which objective thought loses sight of.

Reflection upon the unreflected, not reflection *tout court*. So much becomes apparent from the limitations of classical psychology. Through reflection, classical psychology is able to identify characteristics which serve to distinguish the body from any other object. The body is a centre, a point of view on which I cannot take up a point of view; the body yields double sensations in that I can feel myself touching; the body is the field of kinaesthetic sensations, that is, sensations which are supposed to inform me about my actions. The trouble is that the subjectivity of the body was conceived in terms which simply complemented those of objective physiology. The characteristics in question were thought as characteristics which characterized every body as such. The universality of the 'subjective' traits in question was nothing but the essential complement of the universality of objective thought. And nothing brought out this limitation more clearly than the blindness of the psychologist to the fact that he was *himself* the very being whose being was in question. 'But as a psyche speaking of the psyche, he *was* all that he was talking about' (p. 96). It is the essential reflexivity of any genuinely existential analysis which gives the lie to the psychological correction of the limitations inherent in the physiological explanation of the organism.

If the first two chapters of Part One offer a sort of static critique of the prejudices of physiology and psychology, Chapter 3 develops this critique into a new dynamic. The concept of 'body image' is introduced first to correct the deficiencies of any associationist (empirical) or representational (intellectualist) conception of the body. But it is rapidly developed into the new dimension of a dynamic motility. What this means is that the body can no longer be regarded as an entity to be examined in its own right but has to be placed in the context of a world. Moreover, being-in-the-world cannot itself be understood as a certain relation which obtains between a central body and a surrounding world but has to be understood in terms of tasks, actions to be accomplished, a free space which outlines in advance the possibilities available to the body at any time. In turn these possibilities have to be understood not as the possibilities of a perceptual presentation or conceptual representation of the world but as the possibilities of action in a world. In addition therefore to the homogeneous space assumed by both empiricism and intellectualism we find an oriented space which, moreover, has to be regarded as the ground or foundation of the former.

Merleau-Ponty brings out the need for such a primary concept of oriented space with a series of beautifully conducted critical analyses of the distinction between *concrete* and *abstract* actions. A concrete action is one in which the movements of the body are spontaneously integrated into a task; an abstract action is one in which these same movements are reproduced independently of any such context. Normally, an agent is capable both of raising its hand to reach for an object and of simply raising its hand in response, for instance, to a command. The cases which interest Merleau-Ponty (abnormal cases recorded at length in the work of Gelb and Goldstein) are cases in which a patient who is perfectly capable of undertaking concrete actions is nevertheless incapable of accomplishing the same actions in the abstract. He can reach for an object but has difficulty obeying the command to raise his hand. He can grasp his nose but has difficulty pointing to his nose. Clearly this anomaly cannot be explained in terms of any physiological deficiency, for otherwise the concrete action could not be performed. But nor can it be explained in terms of an inability to arrive at an adequate representation of the world – and for the same reason. 'The patient is conscious of his bodily space as the matrix of his habitual action, but not as an objective setting; his body is at his disposal as a means of ingress into a familiar surrounding, but not as the means of expression of a gratuitous and free spatial thought' (p. 104).

We shall not go into the details of Merleau-Ponty's critique of the attempts made by both intellectualism and empiricism to come to terms with the distinction between concrete and abstract actions. Needless to say, his critique consists in pointing out that neither the one nor the other are capable of adequately accounting for the existence of such a distinction in the specific cases in question. Instead, we shall take account of the new concepts introduced to make sense of this distinction. The first is that of the 'phenomenal body'. An agent (including thereunder the patients in question) possesses an immediate knowledge of the relations between the several parts of his body, that is, a knowledge which is not reducible to a perception of these relations, from without, nor to an association of images, from within. More than this, an agent engaged in a simple action is already at the end and in such a way that the means (the constituent acts) are, as it were, retrospectively organized after the event rather than being presented as steps along the way to the end.

The difficulty the patients in question experience lies in the disconnection of abstract actions from their concrete foundation. Curiously, the patient behaves like an empiricist or intellectualist, and this is the source of his difficulty. Instead of simply assuming his body as the very basis of action, he first has to construct for himself a picture of his body, find the part in question and learn to move it as one learns to manipulate an instrument. 'What he lacks is neither motility nor thought, and we are brought to the recognition of something between movement as a third person process and thought as a representation of movement' (p. 110).

Strictly speaking, this 'between' should be presented as a 'beneath', calling for a new 'genetic phenomenology' capable of moving back beyond any objective conception of the body and the world to its root in a more primordial realm. This regression to the origin in turn makes possible a new 'existential analysis', an analysis which 'goes beyond the traditional alternatives of empiricism and rationalism' (p. 136). To put it more exactly, such an existential analysis goes *on* beyond only because it is capable of going *back* beyond. It is capable of rendering intelligible what neither empiricism nor rationalism can account for only because it is capable of getting back to an origin on which both these two derivative forms of thought tacitly depend but which they have both forgotten. Prior to the 'I think' it is therefore necessary to admit an 'I can' (p. 137), a practical *cogito* which informs my being-in-the-world and which manifests itself in the cultivation of habits.

Habit is a knowledge in the body which is reducible neither to reflex reactions nor to any kind of representation of what is to be done. An organist needs only a short time to familiarize himself with a new instrument. The time is too short for him to develop a completely new set of conditioned reflexes and the spontaneity with which he must command the instrument precludes any objective representation of the manuals and their registers. Rather, his familiarity with organs in general permits him to project a potential space which can be rapidly modified to accommodate specific differences.

Chapter 4 merely resumes and generalizes the findings of the previous chapters. Prior to, and as the ground of, objective space and the objectified body, we find a body consciousness integrated in a bodily space. The body is first and foremost a unity which antecedes any representation of its several parts. This original coincidence of consciousness and the body means that, in action, the body projects a primordial spatiality which is itself, like the body, a unity which antecedes any representation of its several parts. Moreover, the relation of the body to the world in which it finds itself is not to be understood in terms of objective distances but in terms of a sort of primordial coincidence or co-existence of the body with that towards which it enacts itself, mobilizes itself, projects itself. The synthesis of one's own body is therefore, by the same token, a synthesis of the world and a synthesis of the body in the world.

The two final chapters of Part One carry the existential analysis of a primordial body consciousness through to two expressions of embodied existence, sexuality, on the one hand, and speech, on the other. But one would look in vain for anything like a Sartrian examination of sexual relations or a Heideggerian presentation of the ontological significance of language as discourse. Here, as before, the starting point lies in the consideration of malfunctions, in sexual incapacities and speech disturbances. As before, the analysis is somewhat clinical in character even though the aim consists in bringing to light the existential significance of sexuality and language.

The starting point of Merleau-Ponty's examination of sex-

uality is affectivity, more specifically, a critique of two basic
misconceptions of the meaning and function of emotional life.
On the one hand, sexual desire is wrongly depicted as a matter
of conscious representations, on the other, as a matter of
automatic reflex responses. But neither the one conception nor
the other serve to throw light upon cases in which a patient
loses contact with his or her sexuality. On the one hand,
obscene pictures, sexual conversations and the sight of a body
fail to arouse the patient. On the other hand, even close
physical contact loses its erotic power. Basically, what is lost is
neither conscious representations nor a physiological function
but a power of projecting a sexual world, of investing the world
with sexual significance. The intentionality of a sexual relation
is not that of a *cogitatio* which aims at a *cogitatum* but that of a
body which aims at another body and which sees in the other
body the fulfilment of an intention expressed through its own.

It is the very generality of this sexual power which makes it
possible for malfunctions to be symbolically expressed in
specific physiological deficits. Merleau-Ponty takes a case,
presented by Binswanger, of a girl whose mother has forbidden
her to see the young man she loves and who in consequences
loses the use of speech (p. 160). The prohibition cuts the entire
circuit of sexual existence off from its objective and forces it
back upon its origin, the body, where the frustration manifests
itself in the loss of a specific function. The loss of speech has
nothing to do with a physiological disturbance as is shown by
the fact that, permitted once again to see the young man she
loves, she will reacquire the power of speech. But nor is the
silence a voluntary decision, a conscious refusal. The loss of
speech happens to the girl and yet this specific physiological
deficit expresses the frustration of an entire way of being with
others, whereby the inability to 'be with' one other is translated
into a general inability to relate to others in that mode which is
fundamental for human beings, namely, speech. Just as one
other can, in certain exceptional cases, come to stand for others
in general, so the life of the body in general is expressed
indirectly in each and every one of its basic functions, so that
any one of these can come to symbolize a disconnection in the
circuit of existence. 'But', as Merleau-Ponty points out,
'precisely because my body can shut itself off from the world, it
is also what opens me out upon the world and places me in a

situation there. The momentum of existence towards others, towards the future, towards the world can be restored as a river unfreezes' (p. 165).

This chapter on sexuality is of particular interest in that it represents one of the few attempts made by Merleau-Ponty in this work to relate his psychological critique to the findings of psychoanalysis rather than to those of, for instance, reflexology, Gestalt psychology, associationist psychology etc. While recognizing that Freud brought out the extent to which many of our motives have their origin in sources which are not conscious, he does nevertheless refuse to read Freud as a biological or physiological reductionist. The basis for this reading of Freud is to be seen in his concept of *libido*, a concept which is not reducible to the functioning of the genital organs but which is conceived in so very universal a way as to be more or less coextensive with existence itself. Words like 'atmosphere', 'odour', 'haze' are employed to render the ambiguous generality of a sexual projection rooted in a metaphysical conception of the body which resists assimilation to the sphere of either the psychic or the physical. Thus, for Merleau-Ponty, psychoanalysis must be wary of making either one of two basic mistakes: refusing to recognize any psychic contents but those which are conscious and so susceptible to explicit representation, on the one hand, and, on the other, duplicating the sphere of conscious contents with a second sphere of unconscious contents. The basic meanings which psychoanalysis uncovers (and which are not ordinarily directly available to the patient) are expressions of the life of the body, expressions which, as such, are inherently ambiguous, capable of accommodating many alternative interpretations, expressions which, because they antecede the bifurcation into subject and object, mind and matter, the psychic and the physical, give expression to a process whereby the hitherto meaningless takes on meaning, a meaning which, in so far as it symbolizes the assumption of a given situation by a particular body, is always quite unique and individual.

The importance of the chapter on the body as expression and speech lies in the fact that, obviously, speech is the locus of meaning and expression. But, for Merleau-Ponty, meaning and expression are by no means reducible to language, even though language is clearly their most obvious sphere of manifestation.

The author's aim here, as elsewhere, is to get beyond the subject–object dichotomy by going back before the bifurcation which symbolizes this very split and to do so by seeing in the body-subject or *own body* the originary source of meaning and expression. Again, here as elsewhere, the critical method employed is the mutual and reciprocal destruction of both empiricist and intellectualist theories of language and language disturbances. For the former, the word is evoked either by the physical laws of neurological mechanics or by psychological laws of association. For the latter, the expressed word is only the overt sign of a concept or category whose true locus is the covert sphere of the mind. But, as Merleau-Ponty points out, there is a deep-rooted affinity between the empiricist and the intellectualist view of language, an affinity which can best be described by saying that, in both cases, the word has no significance (p. 176). The meaninglessness of the word is obvious in the first case since the word is not supposed to be consciously evoked by a concept. But although meaning is supposed to pre-exist its expression in words in the case of an intellectualist interpretation, this only means that the word, in itself, is meaningless. In the first case, the concept of meaning is redundant whereas, in the second, only an external relation can be supposed to obtain between the word and its meaning. 'Thus we refute both intellectualism and empiricism by simply saying that the word has a meaning' (p. 177).

Merleau-Ponty analyses the meaningfulness of words in terms of what he calls 'gestural meaning'. Like Heidegger, therefore, Merleau-Ponty concentrates his attention upon language as *discourse* rather than upon language as *writing*. And, in order to emphasize still further the meaning-giving function of speaking, he will even draw a further distinction between speaking speech (*parole parlante*) and spoken speech (*parole parlée*) (p. 197), the former capturing the moment of meaningful initiation, of the bringing into being of meaning through speaking. Just as a gesture is an expression, and not the translation into some externally available form of an internally inaccessible meaning, so speaking is meaning. And just as I read anger into the expression of someone else's face, so I read meaning into the sounds that the other articulates.

Thus in the context of Merleau-Ponty's existential analysis, language becomes an action but an action of a quite peculiar kind. For although action is of its very nature an expression of motives and intentions and a way of being in the world, as such it is, at least in principle, capable of operating within the limits of a solipsistically circumscribed sphere. But language is, by its very nature, an action which presupposes a community, a community moreover which shares a language and whose common language makes up a great part of the commonness of that world which underlies and so upholds the very notion of a community. Thus the last chapter of Part One prepares the way for the last chapter of Part Two, the chapter on Other People and the Human World.

Part Two

'The theory of the body is already a theory of perception.' This, the theme of the introduction to Part Two, bridges the gap between Part One and Part Two. The overall theme of Part Two is 'The World as Perceived' or, in other words, the being-in-the-world of a subject defined in terms of its being a body. The first two chapters on 'Sense Experience' and 'Space' present the theory of perception which follows from the discovery of embodied consciousness in its essential generality, first from the standpoint of experience and then from that of the form which characterizes such an experience. We then move into the realm of the specific, first with an account of those specific alterities which do not have the mode of being of a human being (the Thing) and then with those that do (Other People).

The procedure adopted here is rather similar to that applied earlier. First, Merleau-Ponty takes the dogmatic standpoints of empiricism and intellectualism. The *empiricist* believes that there is a world in itself, a world governed by causal relations, a world in which the body itself features as a thing among things and upon which worldly objects are therefore able to impinge in such a way as to reproduce, in the subject, an idea of this world, thereby generating a corresponding psychological world, an internal world characterized by states of consciousness together with the laws of their association. The *intellectualist* holds that there is a world for itself, thereby effecting a reversal of the empiricist thesis. The world becomes what consciousness is conscious 'of'. The already constituted world through which, for the empiricist, consciousness is itself constituted becomes a world to be constituted by a constituting consciousness. The state of consciousness becomes the consciousness of a state. Consciousness of a unified world becomes a consciousness of the unifying power of consciousness, a self-conscious consciousness which is conscious not only of itself but of its responsibility for constituting the very world in which it finds itself (pp. 208 and 237).

And yet behind this apparent disagreement we find a very real agreement. In both cases the already constituted world forms the point of departure for an analysis which either explains consciousness in terms of the world or explains the world in terms of the unifying power of consciousness. In both cases we find a subject set over against the object, the former in the first instance being explained in terms of the latter and the latter in terms of the former in the other instance. In neither case is the analysis in question capable of explaining the genesis of this very opposition of subject and object, which is simply taken to be a self-evident feature of our experience. But in failing to explain the genesis of the world neither empiricism nor intellectualism are capable of offering a rationale for the kind of (abnormal) phenomena which psychology brings to light, the reports given by those who are the victims of physiological disorders of one kind or another, the reports given by those who receive the gift of sight for the first time, the reports given by those who are given drugs such as mescalin. These reports prove conclusively that there is an experience prior to the polarization of experience around the subject–object dichotomy, a primordial experience which has to be understood if we are even to understand the peculiar details of our everyday experience, an experience characterized by forgetfulness of this more originary experience. It only remains to characterize this primordial experience and, more important still, to bring out the concepts and structures which are required to make sense of it.

Neither empiricism nor intellectualism is capable of doing justice to the fact, and the extent, of the involvement of the body in perceptual experience. In order to give this involvement its due, Merleau-Ponty will talk of a 'coexistence' or 'coincidence' of the embodied subject with the world. This primordial coincidence brings with it a number of implications.

First, affection and sensation can no longer be distinguished by attributing the one to the subject and the other to the object. The world offers itself to the sensory subject who, in turn, responds, thereby qualifying the world in such a way that what he sees is, in part, what he has already put into perception through his affective response to what offers itself. The affective quality of, for example, a colour is not superimposed upon a sense datum which is, in the first instance, simply neutrally apprehended. Rather, action and passion, the receiving and the responding are both parts of one and the same interaction. Second, since the body is a unity, each of the senses operates as a unity, unifying the world in its own distinctive fashion. More, beneath the discrimination of the several worlds opened up by the different senses we find an intersensory unity, a *synaesthesia* which is the sensory counterpart of the synthesis of the body. Originally, the findings of touch do not have to be translated into visual terms or vice versa; rather, there is a tactile dimension to seeing and a visual dimension to touching. And since this original, synaesthetic experience comes before the polarization of experience around the dichotomy of subject and object, it has to be attributed to an agent which is, properly speaking, anonymous in the sense that (s)he is not yet the 'I' which (s)he will later become. The body is that 'natural self' which we each of us are *before* the opposition of self and world effects that de-naturalization of experience which is then taken to be the self-evident foundation of any reasonable understanding both of the self and of the world.

It is in this sense that Merleau-Ponty's *Phenomenology of Perception* is designed to teach us to see, to relearn what perception means *against* the falsification that our mental constructions impose. In one sense this 'learning how to see' is the easiest thing in the world. We simply have to set aside the prejudices of science and common sense and let ourselves be carried along by the current of existence, attending carefully to what reveals ourselves when we remain open to the richness and variety of sensory perception (as, for example, the artist must remain open to that richness and variety). In another sense, however, it is the most difficult thing in the world. For it requires that we first unlearn what we have already taken the trouble to learn, that we become once again the child we once were whilst, at the same time, retaining the critical acumen needed to set this original way of seeing off against the intellectual prejudices of both empiricism and intellectualism. Merleau-Ponty is under no illusions about the difficulty of this operation. And it is for this reason that he gives to the kind of reflection needed to enquire back into the origin, a specific name or set of names. It is 'radical reflection' (p. 241), 'reflection on the unreflected' (p. 213); it appeals to a conception of the *a priori synthetic* which no longer sets the *a priori* off *against* the factual (what the world must be as opposed to what it is) but integrates the *a priori with* the *factual*, shows the incompleteness of *actual* perception to be a *necessary* feature of the perceptual process. And once the primordial realm of an originary experience has been discovered, or better, re-discovered, it then becomes possible, for the first time, to account for the emergence of that very objective world which is ordinarily taken for granted.

What we see here therefore is the completion of a circle – and if I have any complaint to make about Merleau-Ponty's presentation it is that he does not bring out the logic of this essential circularity as clearly as he might have done. We begin with the objective universe, the world as it is ordinarily taken for granted by science and common sense. Empiricism offers the first philosophical analysis of this world. But by seeing the self as a sort of mirror or reflection of the world, empiricism remains blind to the contribution which consciousness makes to the construction of this objectified view of the world. By taking up a stand outside the confines of the universe, intellectualism is able to bring to light the operations of a constituting subject, a subject through whose synthesizing activity the universe acquires its meaning as an objective totality. But then intellectualism has now placed the (transcendental) subject *outside* the world and so remains blind to the involvement of the subject in the very process by which the objectivity of the universe gets built up in the first place. Hence the need for a movement of return, a movement which carries back to the origin the resources of reflection, which is capable of reflecting upon that which antecedes objective thought, and therefore also reflective thought, and which, in so doing, is able to give expression to both the original experience of the world and the process by which this experience is then covered over or forgotten in the very course of our coming to understand it. Thus we end up where we started, with the objective universe; but we now understand it for the first time, understand how it came into being, how it got forgotten and how this forgetting itself became a theme for philosophical reflection, so leading us towards a 'reflection on the unreflected' through which something like a re-membering is accomplished.

The chapter on space offers a beautiful confirmation of Merleau-Ponty's position, again, for the most part, with reference to psychological data. The aim is the same as in preceding investigations: to contrast an empirical with an intellectualist view, to demonstrate both their apparent disagreement and the deeper agreement which in fact links them, to show the inability of either to account for certain critical phenomena and then to open the way to a new understanding of the phenomena which calls for a regression to the originary source of our experience. For the empiricist, space is a physical setting which is passively registered by an embodied subject which has its place in such a space, just like any other thing. For the intellectualist, space is a geometrical construction put together by a disembodied subject who, as such, has no specific location in the spatial construction for which he is responsible. Merleau-Ponty adopts the example of retinal inversion to prove that neither empiricism nor intellectualism is capable of doing justice to the facts. Empiricism relies on an association between head and feet and 'up' and 'down' to explain the correction that eventually takes place when special glasses are worn to correct the retinal images which are ordinarily inverted. The trouble is that the empiricism presupposes precisely what has to be proved, by taking 'up' and 'down' to be given directions. But what the empiricist is actually confronted with is a mosaic of sensational contents which knows no orientational axes outside the body's 'power' to introduce such axes. To invoke this 'power' is to admit the defeat of empiricism. Intellectualism is worse off still. For since the intellectualist confers upon the subject the right to construct space and to do so without reference to the specific location of the subject and since, in such a space, places and directions are all merely relative, each to the other, the intellectualist lacks a point of anchorage which might even make it possible for him to distinguish 'up' from 'down' or 'right' from 'left'.

Both empiricism and intellectualism are in agreement in

denying the possibility of an absolute with reference to which space gets its directions; the empiricist because it puts the body in space from the very beginning, the intellectualist because the construction is accomplished by a subject who is everywhere and nowhere. Thus the necessary point of anchorage can only be introduced by the recognition of the absoluteness of the body as existing at the centre of an oriented space, better, as a centre of action, as the source of a system of actual and possible actions. Once again, therefore, Merleau-Ponty appeals to an 'anonymous', 'pre-personal', 'natural' self which generates space by its own action in a world which antecedes thought.

An analysis of depth perception serves to confirm the above conclusion. Again, both empiricism and intellectualism are in agreement in thinking of depth as 'breadth seen from the side', as a construction which, for this very reason, is capable of dispensing with action, or rather, of replacing the phenomenon of action with that of apparent size, or the angle of eye convergence, and employing the latter either as a rational *sign* or as the *cause* of our inferring *from* a world presented in two dimensions *to* a world into which a third dimension has been introduced. As before, Merleau-Ponty invokes his own notion of a 'motive', not so much to mediate between reasons and causes as to effect a regression to a more original source of significance (p. 259).

The analysis of movement provides a second confirmation of an original, oriented space introduced into the world by the body in action. In fact, since action is a kind of movement, the attempt to analyse the movement of bodies other than one's own in abstraction from the latter leads straight into the kind of paradoxes to which Zeno gave his name. Thus, the attempt to reconstruct movement through the hypothesis of a self-identical object which traverses successive spatial positions through a series of discrete temporal instants has to be given up in favour of a recognition of the irreducible primordiality of what Merleau-Ponty calls 'mobility' or the 'mobile'. The experience of mobility refuses the distinctions between object, space and time which are the elements out of which both empiricism and intellectualism will seek to reconstruct the experience of movement. 'Motion is not a hypothesis, the probability of which is measured as in physical theory by the number of acts

which it co-ordinates. That would give only possible movement, whereas movement is a fact' (p. 277).

The concluding section on being-in-the-world as the ultimate
foundation *of* or, as he prefers to call it, 'anchorage' *for* our
experience of space is important and not just as a reiteration of
a familiar theme. Rather, at the end of his chapter on space,
Merleau-Ponty raises an objection to his procedure which
certainly deserves serious consideration. Yes, it might be con-
ceded, detailed examinations of phenomena drawn from the
world of the child, the primitive, the schizophrenic or the
victim of some abnormal impairment do indeed suffice to bring
to light dimensions of experience which are overlooked in our
ordinary world constructions. But then the insignificance of
these dimensions can be recognized from the fact that the child
learns to grow up, that the culture of the primitive invariably
goes under when confronted with that of more 'advanced'
societies, and that abnormalities are only identified and examined with a view to effecting a cure.

It is of course absolutely fundamental to Merleau-Ponty's
appeal to the primordial that this word should name something
more than just a realm of error and illusion that, in fact, in the
absence of an understanding of this more primordial realm our
supposedly more sophisticated explanations and constructions
would prove groundless, even that these explanations are in
themselves quite incapable of accounting for the phenomena in
question. All of this can be accommodated by a proof to the
effect that a realm of the primordial does indeed antecede, and
so ground, our taken for granted conception of the world,
together with the explanatory theories based upon it. But
more, much more than this is, in my estimate, at stake in *The
Phenomenology of Perception*.

First of all, better perhaps than any other philosopher before
him, Merleau-Ponty has understood the affective significance
of the primordial and, as a result, the primordial significance
of affection. In losing its grounding in a more primordial realm,
objective thought has lost much more than it knows. It has lost
the richness and fruitfulness of an original experience which is
a kind of continual creation, a recreation of the world from
moment to moment in an endless transfusion of thought and
action and emotion. Myths and dreams cannot simply be
dismissed as primitive relics. Rather, they point to a deeper

dimension of the self, to an investment of the self in a world which, to some extent, is its own, a world whose joys and fears, successes and failures, are not to be measured by some common rod but express the peculiar character of the natural self. After a century of psychoanalysis such insights are surely not so unfamiliar; and it is interesting that, following Sartre (though with much better reason than his colleague), Merleau-Ponty too refuses to accept the Freudian concept of the unconscious (p. 296). For the natural self is the unconscious, the pre-reflective *cogito* is that primordial foundation of conscious existence to which Freud had to give the name 'unconscious', but only because Freud was incapable of coming to terms with a consciousness which did not know itself explicitly, a consciousness whose life was a life not of the mind but of the body, not of thought but of action, a consciousness for which therefore myth and dream was not to be equated with error and illusion but to be recognized as the authentic expression of a certain way of being in the world.

The chapter on The Thing and the Natural World represents a restoration of concrecity after the relatively abstract topic of space. But precisely because the thing is, as it were, a concrete determination of space, it has to be considered in relation to its natural horizon, the world. In fact, the movement of this whole chapter is from the specific to the general, from the thing itself (its self-sameness and its qualitative characteristics), through the intersensory synthesis accomplished by the thing, to the world as the general setting in which the thing has to be situated. A final section on hallucination serves to confirm the positions already established by destroying the apparent rationality of the objective world and so bringing to light the pre-logical foundations on which this derivative reality rests.

An object is what it is and this logical condition is supported first and foremost by the supposed constancy of size and shape despite changes in distance and perspective. Merleau-Ponty adopts the more concrete term the 'thing' to characterize the object in its pre-objective constitution. It is therefore in terms of the thing that he first criticizes his opponent's views and then presents his own. The method adopted is the same as previously. Empiricism and intellectualism offer alternative and mutually incompatible explanations for the invariance of the thing. This seeming opposition, through which each destroys the other, is then reduced to an underlying agreement which is, in turn, undermined in order to bring to light the more primordial domain which neither the one nor the other is capable of attaining.

Empiricism assumes a normal distance and perspective and then tries to explain the deviations from the norm. But this not only leaves unanswered the question how one apparent size and shape is adopted as the objective norm, it fails to address the more important, because more general, question how objectivity arises in the first place. Intellectualism relativizes all objective relations and conceives of the thing as the point of intersection of distances and directions each of which varies concomitantly with the other. But in assuming that all possible variations in size and shape are explained in advance by some mathematical formula, intellectualism too presupposes what it is called upon to prove, namely, the coming into being of an objective world in which such an abstract system of relations can even be posited. However, it is not because, with every change of distance and perspective, the thing alters its apparent shape and size that I conclude to the invariance of the thing through its apparent changes. It is because I already perceive the thing with a definite shape and size that changes of distance and perspective can produce corresponding changes in the apparent shape or size. Perceiving the thing already with a definite shape and size, however, is only possible because distances are already translated into tensions, because angles are translated automatically into a felt balance, because, in a word, the body is involved in the positing of the thing and indeed transcends itself in order to break forth into things (p. 303). I am not a spectator beholding a visual panorama but an actor staging an ever-changing scenic drama.

By the same token, the qualities of the thing both do and do not maintain a certain constancy despite changes in lighting and the organization of the field. Both empiricism and intellectualism would like to suppose that there is a real colour which the thing displays and that variations can all be explained in terms of changes in the lighting and the organization of the field. And certainly, changes in the lighting conditions and the setting do change the way the colour is perceived but not in the way the theorists require if their explanations are to be successful. Among other things, the prevailing theories would like to regard the constancy of the colour under changes of lighting and setting as three factors between which correlative relations can be established. In so doing they fail to appreciate what links them, binds them together in one indissoluble synthesis: 'the natural correlation between appearances and our kinaesthetic unfoldings (is) something not known through a law, but experienced as the involvement of our body in the typical structures of a world' (p. 310).

Among other things, Merleau-Ponty's descriptions point up the pointlessness of sense data theories. The supposed primordiality of sense data is shown to be doubly, if not triply, derivative. The patches of colour with which British phenomenalism operates and with which it attempts to reconstruct the objective world are second order abstractions from an object which is itself a construction, a construction moreover which requires that we reproduce, at all times, the whole context in which any given act of perception operates, rather than isolating (as sense data theory does) the particular objects in question from the context in which they are perceived. As an attempt to reach what purports to be primordial, sense data are pure fictions, not just logical fictions but psychological fictions, fictions the unreality of which can be demonstrated by psychological experimentation.

The unreality of sense data theory becomes even more evident when we shift the focus of attention from vision to touch, from the most distancing of the senses to the sense which requires proximity. For in order to touch, the body must be touched; in order to feel, the body must feel itself feeling. Nor is the analogy to be disqualified on the grounds that the two senses operate in a completely different fashion. The activity of vision is recaptured in the exploratory movements required for touch perception; the passivity of touch is recaptured in the invasion of the eye by a dazzling light. And though vision is generally treated as the most 'objective' sense, there is a sense in which the reality of the thing is never more adequately apparent than in touch. Precisely because tactile experience adheres to the surface of the body, the subject of touch cannot suppose that he is everywhere and nowhere, cannot abstract himself from a given perspective, cannot abstract from the activity required to sustain the sensations in question in being.

The key to the analysis of the thing as an intersensory synthesis is to be found in this primordial interaction of the body with the thing. Because the body is itself a unity, because the different senses are set in the context of one and the same body and because the action of the body is the unfolding of a power *both* to integrate the several ways of the senses *and* to open them up into separate realms, the correlation of body and thing means that this very power in the body is recuperated in the thing as a power in the thing to unify and integrate the several findings of the sense. Again, Merleau-Ponty is very careful to refuse any description which replaces the concretity of the phenomenon in question with abstract equivalents. The unity of a thing is not to be thought of as a substratum, an = X, an *in itself*, but rather as a 'unique accent', a 'symbolism in the thing which links each sensible quality to the rest' (p. 319).

But there is a paradox to be taken account of – and this leads us from the theme of the thing to that of the world. On the one hand, the disclosure of a genuinely primordial realm brings to light a dimension of coincidence, a coexistence or communion of perception with the perceived, a 'primary faith' which binds us to the world. Indeed, the world itself can be regarded as 'one vast individual' with which I am in constant communication (p. 328), as that in which our own body is 'as the heart is in the organism' (p. 203). On the other hand, the world not only welcomes and accepts, it also resists and rejects; it is not only that in which I find myself but also that which surpasses any experience I can ever have of it; it is not only that in which I find myself at home, it is that in which I am alienated from myself, in which I find myself estranged – and this is the source of many schizophrenic disturbances. This paradox, however, is mitigated (even if it is not resolved) if we shift the focus from being to time, from the dimension of simultaneity to that of succession, from the presumption of completeness to that of an essential incompleteness. 'There is, indeed, a contradiction, as long as we operate within being, but the contradiction disappears . . . if we operate in time, and if we manage to understand time as the measure of being' (p. 330).

But the world is not just a natural world; it is also, and more importantly, a social and cultural world. The chapter on 'Other People and the Human World' begins with the problem presented by a thinking which takes the objective world for granted. For the correlate of the object is the subject, a subject which is supposed to know itself through and through, whose existence and experience is inaccessible to others and whose own body is, in the first instance, a body like any other body, a body with which the subject simply finds itself to be united in a manner which remains ultimately unintelligible to objective thought. To put it in more technical language, the language which Sartre himself adopted in *Being and Nothingness*: 'there are two modes of being, and two only: being in itself, which is that of objects arrayed in space, and being for itself, which is that of consciousness' (p. 349). From such a standpoint the existence of the other must remain problematic. Even the argument from analogy presupposes what it is supposed to prove. For if I am able to conclude to the existence and experience of others on the basis of observed analogies between their behaviour and my own, this is only because I presuppose a consciousness animating the other body in a manner equivalent to that in which my consciousness is known to animate that body with which I find myself united. But with what right do I make such an assumption?

Merleau-Ponty does not so much undertake a critical refutation of alternative theories or offer a proof of his own as simply point out that all the analyses and descriptions accomplished hitherto point in a direction which resolves (rather than solves) the problem. 'If I experience this inhering of my consciousness in its body and its world, the perception of other people and the plurality of consciousness no longer presents any difficulty. . . . If my consciousness has a body, why should other bodies not "have" consciousness?' (p. 351). If, before and beneath my personal subjectivity, I find a pre-personal, anonymous, amorphous being through whose constituting 'power' a world is sustained in being then I can expect the projection of *this* power to intersect with that of others and so to form a common ground on the basis of which mutual understanding and communication becomes possible.

But this is only one side of the story. Piaget informs us that it is around twelve years of age that the child achieves the *cogito*. And although Piaget, unlike Merleau-Ponty, fails to see that the child's world not only *can* be vindicated against that of the adult but that its primordial rationale *must* be upheld if the world of the adult is to be even comprehensible, still, the arrival of the *cogito* on the scene of human interaction does bring with it that struggle between consciousness through which, as Hegel says, each brings about the development of the other while precisely striving to bring that development to an end. Not only Hegel but also and more particularly Sartre haunts these pages, the Sartre of the objectifying gaze which strips the other of its freedom, which reduces the other to an object (pp. 357 and 361). Only, 'for the struggle ever to begin, and for each consciousness to be capable of suspecting the alien presences which it negates, all must necessarily have some common ground and be mindful of their peaceful co-existence in the world of childhood' (p. 355).

But there is more to it than this. For, true to his own adherence to the *cogito*, Merleau-Ponty will not allow the 'I', even the pre-personal, anonymous subject to be done away with in favour of a universal 'We'. I and the other cannot be subsumed under a collective plurality. If there is a community, it is because there is an other for me. And yet, though I read the meaning of the other's existence into his acts, these same acts are only *displayed* to me whereas they are *lived* through by him (p. 356). Moreover, for true communication to take place there has to be reciprocity. If only one loves then, even if the other passively accepts the love received, it is for the other nothing but a contingent determination of her existence whereas, for the one who loves, it represents a necessary and ineluctable commitment of his whole being. There is therefore an insurmountable solipsism. But it is one which enriches and enhances the prospect of human relations rather than one that denies and limits such relations. Solipsism, as a real experience with affective implications (as opposed to the intellectual problem of solipsism), defeats itself because it is forced to presuppose the other from which it feels itself to be cut off. But to experience oneself as cut off from the other is to hold open the possibility of a transcending of this isolation, an integration of my being with that of the other which, precisely because it is that of an other, permits me to transcend myself in my very being-with-the-other, to experience myself as something more than I am given to be by myself.

Part Three

The substance of Merleau-Ponty's thought is, in my estimate, to be found in Parts One and Two, the parts devoted to the theme of the body and of the world. Part Three deals with themes (Cogito, Temporality, Freedom) needed to make Merleau-Ponty's work a complete philosophy, or at least to look like a complete philosophy. All three topics are topics whose themes have haunted the analyses conducted thus far. The first and the third (the Cogito and Freedom), however, are themes so fundamental to French philosophy that a French philosopher, especially of Merleau-Ponty's vintage, would not rest content until he had tackled them. Moreover, the second (Time) is one which Heidegger's seminal work made it necessary for Merleau-Ponty to treat explicitly in a separate chapter.

For French philosophy, Descartes remains the paradigm thinker. To such an extent is this the case that, as we have seen, Sartre's own ontology can be seen as a revised version of Cartesian dualism. But even figures such as Bergson and Merleau-Ponty who both set out deliberately to overcome Cartesian dualism found themselves undertaking this task in terms which presupposed the very thinking they were seeking to surpass.[2] Rather than undertaking a summary of the contents of the first chapter of Part Three (the Cogito), I would therefore prefer to address the more general question: in what way does the entire work reflect the spirit of Cartesianism, and in what way does it successfully resist, and even overcome, the tendencies of Cartesianism?

Like most French philosophers (and unlike Heidegger or Ryle), Merleau-Ponty subscribes to a version of the philosophy of consciousness. Consciousness is one of the great discoveries of modern philosophy and is quite rightly attributed to Descartes. The form in which the philosophy of consciousness arises in Descartes is, of course, that of dualism. More specifically, Cartesian dualism is founded on two premises, the duality of subject and object and the duality of mind and body. Merleau-Ponty's commitment to Cartesianism is highly ambivalent. On the one hand, he accepts more of Cartesian dualism than he is able later to tolerate – and this explains the shift towards the positions assumed in his later philosophy. On the other hand, *The Phenomenology of Perception* represents one of the great contemporary attacks on Cartesian dualism.

The residual retention of Cartesianism is apparent in his acceptance of the very terminology of the *cogito*. He will even connect the excesses of the *cogito* with the postulation of its apparent opposite, the notion of the unconscious; thus, in an odd way, undermining the legitimacy of the Freudian concept of the unconscious in favour of some revised version of the philosophy of consciousness (p. 381). The retention of the language of consciousness makes Merleau-Ponty's massive attack on mind–body dualism more ambiguous than it might at first sight seem. For although the point of this work is to conceive of consciousness as embodied or to conceive of the body as animate (and therefore as already, potentially, a consciousness), a Heideggerian might very well object that even to talk of consciousness (or the body) is to imply a duality. The refusal of the Heideggerian project (which, in a certain sense, inspires the whole of this work) is particularly evident in his virtual reversal of the Heideggerian terminology. The word 'being', when it is used at all, is taken by Merleau-Ponty to mean much the same thing as Heidegger's 'ontic'. 'Here as everywhere, the relation of having, which can be seen in the very etymology of the word habit, is at first concealed by relations belonging to the domain of being, or, as we may equally say, by ontic relations obtaining within the world' (p. 174).

Much more equivocal, in my estimate, is his retention of the language of subjectivity. The body with which he is concerned is a body subject or a bodily subject. And although Merleau-Ponty will talk of a 'pre-personal', 'pre-reflective', 'anonymous', 'amorphous', subject which grounds, and so comes prior to, the emergence of Cartesian subjectivity, nevertheless, his commitment to the language of subjectivity is all-pervasive. This commitment is all the more serious in that he is not equivalently committed to what might appear to be the correlate of the subject, namely, the object. Rather, talk about the object, the object as it exists both for realism and for idealism, is explicitly contrasted with talk about the 'thing'. The thing is the primordial, or the prototypical, object and the genesis of the object out of, and on the basis of, the thing is a move in the direction of the abstract, therefore a move away from the concrete reality of being-in-the-world.

It is for his attack on Cartesian dualism, however, that Merleau-Ponty is best known. His critique of the Cartesian *cogito* goes along with his critique of self-evident truth, of eternal truths, of definitive laws of thought. So the critique of transparent thought is at the same time a reassessment of the significance of contingency, of facticity, of transcendence or rather of that awareness of contingency, facticity and transcendence which is itself an expression of the *cogito* in some new sense. This new sense is given many names, the *'pre-reflective cogito'*, the *'practical cogito'*, the *'tacit cogito'*. But the analyses to which these names lead all point in the same direction, in the direction of a primordial truth which, for Merleau-Ponty, is the ultimate truth – to the extent that he will even accept such a traditional concept as 'ultimate' truth.

Philosophy for Merleau-Ponty, and in complete accord with the entire tradition which took its start in Descartes, is, by its very nature, a reflective discipline. But what distinguishes Merleau-Ponty's brand of reflection is that it is directed towards the unreflected, exists as a reflection upon that which the traditional concept of reflection tends to overlook, precisely because it is a thinking which looks over (*survol*), supervises, seeks to assume a God's eye view of the world. Reflection upon the unreflected therefore takes its start in a reflection upon the inadequacy of the traditional concept of reflection, in a reflection upon the impossibility of assuming the very disembodied stance which characterizes Cartesian reflection and which is even more clearly embedded in transcendental philosophy. But it culminates in a movement of regression, a movement whereby the resources of reflection are carried back to the origin, to that origin which we still carry with us in sedimented form, the meaning of which we can therefore re-vive in the literal sense of that word, that is, 're-live' through a 'radical reflection' which lives its thinking and thinks its living.

The tactic employed in the chapter on Temporality should, by now, be familiar to us. Merleau-Ponty begins with a critique of objective time, or the empiricist's conception of time, moves on to a critique of reflective time, or the intellectualist's conception of time, before moving back to an existential conception of time, which is effectively nothing more than a reflective recuperation of time as originally lived out by an embodied consciousness situated in a world. However, there are a few unusual twists and turns which give this chapter its intrinsic interest.

Merleau-Ponty opens his descriptions with a restatement of the Bergsonian position. There is no time to be found in the world, only one indivisible and changeless being. Time exists only because there are subjects situated in a world. But precisely because the world itself is timeless, and because the subject finds itself given over to being in the world, the subject is inclined to introduce the timeless instant into consciousness and to make of it the foundation of an objective succession by means of which time is measured and defined. In other words, objective time is the result of the spatialization of an original flux, time refracted through the form of space. It is this spatialized time which we find at the root of the empiricist's conception of time, empiricism being that philosophy which, typically, conceives of the subject in terms derived from the object. But then, in conceiving of time in this way, temporality, what makes time temporal, has been lost. To put it another way, time has become space, or rather, a spatial representation of time has taken the place of time.

The move from objective to reflective time effects a significant advance in the direction of an understanding of temporality. Time is now linked explicitly to the subject. The subject is understood as constituting time. A flux of inner time consciousness is posited as the ultimately constitutive flux through which all temporal moments and stretches arise and acquire the temporal identity which belongs to them. But Husserl's attempt to develop a time of inner time consciousness also undergoes a critical dissolution. If a sort of eternity is to be admitted it is one which will be found at the very heart of time, not one assumed by an atemporal, transcendental subject. And if this same subject is, for the purposes of a time analysis, reduced to a flux, then, inevitably, it will be found that the flux outruns itself and so makes impossible the purity of a reflection which would be both the reflecting and the reflected at one and the same time. In this sense, even our purest reflection is condemned to being retrospection, for 'our reflection on the flux is actually inserted into that flux' (p. 426). Moreover, an inner time consciousness which seeks to constitute time in the present of reflection must needs fail to comprehend the pastness of the past and the futureness of the future. Recollection, for instance, takes place in the present and is therefore incapable of situating the past event there where it belongs, in the past. Husserl, Merleau-Ponty suggests, was himself aware of the limitations of his own conception of time, limitations already announced with the introduction of such new concepts as operative intentionality (to replace act intentionality) or passive synthesis (to replace active synthesis).

This is the point at which the Heideggerian conception of time begins to take hold. Time is not temporalized by a constituting subject; time temporalizes itself and, in so doing, always outruns any possible constitutive synthesis. 'There is no need for a synthesis externally binding together the *tempora* into one single time, because each one of the *tempora* was already inclusive, beyond itself, of the whole open series of other *tempora*, being an internal communication with them, and because the "cohesion of a life" is given with its ek-stase' (p. 421). But this is the point at which Merleau-Ponty takes his leave of Heidegger and in a most interesting and significant way. For although he accepts that each dimension of time is inextricably bound up with the rest, it is to the present, not the future, that he accords the privilege (p. 424).

Merleau-Ponty's way through to the privilege of the present is startlingly unorthodox. Eternity, the very term which is rejected as the index of a God's eye view of the world, of the assumption of an atemporal, transcendental stance, is *reinstated* at the heart of time, which means the heart of existence, where it assumes the form of the 'eternal present', of a presence (or better still a presencing) which is the very action of time creation, of a flux which continually outruns itself and so can never catch up with itself, of a transcending which, because it is always beyond itself, can never come to terms with itself and so represents a time before time (in the ordinary sense) ever comes into being. But this 'time before time' is so far from being atemporal that it is time itself in its on-going dynamic, that dynamic without which there could be no consciousness of time. This is the paradox of time of which Augustine wrote: If no one asks me what time is, I know; if I am asked, I do not know.

This original and fundamental time is, of course, the time of an incarnate consciousness living out its life in a given situation. It is the time of a being which acts and affects itself by its own action, a being that ex-ists beyond itself and which still drags its past behind it like a comet's tail, a being which is time and for which, nevertheless, the whole of life is but one eternal present, a creator who is, at the same time, a creature condemned by birth to death.

The final chapter on Freedom confirms the analyses devoted to time. Merleau-Ponty begins by refusing determinism since determinism is that view which takes up, with regard to the subject, the point of view of the object, for which therefore, in the proper sense of that word, there is no subject. The refusal of the empiricist's thesis of determinism would seem to leave the way open to the assertion of an absolute freedom, the kind of assertion we find in the history of modern philosophy from Descartes to Sartre. 'There is, then, ultimately nothing that can set limits to freedom, except those limits that freedom itself has set in the form of its various initiatives, so that the subject has simply the external world that he gives himself' (p. 436). This parody of the Sartrian position is no sooner stated than it is rejected. For freedom is doing, and doing means the action of an incarnate consciousness whose very body sets limits to any project which it might set out to accomplish. Nor will Merleau-Ponty permit the Sartrian retreat into a trying whose absolute and unlimited freedom is exhibited in deliberate proposals, no matter how impossible it might be to transform such proposals into doable projects. And this not because the trying is an inadequate substitute for doing but because the shift from the deliberate project (doing) to the deliberate proposal (trying) fails to uncover the impersonal and therefore non-deliberate ground in which all our deliberate decisions are rooted.

From his preliminary refusal both of the freedom–determinism debate and of any affirmation of an absolute, unqualified freedom, Merleau-Ponty proceeds on to the final step, an acknowledgment of the mutual and reciprocal determination of freedom and facticity. Freedom and facticity are not dialectically opposed, nor is one affirmed at the expense of the other.

Rather, they are inextricably interwoven. If freedom lies in doing then freedom is necessarily conditioned by an incarnate existence which sets limits to freedom. I cannot be free without doing and I cannot do without being a body. But if, at the same time, my being a body sets limits to my freedom, then freedom is conditioned by that which sets limits to it. Freedom cannot be saved by being limited and constrained, by being the freedom of an incarnate being in a given situation. Torture brings out most effectively the cruel paradox inherent in freedom. The torturer works upon the body of his victim. The victim, we say, is 'free' to give or not to give the names and addresses which it is desired to extract from him. But this freedom is not the freedom of a bare consciousness, a consciousness which is capable of denying with respect to itself that it is this body which is presently being tortured. The extent of the commitment to freedom is measured by the very pain which the victim chooses to withstand and is incomprehensible outside the parameters of a consciousness *become* pure and simple pain.

The emphasis of Part Three has been upon those dimensions of human reality which are more intimately aligned with consciousness, with the *for itself*, with the subject. Beginning with the Cartesian theme of the *cogito*, a theme which, in a certain historical sense, opens the way to the whole new dimension of consciousness and subjectivity, we move on to the theme of time which, as Kant tells us, is the form of the mind as opposed to the form (space) of that which exists 'outside' the mind, only to conclude with the theme of freedom, a theme which, historically, has been invoked to mark out for Man a sphere of inalienable spontaneity, a sphere within which he is able to escape the general condition of all incarnate existence, be something more than a body, shape and form his own life in accord with his own aims, ambitions and ideals. But the upshot of his analyses is a disappointment for modern philosophy, a rejection of that self-conception which made of man a creature created in the image of God, a self-made Man, a God-man – even a Superman. A disappointment or a promise? Surely, a promise. The promise of a richness and a fullness of existence which modern philosophy never knew, the promise of an atunement with being and with nature which modern philosophy undermined, the promise of a new spirituality which does not leave the body behind but plunges into the body in order to find therein a depth and a wisdom which mind never knew.

What is the distinctive contribution made by Merleau-Ponty? In my estimate, it is the grounding of the being of human being in its being a body – with all that follows therefrom. And a very great deal does follow therefrom. Heidegger's refusal of the category of embodiment goes along with a refusal to take account of the findings of the human sciences – let alone the natural sciences. Whether today it is possible for a philosopher to even attempt to integrate developments in the natural sciences into the main body of his philosophical thinking is a matter which might be disputed. But if philosophy can no longer claim to be the 'Queen of the Sciences', a place still remains open for a conception of philosophy as the 'Queen of the Humanities'.

The significance of the general procedure of an uncovering of the originary ground for such a conception of ontological phenomenology is obvious. Indeed, Merleau-Ponty's own almost exclusive concentration upon experimental psychology must appear peculiar in the light of the fact that, even within the discipline of psychology, other branches of this discipline would seem to lend themselves more happily to a reflection upon the unreflected – child psychology and psychoanalysis in particular. Aside from psychology, however, anthropology (the study of primordial man) and mythology (the study of the most primordial cultural expression of man's being-in-the-world) immediately recommend themselves as disciplines relevant to the disclosure of the originary, disciplines whose foremost practitioners today seem concerned to counter the traditional conception of the primordial as the 'primitive' – in the most deficient sense of that word.

The course of the history of the twentieth century has destroyed that faith in 'progress' which characterized the intellectual attitudes of the nineteenth century. As the destructiveness inherent in progress becomes ever more apparent so we are becoming ever more attuned to recognize in the regression to an originary ground the disclosure of a creative (or even a recreative) source which our contemporary civilization stands in need of. In the words of Friedrich Nietzsche: 'There is more reason in thy body than in thy best wisdom. And who can know why thy body needeth thy best wisdom?'[3]

NOTES

1 Maurice Merleau-Ponty, *La structure du comportement*, précédé de: Une philosophie de l'ambiguïté par Alphonse de Waelhens (Presses Universitaires de France: Paris, 1963).

2 For instance, Bergson's *Matter and Memory* seeks to overcome dualism through the introduction of concepts of the body and of action. But it does so by first presupposing the very dualism it seeks to surpass. To take only the very first words of the Introduction to this work: 'This book affirms the reality of spirit and the reality of matter, and tries to determine the relation of the one to the other by the study of a definite example, that of memory. It is, then, frankly dualistic. But, on the other hand, it deals with body and mind in such a way as, we hope, to lessen greatly, if not to overcome, the theoretical difficulties which have always beset dualism.' (Henri Bergson, *Matter and Memory*, trans. Nancy Paul and W. Scott Palmer (George Allen & Unwin: London, 1911), p. xi.

3 Friedrich Nietzsche, *Also sprach Zarathustra*, Part One: On the Despisers of the Body, Taschenausgabe B7 (Naumann: Leipzig, 1906).

Conclusion

Merleau-Ponty opens his *The Phenomenology of Perception* with the question: What is phenomenology? But his answer to this question is equivocal, to say the least. Phenomenology is *both* a philosophy of essences *and* a philosophy of existence, *both* a transcendental *and* an ontological philosophy, *both* a 'rigorous science' *and* a hermeneutics. As it stands, this 'both . . . and' clearly fails to do justice to the disparity between the Husserlian and the Heideggerian way of doing phenomenology. Hence some phenomenologists have decided to take their stand on one of the two sides – to the exclusion of the other. And yet both Husserl and Heidegger claimed to be doing 'phenomenology'!

It is for this reason that some of the best critics, while refusing the Merleau-Pontian conjunction, have nevertheless stressed the continuity rather than the discontinuity of transcendental and ontological phenomenology. Taking the theme of truth as his guide, Ernst Tugendhat, in his *Wahrheitsbegriff bei Husserl und Heidegger*, seeks to present the transition from a transcendental, or even a proto-transcendental, to an ontological conception of truth as a legitimate extension which was not, however, carried through by Heidegger in as profitable a manner as might have been possible.[1] Michael Theunissen's *Der Andere* undertakes a similar investigation of the transition from the standpoint of the theme of intersubjectivity.[2] Again, Klaus Held has taken the theme of the 'World' as the basis for his own conception of the transition as consisting, essentially, in a radicalization of the transcendental phenomenology of Husserl.[3]

Studies of this kind certainly do help us to understand the

common ground that lies beneath the thinking of both Husserl and Heidegger but, in so doing, they tend to minimalize the essential differences. It is for this reason that, in my own study of Husserl's philosophy, I have tried to account for both the underlying similarity and the difference between the two projects of a transcendental and an ontological phenomenology by focusing upon a structure which I call the 'ontological transposition'.[4] By virtue of a 'logic' intrinsic to the development of phenomenological thinking, the *highest* eventually becomes the *lowest*, the *last* becomes the *first*, the most *abstract* is transformed into the most *concrete*.[5] In this way, *both* the element of continuity *and* the element of discontinuity can be preserved.

However differently Husserl's transcendental and Heidegger's ontological phenomenology might have undertaken the task of founding or grounding, they both share a common point of departure – in Husserl's case, the world of the natural attitude; in Heidegger's case, the realm of the ontic. Thus, in §5 of *Basic Problems of Phenomenology*, the text in which Heidegger first starts thinking about what he had accomplished in *Being and Time*, he describes his procedure as an inversion of the Husserlian: '*For Husserl*, phenomenological reduction . . . is the method of leading phenomenological vision from the natural attitude of the human being whose life is involved in the world of things and persons back to the transcendental life of consciousness and its noetic–noematic experiences, in which objects are constituted as correlates of consciousness. *For us*, phenomenological reduction means leading phenomenological vision back from the apprehension of a being, whatever may be the character of that apprehension, to the understanding of the being of this being (by projecting upon the way it is unconcealed).'[6]

This conception of ontological phenomenology as an inversion of transcendental phenomenology makes it possible to distinguish three levels: the intermediate level of the natural attitude (Husserl) or the ontic (Heidegger), the conclusive, transcendental level and the primary, ontological level. But a further question still remains. Does the ontological level come first or last? In order to answer this question we need to remind ourselves of Heidegger's distinction between a pre-ontological way of being of Dasein and the discipline of ontology. Dasein is ontological in its very being. But precisely because, in being ontological, it is so very close to that way of being which characterizes its self, Dasein first has to lose itself (by absorption in the 'They') before it can finally recover itself again, this time in the form of an explicitly ontological analysis of that way of being which characterizes Dasein from the first.

Hence the following conclusion: the ontological level is the first *in the order of being* but, for this very reason, it is also the last *in the order of analysis*. In other words, that way of being which characterizes human being from the outset is something which it *is* in so very immediate a way that it can only be rendered *susceptible to analysis* at the outcome of a long and laborious detour which eventually brings thinking back to its original point of departure.

Thus we are left with four rather than three levels: (1) the ontological (which also counts as the fourth or last level); (2) the ontic level or the level of the natural attitude; and (3) the transcendental level.

It would be tempting to say that only three of these levels, the first, the third and the fourth, are properly phenomenological levels of investigation while the second is phenomenologically insignificant. After all, Husserl typically only offers a sketch of the natural attitude as a prelude to carrying through a reduction to the properly transcendental level, while Heidegger's starting point on the ontic plane is only assumed in order to assemble the requisite phenomenal data, data whose properly phenomenological comprehension will then call for a regressive movement back to the underlying ground. But then Sartre's ontological phenomenology, as we have already seen, would seem to operate upon the very (Cartesian) plane which Husserl and Heidegger feel it necessary to abandon in order to inaugurate their own phenomenological analyses.

In my estimate, *Being and Nothingness* can best be understood as having furnished an existential phenomenology which operates exclusively upon the second level. Given the dominance of science and technology in the contemporary world view, it is not surprising that the 'natural attitude' should have become the *natural* attitude, even for philosophy.[7] Indeed, I would suggest that science and common sense (the two essential components of the natural attitude) still feature as the paradigm for analytical philosophy. Of course, Sartre does not operate within the parameters of analytic philosophy, the philosophy most closely associated with the 'natural attitude'. What he has done for us is something more important. He has made us aware of the existential implications of that world view which most of us assume as *the* truth, whether or not we do so explicitly. He has made us aware that if consciousness is regarded as nothing more than a supervenient property, a superfluous excrescence which, for purely accidental reasons, just happens to occur here and there and from time to time, then the physical universe in which we find ourselves is one in which it is absurd even to *seek* a human meaning or a truth which justifies and validates the contingent occurrence of conscious beings. He has made us aware that if the self is defined as a consciousness for which the other is, in the first instance, nothing but an object for consciousness, then human relations can only be characterized, along Hegelian lines, as a 'struggle to the death'. This tragic conception of human existence is qualified by a certain Stoic resignation, and a humanistic readiness to work for the improvement of the human lot.

Let us see if we can apply this three (or, more correctly, four) level theory to order and connect the thinking of our four phenomenological philosophers. With a view to sharpening the distinctions we have drawn, we might also seek to assign a specific methodology to each of the levels in question: to the first (as the last) level, the methodology of *ontology*, to the second level, the methodology of *epistemology*, to the third level, the methodology of *transcendental philosophy*.

It is perhaps fitting that the founding figure should be the only one whose life's work can actually be regarded as moving through each and every one of the three methodologies we have distinguished. Coming to philosophy from mathematics, Husserl began by gravitating towards the logical end of the philosophical spectrum and therefore towards an *epistemological* philosophy. As we have seen, it was the difficulties to which his epistemology led him which motivated him to make the break into *transcendental* philosophy. In turn, the attempt to carry through his transcendental programme forced his thinking, at the limit, into contradiction with itself and so provided him with a rationale for the final period of his *'genetic'* phenomenology, a phenomenology whose regressive questioning is already, implicitly, ontological in character.

With *Being and Time*, the thematic of a regression to the ground is carried through without reference to anything like a transcendental consciousness, thereby introducing an explicit break with Husserlian phenomenology. This break can be summarily presented as a threefold quest for concrecity. In place of the *transcendental subject*, Heidegger proposes an analysis of Dasein. In place of the being *out* of the world of the transcendental subject, Heidegger proposes the *being-in-the-world* of Dasein. And in place of a time of *inner time consciousness*, Heidegger proposes an *existential time*.

Sartre's existential philosophy breaks both with Husserl's phenomenology and with Heidegger's ontology. For Husserl, at least the Husserl of the middle period and on, phenomenology is, and can only be, transcendental in character. But one of Sartre's very first publications (*Transcendence of the Ego*) refuses the concept of the transcendental subject and aims at a pre-transcendental phenomenology of the subject. At the same time, the avowedly dualistic ontology of *Being and Nothingness* makes it impossible for Heidegger to see in Sartre a legitimate advocate of ontological phenomenology.

Like Husserl, but unlike early Heidegger and Sartre, Merleau-Ponty's thinking covers all three planes. However, it is not so much a matter of developing an epistemological and a transcendental as well as an ontological phenomenology. Rather the contrary, like Heidegger, Merleau-Ponty is exclusively committed to the exploration of the originary realm. But he gets there by employing a tactic whereby the other two stages are taken account of in terms of their nominal representatives – the realists and the idealists, the empiricists and the intellectualists. Moreover, this nominal representation not only groups together a diversity of philosophical figures; the net is cast widely enough to cover different schools of psychology. What is missing (though it is implicit) in Merleau-Ponty's analyses is the development of a logic whereby empiricism and intellectualism would no longer be placed side by side in an antinomical relation but in an order which, in my estimate, corresponds to a logic inherent in the evolution of the schools in question. What is also missing (though again it is implied) is an extension of the scope of the human sciences to cover disciplines such as psychoanalysis, child psychology, anthropology, mythology – in other words, disciplines whose theme is that of the originary.

To sum up and to situate each of our phenomenological philosophers in terms of the format established initially: Husserl operates upon all three levels – though in a development which proceeds *from* the second *through* the third and so on *to* the fourth. Heidegger confines himself to a movement *from* the second *back to* the first (in the order of being) as the last (in the order of analysis). With Sartre we remain from first to last upon the second plane – though in such a way that both the ontological and the existential implications of such a stance are made explicit. Finally, with Merleau-Ponty, all three planes are covered but in such a way that two of these three (the second and the third) are subjected to a mutually destructive critique which leaves the way open for the last (the fourth as 'reflection upon the unreflected', that is, upon the first).

This three (or four) level framework does help to order and situate the thinking of our four phenomenological philosophers. In so doing, however, it might be objected that we have obscured rather than clarified the situation. Why not return to the example set by the founding father and replace the bewildering multiplicity of ontological and existential positions with the neutral unity of a method? The business of the phenomenological philosopher, it might be argued, is simply that of applying the already established methodological principles to new domains. There is of course a great deal of respectable philosophical labour that can be accomplished under these auspices; but they are auspices which, as it stands, labour under a grave misconception, namely, that the fundamental principles of phenomenological philosophy have already been laid down in a more or less definitive fashion – or could ever be so laid down.

Definitively established principles! What definitively established principles? Even if one turns to Husserl one cannot find any such set of principles, since Husserl kept on redefining what he meant by 'phenomenology'. Turn from Husserl to those figures who might be called his followers and the situation gets much worse – as we have already seen. In the end, what distinguishes our four phenomenological philosophers is that they each and every one of them defined *for themselves* what they took phenomenology to be and then, at

least in the the case of Husserl's three successors, went on to
establish a definite philosophical position in accord with the
method they had devised.

But if Husserl's three most famous successors only adopted
the methodology in order to establish and so to justify the
assumption of a philosophical position, then one is bound to ask
what phenomenology of this kind implies with regard to our
conception of the nature and purpose of philosophy. The
answer to this question is, in my estimate, quite
straightforward. First, in all three cases what we find is a
philosophical construction defined in terms of a threefold
intellectual configuration – a *methodology* drawn from *phenomenology*, an *ontological* grounding principle which could be called
ontological and a view of *human existence* which should be called
existential. But second, in so far as questions of existence can
only be answered through existing, the development of an
existential philosophy necessarily assumes something of the
character of a *Weltanschauung*.

This view of philosopy as *Weltanschauung* is one which was
upheld and defended by Karl Jaspers, for instance, in his
Psychologie der Weltanschauung. In a well known review of this
work, Martin Heidegger attacked the notion of philosophy as
Weltanschauung.[8] And yet it seems that the hermeneutical
revolution inaugurated by Martin Heidegger ought to lead in
this direction. Nothing confirms this position more conclusively than the claim made on behalf of his philosophy *by the
author himself* that *Being and Time* was in accord with Nazi
ideology,[9] not merely a *Weltanschauung* in the most obvious sense
of that word but one which proved to be lamentably biased and
destructive.

Adopting this idea as a working hypothesis, we find that it
makes good sense of the work of at least two of our four
phenomenological philosophers. Heidegger was certainly aware
of the currents of thought and feeling which eventually found
their way into politics in the form of a Nazi government. And
to the extent that *Being and Time*, first published in 1927, can be
aligned with Nazi ideology, his book was prophetic.[10] Further, it
could be said that Sartre's existential philosophy was in large
measure a response to the threat of Nazism. If the basis of
Nazism lies in the possibility of harnessing what Nietzsche
called the 'herd instinct' to political ends, then the formulation

of an existential philosophy which insists upon the freedom and uniqueness of the individual could be seen as an attack on the mentality which makes Nazism possible. Developed no doubt as a reaction to the authoritarianism of Nazi ideology, Sartre's own determination to '*épater la bourgoisie*', to mock at and to scandalize the values of the bourgeois society in which he was brought up, in turn became prophetic, leading as it has done to that breakdown in the social order from which our 'democratic' societies presently suffer.

The times have changed. So surely, it is time to rethink the meaning of being, to think the meaning of being in such a way that a viable and justifiable ethics becomes possible, to rethink the relation of the mental and the physical in such a way that the two no longer remain in an irreconcilable opposition, to rethink the question of God so that the spiritualism of Eastern philosophy no longer stands out in opposition to the materialism of Western philosophy. And yet, since the 1960s, as fashion has succeeded fashion, often with bewildering rapidity – structuralism, de-constructivism, post-modernism, relativism – not only does the presence of phenomenology seem to have receded, it appears to have been replaced by schools which refuse to admit the very possibility of establishing a philosophical position.

This refusal has taken three distinct forms. The first of these is an ever increasing commitment to historical research, *pure and simple*. If you look at the writings of our four phenomenological philosophers you will find that historical research, *per se*, plays only an incidental role – which is not to say that they were not enormously knowledgeable about the history of philosophy. To turn to the classics of British post-war philosophy, Ayer's *Language, Truth and Logic* contains few notes, Ryle's *Concept of Mind* and Strawson's *Individuals* virtually none while it goes without saying that Wittgenstein's *Philosophical Investigations* makes no use of supplementary notes since it, in itself, consists of nothing but notes.

Where contemporary philosophers move beyond historical research they tend to do so in the direction of meta-theoretical speculations *about* the works of those who did precisely establish such positions. The contribution of the *Frankfurt Schule* is a case in point, since the task of Critical philosophy consists very largely of subjecting major works of philosophy to critical review – and the same goes of relativism, the essential aim of which it is to place the thinking of the great philosophers in relation to the historical and social contexts in and out of which they arose.

But there is a third tendency which is, in essence, much more destructive, since it leads to the conclusion that the only task available to philosophy today consists in a reflection upon the impossibility of doing philosophy in the manner in which it has always been done, namely, as the establishment of a philosophical, even metaphysical, position. There is nothing new about the thesis with respect to 'the end of philosophy'. Time and time again, great philosophers, and especially great German philosophers, have held that the history of philosophy had been brought to a close and, on each occasion, what might have appeared as an end turned out to be nothing more than a new beginning.[11]

The destructive implications of the thesis with regard to the 'end of philosophy' have their counterpart in the analytic tradition. A major component in that configuration which went by the name of 'linguistic philosophy' (whose intellectual ancestry can be traced to the work of later Wittgenstein) implied, or at least suggested, that the history of philosophy was the history of the grammatical (or categorial) errors committed by the great philosophers of the past. In response to the destructive implications of both the Heideggerian and the Wittgensteinian version of this thesis (and therefore with respect to the value and significance of philosophy itself), I can do no better than quote from a paper by Karl-Otto Apel, a philosopher who has subjected this phenomenon to a long and laborious critical examination.

> Briefly, the reduction of philosophy to self therapy, a reduction which Wittgenstein's critique of language and meaning linked with the pseudo-problems of traditional metaphysics, was paradoxical from the very beginning; for it represented a negation of critical philosophy's own claims to meaning and truth. Precisely this tendency created its own disciples. Moreover, in Heidegger's ever more radical 'Destruction' of Western metaphysics (and more completely in Derrida's 'Deconstructivism' and in Lyotard's 'Post Modernism', which refer back to Heidegger and Wittgenstein) this tendency is strengthened to the point of attesting to something like the *self-destruction of philosophical reason.*[12]

In a more positive vein, I would like to advance a claim which it will not be possible to defend here. It runs as follows. No theme which has dominated philosophical attention for more than, let us say, a century can lightly be dismissed as an 'error' or an 'illusion'. Such a claim bears with particular force upon two themes which contemporary philosophy tends either to ignore altogether or to dismiss as a historical error. Medieval philosophy was dominated by the theme of *God* and modern philosophy by that of *consciousness* or subjectivity – and 'dominated' is the operative word. Such is the oblivion into which the question of God has fallen in contemporary philosophical circles that I shall not say any more about the former and simply conclude with a few remarks about the latter.

Husserl's achievement has often been called the 'triumph of subjectivity' – and rightly so. It is, however, part of the 'triumphalism' of contemporary philosophy that it should think of itself as having finally reached a vantage point from which it becomes possible to dismiss such archaic concepts as 'interiority', 'subjectivity', 'consciousness', 'spirituality' etc. from the roster of relevant philosophical categories. It may well be that these categories need re-thinking and re-defining, but I would like to suggest that whenever, and wherever, anything approaching civilization has emerged in human affairs, it has been due to something which deserves to go by one or other of these currently disreputable names.

No one understood this better than Husserl whose *Crisis* assumes, in its historical perspective, the proportions of an extended cry of pain as the founder of phenomenological philosophy watched his cherished ideal of philosophical rationality collapse into the abyss of Nazi irrationalism. So it is simply not possible to overestimate the prophetic grandeur of the following, uncharacteristically rhetorical, passage with which Husserl concludes his Vienna Lecture of May 1935:

There are only two escapes from the crisis of European existence: the downfall of Europe in its estrangement from its own rational sense of life, its fall into hostility towards the spirit and into barbarity; or the rebirth of Europe from the spirit of philosophy through a heroism of reason that overcomes naturalism once and for all. Europe's greatest danger is weariness. If we struggle against this greatest of all dangers as 'good Europeans' with the sort of courage that does not fear even an infinite struggle, then out of the destructive blaze of faithlessness, the smouldering fire of despair over the West's mission for humanity, the ashes of great weariness, will rise up the phoenix of a new life-inwardness and spiritualization as the pledge of a great and distant future for man: for the spirit alone is immortal.[13]

Have we, in the West, *already* (within fifty years of a crisis which brought the world to its knees) disqualified that phoenix of a new life-inwardness and spiritualization which, according to Husserl, holds forth the pledge of a great and distant future for man?

NOTES

1 For an excellent discussion of this subject see Tugendhat's paper 'Heidegger's Idea of Truth', in *Martin Heidegger: Critical Assessments*, ed. C. Macann (Routledge: London, 1992), vol. III.

2 Michael Theunissen, *Der Andere*, trans. C. Macann, as *The Other*, (MIT Press: Cambridge, MA, 1984).

3 See Klaus Held's paper 'Heidegger and the Principle of Phenomenology', trans. C. Macann, in *Heidegger: Critical Assessments*, vol. II.

4 *Presence and Coincidence: The Transformation of Transcendental into Ontological Phenomenology*, Phaenomenologica 119 (Kluwer: Dordrecht, 1991).

5 The concept of an 'ontological transposition' has been employed in my interpretive studies of the transcendental philosophy of both Kant and Husserl. *Kant and the Foundations of Metaphysics* (Winterverlag: Heidelberg, 1981) adopts a completely different route to the originary ground from that adopted by Heidegger in his *Kant and the Problem of Metaphysics*. Whereas the Heideggerian interpretation focuses upon the 'lower' faculty of imagination at the expense of apperception, I focus my interpretation upon the highest (transcendental) faculty of apperception which, by virtue of the 'ontological transposition', eventually becomes the 'lowest' (ontological) faculty. In *Presence and Coincidence* the same issue is differently articulated. I show here that with regard to four critical themes, the transcendental ego, time, the own body and the other subject, the attempt at a transcendental constitution falls into contradiction with itself, a contradiction which is expressed (implicitly) in the replacement of the 'doctrine of presence' by an alternative 'doctrine of coincidence'.

6 Heidegger, *Gesamtausgabe*, vol. 24, p. 29.

7 The single most important attribute of the 'natural attitude' is that it takes the real, qua material, as an unquestioned and unquestionable *given* and this whether the givenness of the 'object' is or is not complemented by an equivalent givenness of the 'subject'. For phenomenological philosophy, this givenness of the real becomes

questionable and, in the end, has to be constituted in one way or another.

8 Reproduced in *Wegmarken, Gesamtausgabe*, vol. 9.

9 A statement to this effect is reported by Karl Löwith who met him in Rome, in 1936, wearing the Nazi insignia. 'Heidegger . . . led me to believe that it was his concept of "Historicality" which lay at the root of his political stance' (Karl Löwith, 'Letztes Wiedersehen mit Heidegger', in *Antwort: Martin Heidegger im Gespräch* (Neske, 1988), p. 171).

10 This claim is of course heavily disputed. In my estimate the link between *Being and Time* and Nazism is to be sought not, as the author once suggested to Löwith, in the theme of historicality but in that of resoluteness, a resoluteness unrestrained by ethical considerations. On this, see my paper: 'Who is Dasein?: Towards an Ethics of Authenticity', in *Heidegger: Critical Assessments*, vol. IV.

11 Kant, for example, held that the Critical philosophy had successfully solved all the traditional problems with which philosophy had been beset and that it only remained to apply the principles of his Critical philosophy to the different domains of human thought. What actually happened was the very reverse of the sort of closure Kant had in mind, a veritable explosion of creative philosophical thinking. A similarly premature declaration is to be found with Hegel as also, and in a very different way, with Heidegger. See my Introduction to *Martin Heidegger: Critical Assessments*, vol. II.

12 Karl-Otto Apel, 'Language Games and Life Forms', trans. C. Macann, in *Martin Heidegger: Critical Assessments*, vol. III.

13 Edmund Husserl, *The Crisis of European Sciences and Transcendental Phenomenology*, trans. David Carr (Northwestern University Press: Evanston, IL, 1970), p. 299.

14 My own ontological phenomenology, entitled *Being and Becoming*, seeks to reintegrate ontological and transcendental phenomenology with analytical philosophy by employing a four stage genesis of the kind summarily presented in this conclusion. The complete project is planned to take up four volumes: a first volume devoted to the genetic theory of consciousness, a second to Natural Philosophy (Time/Space/Causality), a third to Social Philosophy (Personal Relations/Language/Culture) and a fourth to Practical Philosophy (Freedom/Ethics/Politics). Rather than dismissing such conceptions as 'interiority', 'subjectivity', 'spirituality', these conceptions will be integrated into the developmental theory of the being of human being, but in such a way as to circumvent the philosophical difficulties associated with 'solipsism', 'private languages' and so on. In the context of *Being and Becoming*, the very spirituality which contemporary philosophy seems bent upon eradicating will feature as the 'saving grace' without which our species can have little to look forward to but a perpetual repetition of the ghastly horrors that have already characterized the history of this century, aggravated, of course, by the ever increasing destructive potential of our technology.

Select bibliography

PRIMARY TEXTS

Edmund Husserl

Logical Investigations, vols I and II, translated by J. N. Findlay, Routledge: London, 1976.

The Idea of Phenomenology, translated by W. Alston and G. Nakhnian, Martinus Nijhoff: The Hague, 1964.

The Phenomenology of Internal Time Consciousness, edited by Martin Heidegger and translated by James Churchill, Indiana Unversity Press: Bloomington, Indiana, 1966.

Ideas I, translated by Boyce Gibson, Allen & Unwin: London, 1931. Newly translated by F. Kersten for Martinus Nijhoff: The Hague, 1982.

Ideas II, translated by R. Rojcewicz and A. Schuwer, Kluwer: Dordrecht, 1989.

Ideas III, translated by Ted Klein and William Pohl, Martinus Nijhoff: The Hague, 1980.

Formal and Transcendental Logic, translated by Dorion Cairns, Martinus Nijhoff: The Hague, 1969.

Cartesian Meditations, translated by Dorion Cairns, Martinus Nijhoff: The Hague, 1960.

Experience and Judgment, translated by J. Churchill and K. Ameriks, Routledge & Kegan Paul: London, 1973.

The Crisis of European Sciences and Transcendental Phenomenology, translated by D. Carr, Northwestern University Press: Evanston, Illinois, 1970.

Martin Heidegger

Being and Time, translated by John Macquarrie and Edward Robinson, Harper & Row: New York, 1962.

Basic Problems of Phenomenology, translated by Albert Hofstadter, Indiana University Press: Bloomington, Indiana, 1982.

Kant and the Problem of Metaphysics, translated by James Churchill, Indiana University Press: Bloomington, Indiana, 1962.
An Introduction to Metaphysics, translated by Ralph Manheim, Doubleday: New York, 1961.
Existence and Being, Introduction and analysis by Werner Brock, Henry Regnery: Chicago, Illinois, 1949.
Nietzsche, translated by David Krell, Harper: San Francisco, California, 1979.

Jean-Paul Sartre

The Transcendence of the Ego, translated by F. Williams and R. Kirkpatrick, Farrar, Straus & Giroux: New York, 1957.
The Psychology of Imagination, translated by Bernard Frechtman, Washington Square Press: New York, 1966.
Being and Nothingness, translated by Hazel Barnes, University Paperbacks, Routledge & Kegan Paul: London, 1969.
Existentialism and Humanism, translated by Philip Mairet, Methuen: London, 1948.
The Critique of Dialectical Reason, translated by Allan Sheridan-Smith, New Left Books: London, 1976.

Maurice Merleau-Ponty

The Structure of Behaviour, translated by A. Fischer, Beacon Press: Boston, Massachusetts, 1963.
The Phenomenology of Perception, translated by Colin Smith, Routledge & Kegan Paul: London, 1962.
The Visible and the Invisible, translated by Alphonso Lingis, Northwestern University Press: Evanston, Illinois, 1968.
Signs, translated by Richard McCleary, Northwestern University Press, Evanston, Illinois, 1964.

SECONDARY LITERATURE

Bachelard, Suzanne, *A Study of Husserl's Formal and Transcendental Logic*, translated by Lester Embree, Northwestern University Press: Evanston, Illinois, 1968.
Biemel, Walter, *Martin Heidegger*, Routledge & Kegan Paul: London, 1977.
Carr, David, *Phenomenology and the Problem of History*, Northwestern University Press: Evanston, Illinois, 1974.
Catalano, Joseph, *A Commentary on Jean-Paul Sartre's Being and Nothingness*, University of Chicago Press: Chicago, Illinois, 1980.
Edie, James, *Edmund Husserl's Phenomenology*, Indiana University Press: Bloomington, Indiana, 1987.

Faber, Marvin, *The Foundation of Phenomenology*, State University of New York Press: New York, 1943.

Gelven, Michael, *A Commentary on Heidegger's Being and Time*, Harper & Row: New York, 1970.

Held, Klaus, *Lebendige Gegenwart*, Phaenomenologica 23, Martinus Nijhoff: The Hague, 1966.

Jeanson, Francis, *Sartre and the Problem of Morality*, translated by Robert Stone, Indiana University Press: Bloomington, Indiana, 1980.

Kockelmans, Joseph, *Martin Heidegger*, Duquesne University Press: Pittsburgh, Pennsylvania, 1965.

Kockelmans, Joseph, *On the Truth of Being*, Indiana University Press: Bloomington, Indiana, 1984.

Langer, Monika, *Merleau-Ponty's Phenomenology of Perception: a guide and commentary*, Macmillan: London, 1989.

Lauer, Quentin, *Phenomenology: Its Genesis and Prospect*, Harper & Row: New York, 1955.

Levinas, Emmanuel, *The Theory of Intuition in Husserl's Phenomenology*, translated by André Orianne, Northwestern University Press: Evanston, Illinois, 1973.

Macann, Christopher, *Presence and Coincidence: The Transformation of Transcendental into Ontological Phenomenology*, Phaenomenologica 119, Kluwer: Dordrecht, 1991.

Macann, Christopher (ed.), *Martin Heidegger: Critical Assessments* (four volumes), Routledge: London, 1992.

Macomber, William, *Anatomy of Disillusion*, Northwestern University Press: Evanston, Illinois, 1967.

Miller, Izchak, *Husserl, Perception and Temporal Awareness*, MIT Press: Cambridge, Massachusetts, 1984.

Mohanty, J. N., *The Possibility of Transcendental Philosophy*, Phaenomenologica 98, Martinus Nijhoff: The Hague, 1985.

Richardson, William, *Heidegger: Through Phenomenology to Thought*, Phaenomenologica 13, Martinus Nijhoff: The Hague, 1963.

Ricoeur, Paul, *Husserl: An Analysis of his Phenomenology*, Northwestern University Press: Evanston, Illinois, 1967.

Schmitt, Richard, *Martin Heidegger on being Human*, Random House: New York, 1969.

Sokolowski, Robert, *The Formation of Husserl's Concept of Constitution*, Phaenomenologica 18, Martinus Nijhoff: The Hague, 1964.

Steiner, George, *Martin Heidegger*, University of Chicago Press: Chicago, Illinois, 1978.

Theunissen, Michael, *Der Andere*, translated by Christopher Macann as *The Other*, MIT Press: Cambridge, Massachusetts, 1984.

Tugendhat, Ernst, *Der Wahrheitsbegriff bei Husserl und Heidegger*, De Gruyter: Berlin, 1967.

Index

abstraction 3, 7, 9, 15, 104, 154, 166, 170, 185; categorial 16; doctrine of 9; from the body 43, 53; ideational 9, 10

action 52, 53, 98, 121, 145, 149, 152, 154, 156, 164, 170, 173, 174, 175, 176, 179, 180, 182, 185, 186, 187, 190, 198

anxiety 87, 88, 92, 93, 97, 98, 102, 103, 119, 128

apperception 11, 48, 49; analogizing 48, 49; mundanizing 47

Aristotle 56, 58, 73, 107

association 46, 164, 166, 173, 175, 178, 179, 180, 184

Augustine 54, 197

authentic 61, 65, 70, 84, 85, 91, 93, 97, 98, 99, 100, 101, 102, 105, 124, 169, 187; inauthentic 61, 70, 84, 86, 91, 101, 102, 103, 104, 105, 121

bad faith 121, 122, 123, 124, 136, 155, 156

de Beauvoir 110, 172

being, 7, 14, 15, 18, 25, 26, 29, 30, 31, 34, 36, 40, 41, 42, 47, 48, 49, 52, 53, 57, 58, 59, 60, 61; in general 60, 80, 105, 106, 116, 157; meaning of 60, 80, 105, 106, 209; question of 105

being-with 83, 84, 85, 90, 155, 192

Bergson 20, 82, 104, 132, 136, 169, 193, 196

Berkeley 9, 113

body: image 173; other 49, 141, 144, 146, 149, 152, 153, 177, 191; own 41, 42, 43, 44, 47, 48, 49, 52, 53, 111, 124, 128, 140, 141, 144, 145, 146, 147, 148, 149, 150, 152, 153, 156, 160, 161, 170, 172, 173, 174, 175, 176, 177, 178, 179, 180, 182, 185, 188, 189, 190, 191, 193, 194, 198, 199, 200; phenomenal 175; physical 11, 41, 42, 44, 48, 49, 86, 144, 152, 160, 171, 176, 185, 191; psychic 146

Brentano 3, 4, 20

care 59, 83, 84, 92, 93, 94, 96, 97, 99, 100, 101

cogito 19, 58, 79, 114, 142, 145, 191, 192, 193, 194, 195, 199; practical 52, 164, 195; pre-reflective 113, 114, 115, 126, 176, 187, 195; tacit 195

coincidence 13, 16, 23, 44, 126, 145, 169, 176, 181, 190

conscience 96, 98, 99

constitution: of animal nature 41; of the ego 45, of the flux 20; genetic 51; of immanental time 23; intersubjective 42, 43; of material nature 41, 42, 44; of the other subject 47; of the